Reader,

At the hazard of being dismissed by you we imprudently ask you to undertake certain obligations on receiving this book. Prudence, we feel, is not the proper response to impending catastrophe which, if it is to be averted, had better be met with acute foresight, with critical appraisal, with courageous action. This book is addressed to what the author considers the critical problems of all Humanity in our time. The problems are the current misery of mankind, and the threat of a genocidal war. The misery cannot be alleviated, nor the destruction averted, by men who are not conscious of the threat or of its causes.

The purpose of this book is to communicate the author's understanding of these problems to readers. We feel convinced that such communication cannot be accomplished by a publishing network whose primary purpose is not communication but profit.

In view of these considerations, we turn to you, reader, and ask you to make yourself responsible for the life or the death, the enjoyment or the misery, of all humanity. We ask this by placing a small task before you, a task which is not intended to be the end of your endeavors, but merely the cue which we hope will inspire you to devise far greater projects of your own.

We do not ask you to agree with the analysis contained in this book, in whole or in part; but we do ask you to read the book and to share at least our concern.

We further ask you to share our concern over the lack of unfettered media of communication in a land where the press is a business. You and I are, we feel, responsible to devise ways of circumventing this lack. We want you to join us in a search for a free press and a free literature whose sole aim is communication.

If you share our concern, if not our interpretation, we ask you either to see to it that this book is reproduced again, and yet again, and distributed without charge, or that your own interpretation of the problem is reproduced and distributed free of charge. If you do this, reader, the business press will have been circumvented.

If you feel yourself better suited to different forms of communication, allow us to suggest free plays, free novels, posters, pamphlets; allow us to suggest that you organize your community for lectures, forums, pickets, strikes....

If you do none of these things, and if you do not engage yourself in any of the infinite number of projects which have not occurred to us, then know, reader, that in our eyes you will have abdicated your responsibility to all living humanity, and to all the dead who have made you what you are, given you what you have, and taught you what you know.

Fredy Perlman

John E. Riehl

The New Freedom
CORPORATE CAPITALISM

Fredy Perlman

The New Freedom: Corporate Capitalism

Fredy Perlman

Cover art and woodcuts by John Ricklefs.

Cover design by Factory School.

Originally published in 1961.

Factory School, 2007
Queens, New York

ISBN 978-1-60001-999-9

No Copyright

This book shall not be part of any financial transaction. The book, in whole or in part, may be reproduced in any form only on condition that the reproductions are distributed free of charge.

Factory School is a learning and production collective engaged in action research, multiple-media arts, publishing, and community service. For more information, please visit factoryschool.org.

CONTENTS

1. Golden Age   11
2. Democratic Experiment   27
3. Growth of Capitalism   63
4. Ideology and Manipulation   96
5. Corporate Dispensation   144

NOTES   211

BIBLIOGRAPHY   222

Golden age

"Happy the age and happy the times on which the ancients bestowed the name of golden, not because gold, which in this iron age of ours is rated so highly, was attainable without labour in those fortunate times, but rather because the people of those days did not know those two words *thine* and *mine*. In that blessed age all things were held in common. No man, to gain his common sustenance, needed to make any greater effort than to reach up his hand and pluck it from the strong oaks, which literally invited him to taste their sweet and savoury fruit. Clear springs and running rivers offered him their sweet and limpid water in glorious abundance. In clefts of the rock and hollow trees the careful and provident bees formed their commonwealth, offering to every hand without interest the fertile produce of their fragrant toil. Spontaneously, out of sheer courtesy, the sturdy cork trees shed their light and broad bark, with which men first covered their houses, supported on rough poles only as a defense against the inclemencies of the heavens. All was peace then, all amity, all concord. The crooked plough had not yet dared to force open and search the kindly bowels of our first mother with its heavy coulter; for without compulsion she yielded from every part of her fertile and broad bosom everything to satisfy, sustain, and delight the children who then possessed her. Then did the simple and lovely shepherdesses go from valley to valley and from hill to hill, with their tresses loose, and without more clothes than were needed to cover modestly what modesty requires, and has always required, to be concealed. For were there such ornaments as are in fashion today, all trumped up with Tyrian purple and silk in so many contorted shapes. Yet, with only a few green loaves of dock and ivy plaited together, they must have looked as splendid and elegant as our court ladies with the rare and outlandish inventions which idle curiosity has taught them.

In those days the soul's amorous fancies were clothed simply and plainly, exactly as they were conceived, without any search for artificial elaborations to enhance them. Nor had fraud, deceit, or malice mingled with truth and sincerity. Justice pursued her own proper purposes, undisturbed and unassailed by favour and interest, which so impair, restrain, and pervert her to-day. The law did not then depend on the judge's nice interpretations, for there were none to judge or to be judged...."[1]

Generous goatherds sat around a rustic table and listened to their eloquent guest, Don Quixote de la Mancha, as he told them of an age long past and someday to return. The goatherds were not as familiar as the Don with the feudal world of fraud, deceit and malice. To them the description of the Golden Age was a fascinating harangue. They did not know the Don was holding up an ideal to his Western European contemporaries. That the goatherds understood him no better than his other contemporaries is not surprising. Don Quixote himself didn't fully understand his vision, nor his mission with relation to it. He knew that the world of noblemen and painted ladies was passing away. He hoped this world would give way to an age of creative cooperation and communal sharing. Yet all around he saw an increase of plunder and repression, fraud and deceit. He did not know to whom to address his complaint, to whom to appeal for the realization of his ideal. So he relegated his ideal to a long-forgotten past. He prepared to build the new world by taking up the role of Knight—a version of knighthood that had never existed. He sought to implement a dream and negate the corruption of an era by reviving the era's most corrupt and repressive institution. And then he could not find the giants who were responsible for the misery and repression. But he was determined to find them and root them out, and in his determination he charged bravely with his horse and lance at indifferent windmills.

Shakespeare's Gonzago also held up the image of a Golden Age.

> ... no kind of traffic
> Would I admit; no name of magistrate;
> Letters should not be known; riches, poverty,
> And use of service, none; contract, succession,
> Bourn, bound of land, tilth, vineyard, none;

> ....
> All things in common nature should produce
> Without sweat or endeavour: treason, felony,
> Sword, pike, knife, gun, or need of any engine
> Would I not have; but nature should bring forth,
> Of it own kind, all foison, all abundance,
> To feed my innocent people.[2]

But Gonzago, too, speaks to deaf ears and decayed imaginations. The noblemen who listen find only an image of their own reality in Gonzago's dream.

> Sebastian.   No marrying 'mong his subjects?
> Antonio.   None, man; all idle; whores and knaves.

Prospero, familiar with the new knowledge and new power being made available to Western man in the Renaissance, wanted to use the knowledge and power to benefit and educate mankind.

And in Miranda, Shakespeare expressed hope that the New World so visibly replacing the old would fulfill its promise and truly abound with good will, plenty, and beauty.

> O, wonder!
> How many goodly creatures are there here!
> How beauteous mankind is! O brave new world,
> That has such people in't!

Gonzago and Don Quixote located their vision in an age long past. But there were men who, ever since the Middle Ages, had demanded that a just and humane society be established within their own lifetimes. The Anabaptists learned from priests about a Kingdom of God which became accessible to men after they reached their graves. The Anabaptists compared the vision with the misery allotted to living men. Their spokesman Thomas Münzer spoke of the "courage and strength to realize the impossible,"[3] and the hopeful peasants rose in revolt against the priests who promised salvation but dispensed oppression, the Anabaptists demanded the establishment of the Kingdom of God among the living. When Luther proclaimed that priests and Church were irrelevant to Salvation, the Anabaptists thought they had an important ally. But Luther, rejecting priests, turned to the Princes of the old regime: "Whoso can, strike, smite, strangle, or stab, secretly or publicly ... such wonderful times are these that a prince can better merit Heaven with bloodshed than another with prayer..." "...stern hard civil rule is necessary in the world, lest the world become wild, peace vanish, and commerce and common interests be destroyed.... No one need think that the world can be ruled without blood. The civil sword shall and must be red and bloody."[4] And Luther praised the brutal and bloody repression of the hopeful peasants. "I would rather suffer a prince doing wrong than a people doing right."[5]

In mid-seventeenth century England a group of men who called themselves the "True Levellers" attempted once more to make the Kingdom of God a human reality. At that time, the common lands of England were being enclosed—the lands were taken from the men who used and worked them and given to rich men. However, a small group took some unenclosed land and cultivated it, with the purpose of distributing the fruits of their work among the poor.[6] Landlords, lawyers, officials and mobs suppressed this experiment, and the group became notorious under the name of "Diggers." The spokesman of the Diggers, Gerrard Winstanley, urged that the experiment be adopted as a model for the government of all England.

Men in the dying feudal society dreamt of "those fortunate times" when men "did not know those two words *thine* and *mine*," they dreamt of the "blessed age" when "all things were held in common," because the society in which they dreamt was one where all things were held by very few men; it was an age when most men knew only unbroken misery and found salvation only in the grave. Most men were condemned to labor their entire lives for a bare subsistence. A small number of men enjoyed privileges, did not work, were sustained by the working majority, and conscripted the people who supported them to fight their wars. Within this feudal context, Don Quixote and Gonzago dreamt of a better world. But to support his dream, the Don could only appeal to goatherds who had never been part of the feudal world, and to implement his dream he could only attack windmills. And Gonzago could find no better audience than two cynical politicians whose familiarity with life beyond state-power extended only to "whores and knaves." The agrarian economy of European feudalism was not able to support a socialist commonwealth. There was no longer enough wild fruit to go around and feed the entire population: food had to be cultivated. And even then the surplus was so small that it could support only a small number of men not bound to the soil. In order to support all mankind on a high level of material wellbeing and spiritual sharing, the economy had first to be transformed. But the Don was incapable of perceiving what had to be done, and Gonzago had too narrow an audience.

Years before the birth of Shakespeare or Cervantes, Thomas More had analyzed, in much clearer terms, the cause of feudal "fraud, deceit ... malice." Thomas More was converted into a saint in 1935 by the Catholic Pope. However, in his own time four centuries earlier, in 1535, More was executed and his head was displayed on London Bridge. For Thomas More, author of *Utopia*, had pointed an accusing finger at the institutions that supported privilege for the few and dispensed misery to the many: "...where every man under certain titles and pretenses draweth and plucketh to himself as much as he can, and so a few divide among themselves all the riches that there is, be there never so much abundance and store, there to the residue is left lack and poverty."[7] The few who have a monopoly of wealth and power claim, in addition, to possess a "nobility" which "common" men lack. They consider themselves more intelligent, industrious, and virtuous than other men. According to More, however, the virtue and industry reside rather in the poor who are despised and deprived of the fruits of their labor: "...it chanceth that this latter sort is more worthy to enjoy that state of wealth than the other be, because the rich men be covetous, crafty, and unprofitable. On the other part, the poor be lowly, simple, and by their daily labor more profitable to the commonwealth than to themselves." And yet the noblemen, "not contenting themselves with the yearly revenues and profits that were wont to grow to their forefathers and predecessors of their lands, nor being content that they live in rest and pleasure, nothing profiting, yea, much noying the weal public, leave no ground for tillage: they enclose all in pastures..." And yet the laws of the land do not condemn the criminal. Instead, it is the victim who is convicted as a criminal, and since it is his persecutor who holds the wealth, the power, as well as the lair, the victim must either submit or die. "Therefore, that one covetous and unsatiable cormorant and very plague of his native country may compass about and enclose many thousand acres of ground together within one pale or hedge, the husbandmen be thrust out of their own, or else other by covin or fraud, or by violent oppression, they be put besides it, or by wrongs and injuries they be so worried that they be compelled to sell all: by one means, therefore, or by other, other by hook or crook, they must needs depart away, poor, silly, wretched souls, men, women, husbands, wives, fatherless children, widows, woeful mothers with their young babes, and their whole household small in substance, and much in number, as husbandry requireth many hands. Away they trudge, I say, out of their known and accustomed houses, finding no place to rest in. All their household stuff, which is very little worth, though it might well abide the sale: yet, being suddenly thrust out, they be constrained to sell it for a thing of naught. And when they have, wandering about, soon spent that, what can they else do but steal, and then justly, God wot, be hanged, or else go about a-begging. And yet then also they be cast in prison as vagabonds, because they go about and work not; whom no man will set a-work, though they never so willingly offer themselves thereto."

According to Thomas More's contemporary, Niccolo Machiavelli, "the desire to acquire possessions is a very natural and ordinary thing, and when those men do it who can do so successfully, they are always praised and not blamed..."[8] In the feudal society, fortune (or fate) is the dispenser of reward and misery. By learning to control and manipulate fortune, an aristocracy can derive privilege and push into poverty those whose attention is turned to other things. "...[F]ortune is the ruler of half our actions, but ... she allows the other half or thereabouts to be governed by us. I would compare her to an impetuous river that, when turbulent, inundates the plains, casts down trees and buildings, removes earth from this side and places it on the other; every one flees before it, and everything yields to its fury without being able to oppose it; and yet though it is of such a kind, still when it is quiet, men can make provision against it by dykes and banks, so that when it rises it will either go into a canal or its rush will not be so wild and dangerous. So it is with fortune, which shows her power where no measures have been taken to resist her, and directs her fury where she knows that no dykes or barriers have been made to hold her." The "dykes and banks" by which an ambitious aristocrat in the feudal society "can make provision against" fortune are enumerated by Machiavelli for the aristocrat's guidance. First of all, "the Prince" must be aware of good means, but must be prepared to use bad means if it is in his interest to do so, "for how we live is so far removed from how we ought to live, that he who abandons what is done for what ought to be done, will rather learn to bring about his own ruin than his own preservation. A man who wishes to make a profession of goodness in everything must necessarily come to grief among so many who are not good." Secondly, he must inspire fear in other men, for as Machiavelli said, "one ought to be both feared and loved, but as it is difficult for the two to go together, it is much safer to be feared than loved, if one of the two has to be wanting." Thirdly, the "Prince" must be adept in the use of violence—both kinds of violence, the kind known as law as well as the kind known as brute force. "You must know, then, that there are two methods of fighting, the one by law, the other by force: the first method is that of men, the second of beasts; but as the first method is often insufficient, one must have recourse to the second." He must know when to break faith, for "a prudent ruler ought not to keep faith when by doing it would be against his interest, and when the reasons which made him bind himself no longer exist." Hypocrisy is another indispensable "dyke" by which wealth, power and privilege are consolidated and maintained, and fortune's fury is kept out; "it is well to seem merciful, faithful, humane, sincere, religious, and also to be so; but you must have the mind so disposed that when it is needful to be otherwise you may be able to change to the opposite qualities. And it must be understood that a prince, and especially a new prince, cannot observe all those things which are considered good in men, being often obliged, in order to maintain the state, to act against faith, against charity, against humanity, and against religion. And, therefore, he must have a mind disposed to adapt itself according to the wind, and as the variations of fortune dictate, and ... not deviate from what is good, if possible, but be able to do evil if constrained." And above all, the successful "Prince" must be an opportunist, for, as Machiavelli pointed out, "...fortune varying and men remaining fixed in their ways, they are successful so long as these ways conform to circumstances, but when they are opposed then they are unsuccessful." In short, the virtues of a successful man of wealth, power and privilege are what Don Quixote later called fraud, deceit, and malice.

Machiavelli was concerned exclusively with the "dykes and banks" which, in the feudal era, were designed to protect and benefit an aristocracy of hereditary parasites. Thomas More, however, was concerned with the dykes that would bring comfort, education and political participation to all mankind. The greatest scourge of humanity is privilege, and at the root of privilege is private property. Wherever the laws protect the accumulation of private wealth, there will be public misery. "Wheresoever possessions be private, where money beareth all the stroke, it is hard and almost impossible that there the weal public may justly be governed and prosperously flourish."[9] Not only will there be no justice in a realm where possessions are private; there cannot be justice in such a realm. "Unless you think thus: that justice is there executed where all things come into the hands of evil men, or that prosperity there flourisheth where all is divided among a few; which few, nevertheless, do not lead their lives very wealthily, and the residue live miserably, wretchedly, and beggarly." The only possible way to bring justice among men, to free them from poverty and slavery, to enable each to develop his finest capabilities, is to abolish the institution of private property. "Thus I do fully persuade myself that no equal and just distribution of things can be made, nor that perfect wealth shall ever be among men, unless this propriety be exiled and banished." With Thomas Münzer's "courage and strength to realize the impossible," such a program could have been carried out in Sixteenth Century Western Europe, and fortune need not have been allowed to protect the few and drown the many.

A century after More's execution, Gerrard Winstanley led the Diggers to demand the abolition of the dykes that train fortune's floods on the poor—he demanded new dykes which would control the floods of fortune for the benefit of all. "O you Adams of the earth," said Winstanley to the rich, "you have rich clothing, full bellies.... But know ... that the day of judgment is begun.... The poor people whom thou oppress shall be the saviors of the land.... If thou wilt find mercy ... disown this oppressing ... thievery of buying and selling of land, owing of landlords, and paying of rents, and give your free consent to make the earth a common treasury."[10] Winstanley felt it was a crime for some men to be lords and masters on land which is the "common treasury" of all mankind.

"None ought to be lords or landlords over another, but the earth is free for every son and daughter of mankind to live free upon."[11]

Much later, when the ideals of More, of Winstanley, and of the French Enlightenment, ideals of Liberty, Equality, Fraternity, were betrayed by every turn of the French Revolution, Gracchus Babeuf was paraded in a cage for continuing to defend them. He was condemned as a traitor and conspirator for continuing to insist that "If you follow the chain of our vices, you will find that the first link is fastened to the inequality of wealth."[12] Babeuf pointed out to his murderers that no more had been said by the popular and humane French philosophers Rousseau, Mably, "And Diderot, who said that from the scepter to the crozier, humanity was ruled by personal interest, and that personal interest arose from property, and that it was idle for philosophers to argue about the best possible  form of government so long as the ax had not been laid to the roots of property itself—Diderot, who asked whether the instability, the periodic vicissitudes of empires, would be possible if all goods were held in common, and who asserted that every citizen should take from the community what he needed and give to the community what he could and that anyone who should try to restore the detestable principle of property should be locked up as an enemy of humanity and a dangerous lunatic!"[13] For, according to Babeuf, property is a crime; "it is a crime to take for oneself at the expense of other people the products of industry or the earth. In a society which was really sound, there would be neither poor nor rich. There would be no such system of property as ours. Our laws of heredity and inalienability are 'humanicide' institutions. The monopoly of the land by individuals, their possession of its produce in excess of their wants, is nothing more nor less than theft; and all our civil institutions, our ordinary business transactions, are the deeds of a perpetual brigandage, authorized by barbarous laws."[14]

From the late middle ages on, many men knew that misery and oppression lay in privilege and property. And yet, when a new technology was created by men to contribute to their "common treasury," it was used not only to maintain, but to strengthen the property, power and privilege of the few. Utopia remained an untried dream. Don

Quixote addressed himself to a pre-agricultural past, to a time when "the crooked plough had not yet dared to force open and search the kindly bowels of our first mother with its heavy coulter; for without compulsion she yielded from every part of her fertile and broad bosom everything to satisfy, sustain, and delight the children who then possessed her," a time when "No man, to gain his common sustenance, needed to make any greater effort than to reach up his hand and pluck it from the strong oaks, which literally invited him to taste their sweet and savoury fruit." Such an economy, unfortunately, had supported a small number of men—and that, not very effectively, as they had no control whatever over their destiny and were literally at the mercy of their "first mother." And Gonzago, well-intentioned though he was, could offer his contemporaries nothing but a similar version of a similar age.

> ... need of any engine
> Would I not have; but nature should bring forth,
> Of it own kind ...

But Thomas More did not speak of a past age. Rather he located his ideal society in Utopia—a place whose name means Nowhere. More did not, thereby, intend his Utopia to be a mere literary instrument with which to satirize England, as his interpreters would have men believe. More well knew that all human history consisted of the building of economies that had never existed before, the creation of ideas that had never been thought, the formation of habits that had not seemed possible. He knew that human history was a succession of Nowheres which men tried to realize somewhere. His Church also knew—and feared—the capacity of man to go beyond his condition. So did his king, Henry VIII, who did not want his own convenient innovations to be taken as models by the English population. Both King and Church had privileges at stake, and thus herded into monasteries or burned as heretics those who, by giving men a glimpse of Utopia, undermined men's faith in the feudal hierarchy of priest, property, privilege and power.

The agrarian economy was limited in the amount of food it could produce. In order that all men gain comfort, knowledge, and that all men participate in the creation of cultural values, the privileges of priests and aristocrats would have to be distributed among the poor. Winstanley urged that, if justice be made available to all men, everyone must do productive work. The just society cannot permit itself the luxury of soldiers, aristocrats or priests. Soldiers do nothing but destroy what other men build. Aristocrats waste other men's labor on useless ornaments, elaborate clothing, and gigantic castles, all of which serve no other purpose than to demonstrate their wealth. And priests, according to Winstanley, "make sermons to please the sickly minds of ignorant peoples, to preserve their own riches and esteem among a charmed, befooled, and besotted people."[15] Winstanley urged that priests become schoolmasters, that they teach men of the world in which they live, of human history, of the laws and diversity of nature. In the true commonwealth, there would be no warriors, since there would not be any desire to accumulate private wealth if the world is a "common treasury." There would be no ornamented aristocracy, as there would be no privilege and thus no need to display it. There would be no priests, as there would be no need to make men submit to the inhuman misery required to maintain the wealth and power of the few.

But Gerrard Winstanley did not know that the productive capacities of human beings were in the process of transformation; he knew no more of engines than was known by Don Quixote or Gonzago. Nor did Babeuf dream of the possibilities of the inventions spreading in his time. Babeuf also urged that all men do productive labor, and he coped with the problem of repetitive and unpleasant tasks by relegating them to everybody—unpleasant tasks were to be done by everyone taking his turn. Neither Winstanley nor Babeuf could foresee the possibility of using machines to do repetitive tasks, thus freeing all men for intellectual and imaginative pursuits. Both confined their communal democratic ideal to the conditions of the agrarian economy.

The agrarian form of society has been praised in many current Western writings because of its "unity" and "simplicity" and "integrity," and primarily because of its lack of the evils commonly associated with technology. In this praise, even adulation, it is often forgotten that the agrarian economy is not able to support a large number of people who are engaged in other pursuits than food-growing. Such a society would be unable to support all the anthropologists and philosophers who sing its praises in a technological society. The comfortable philosopher who exhorts men not to stir the happy farmers from their food-growing joy is making a choice for the farmers which he has not made for himself. Agriculture is a highly valued occupation, but clearly not all human beings are inclined to it, and in an agrarian economy they are rarely given a choice. This lack of choice constitutes the "simplicity" of an agrarian economy; its "unity" comes from the fact that most men do much the same thing throughout their lives—a better name for such "unity" is uniformity.

To enable men to follow other pursuits than agriculture, the agrarian economy must either have a very large surplus, or it must transform itself into a machine-based economy. Essentially, the machine is an extension of the human hand: it is a tool which enhances the scope and power of the hand: it enables one man to do the work of five, or a hundred, men. Thus, if a machine on a farm can do the work of five men, then those men are free to follow other pursuits. If the other pursuits available in a society are less attractive and more repetitive than farming, this is clearly not the machine's fault. A tool is not responsible for the way men use it. Peaceful men will use a knife to carve and sculpt, not to kill. Creative men will use a machine to do the repetitive labor while men devote themselves to original tasks, not to increase the amount of repetitive labor to which men are bound as slaves. Such, at least, would have been the possibilities if men had used the new instruments to abolish, not increase, human misery—if men had truly been as they appeared to Miranda when she exclaimed

> O, wonder!
> How many goodly creatures are there here!
> How beauteous mankind is! O brave new world,
> That has such people in't!

But Shakespeare was not as hopeful as Miranda. He knew that other forces than Gonzago's dreams or Prospero's knowledge would shape the world to come. He knew that among the "many goodly creatures" there was also Caliban, the half-beast, the man with "a mind bemired in fact, an imagination beslimed with particulars."[16] Caliban, the personification of lust and greed, knew only hatred and destruction. This inhuman undercurrent, ever-present in Western history, was not to become dominant until the middle of the Twentieth Century, when fascism and militarism took Caliban as the model for a "super-race."

And there is Malvolio the Puritan, earliest representative of the brave new world. Humorless Malvolio. His very presence negates the laughter and debauchery of the dying aristocracy. Sir Toby Belch, the parasitic old Lord who embodies both the enjoyment and the uselessness of the decaying feudal regime, challenged the Efficient Malvolio's intrusion.

> Art any more than a steward? Dost thou
> think, because thou art virtuous, there shall
> be no more cakes and ale?[17]

Temporarily no more than a steward, Malvolio was soon to graduate; he was rise to the world of Business and Industry. And then there were no more cakes and ale—not for a long time to come. English theaters closed down—and when they opened, there were Malvolios everywhere on the stage. Englishmen retained the institution of Monarchy, for old time's sake, but when they beheaded their last monarch they put a succession of Malviolios on the throne. The Feudal world of fraud, deceit and malice did in fact collapse, but it was not replaced by a Golden Age of music and harmony. The Malvolios brought only drabness, calculation, and the naked search for wealth and power. The writings of Cervantes were carefully channeled to children and pedants. Shakespeare was left to gather dust for almost a century, and when at last he was unearthed, the tragedies were shown with happy endings and the dreams were presented as comedies.

The transition from the agrarian to the technological economy was to pass through the humorless Malvolio. And it literally *passed through*, for though he was the carrier of the change he neither understood it, nor experienced it, nor enjoyed it. Unlike Don Quixote, Malvolio didn't have a yearning for Justice; unlike Gonzago, he didn't dream; unlike Prospero, he had no passion for knowledge. He had little use for reason except as calculation, and his ideals extended only as far as his avarice. Under the tutelage of capitalists, the industrial revolution was born without love, formed without understanding, built without passion.

The small amount of surplus produced by the agrarian economy had gone to support a minority of elaborate warriors and churchmen. The majority of men got little more than misery from those they supported. Imaginative creation is hard put in such conditions. Men whose time and leisure depends on the misery and enslavement of others find their own imaginations shackled. The development of technology made it possible for more men to leave the land—technology in time made it possible for all men to be fully educated and to participate in the sharing and creation of human art and knowledge. Technology changed the human economy: it made man's oldest dream a possibility. The machine took care of the repetitive tasks and freed men from bondage to economic activity. But capitalism left the feudal structure of privilege intact. The doctrine of private property decreed that the new surplus was not to support mankind, but merely a new minority. The collapse of feudal privilege did not usher in a Golden Age where all the where all the earth's yield would be shared by men in common, where men would work together to put the finest human ideals into practice. The disintegration of feudal privilege ushered in a new age of privilege, an Age of Gold where "gold" was not a metaphor but a thing. The propelling motive of the new age was greed. The gold filled the coffers of the few and increased the misery of the many. Wealth, knowledge and power opened the gate of the Golden Age, but in front of the gate was built a grotesque obstruction: The Market. Revolutions for liberty, equality, fraternity, did take place, both in France and in America—and men were called on to support them. But the revolutions betrayed their initiators as well as their supporters; they were revolutions that suppressed liberty, increased privilege, sanctioned property, and banished fraternity. In the cafes of Paris men sang a song written by a member of Babeuf's Society of Equals: "Dying of hunger, dying of cold, the people robbed of every right … newcomers gorged with gold, who have given neither work nor thought, are laying hold on the hive; while you, the toiling people, eat iron like an ostrich…. A brainless double council, five frightened directors; the soldier pampered and petted, the democrat crushed: voilà la République!"[18] The "brave new world" became a ludicrous caricature of Miranda's expectations. Her outcry of wonder and admiration was taken up at a later date in Western history with bitter irony.

Men were indeed freed from bondage to the soil. But from the land they were pushed into the factories. And there they were not allowed to consciously participate in the exciting creation of a new economy. Nor were they given a share of the new wealth they produced. The men became a "work force." They were given only so much as would keep them alive—and that much only because dead they were no use to the factories. They were freed from the land, but not from economic activity. Men who only have a bare minimum of what keeps them alive will be constantly preoccupied with keeping alive. Their preoccupation with economic needs was actually intensified in the factory. On the soil they had had "bad years," but they had also had "good years": times for reading and ceremony and enjoyment. In the factories there were only bad years—and if they lost their work they starved. Men to whom much had been promised became beasts of burden for new masters.

The feudal world of privilege was replaced by the capitalist world of privilege, not by the Golden Age. The aristocracy of rank was replaced by the aristocracy of wealth. Inequality was increased, violence was glorified, and the limits of misery were extended. Gracchus Babeuf, who had been hunted as a heretic under the old aristocracy, was put to death as a conspirator under the new. Before going to the guillotine, Babeuf accused his accusers: "Diderot ... asserted that ... anyone who should try to restore the detestable principle of property should be locked up as an enemy of humanity and a dangerous lunatic!—Citizens, 'dangerous lunatic' is precisely what you have called *me* for trying to introduce equality!"

The ideal of the new world was not wellbeing, but accumulation. Through a complex interaction of legality and violence, a few men gathered all the new wealth into their hands. Land, even what had formerly been common land, was channeled into the private property of a few. A few men became owners of the factories, the machines, the resources, the food, the knowledge. Whatever could possibly be accumulated was accumulated. The new wealth came from the impoverishment of people all over the world. The new power was used not to benefit men, but to repress them. The new knowledge was put to the service of power.

Thomas More came to be worshiped as a saint: men turned their attention away from his ideal and to his person, away from his spirit and to his body; and More's Utopia was left to gather dust. Babeuf was guillotined. He was not permitted to see his children before he died. He nevertheless called out to them. "I have only one bitter regret to express to you: that, though I have wanted so much to leave you a heritage of that liberty which is the source of every good, I foresee for the future only slavery, and that I am leaving you a prey to every ill. I have nothing at all to give you! I would not leave you even my civic virtues my profound hatred of tyranny, my ardent devotion to the cause of Liberty and Equality, my passionate love of the People. I should make you too disastrous a present. What would you do with it under the monarchic oppression which is infallibly going to descend on you? I am leaving you slaves, and it is this thought alone which will torture my soul in its final moments. I should equip you, in this situation, with advice as to how to bear your chains more patiently, but I do not feel that I am capable of it."[19]

DEMOCRATIC EXPERIMENT

On the American continent, on fresh ground unsoiled by the "fraud, deceit ... malice" of Western Europe, independent farmers and left wing intellectuals dreamed of attempting a democratic experiment. They dreamed of a government in which every man, whether farmer, artisan or lawyer, would have a voice. It was to be a government where force or the threat of force would be replaced by rational discussion and decisions based on common consent. The decisions of the King's Private Chamber were to be placed into the hands of the public who are affected by them. All men were to receive a thorough education which would familiarize them with the problems and projects of the world in which they live, of the past experience of mankind, of the laws of nature. They would be fully informed on all important social and political issues, for only thus could they participate intelligently in forming public policy, reaching decisions, interpreting criticism.

To gain their right to attempt the democratic experiment, the Americans dissolved their colonial relationship with the British.

> We have reminded them of the circumstances of our emigration and settlement here. We have appealed to their native justice and magnanimity, and we have conjured them, by the ties of our common kindred, to disavow these usurpations, which would inevitably interrupt our connections and correspondence. They ... have been deaf to the voice of justice and consanguinity....
>
> We, therefore, the representatives of the United States of America, in general Congress assembled ... do, in the name, and by the authority of the good people of these colonies, solemnly and declare, that these united colonies are, and of right ought to be, free and independent states.[1]

For the British, the function of colonies was to increase the privileges of England's wealthiest men: "...not contenting themselves with the yearly revenues and profits that were wont to grow to their forefathers and predecessors of their lands, nor being content that they live in rest and pleasure, nothing profiting, yea, much noying the weal public, leave no ground for tillage: they enclose all in pastures..."[2] and they establish colonies in all parts of the world to increase yet further their yearly revenues and profits. If as a result of this avaricious accumulation, the colonial subjects suffer misery and hardship, the wealthy Englishmen can hardly feel pity, removed as they are from them by oceans.

In order to convince the British that they'd had enough of the oppression necessary to support a privileged class, the Americans fought a war with England, by means of passive resistance as well as by violence. The only goal the American revolutionaries had in common was to put an end to privilege and oppression. None fought to exchange foreign for domestic oppressors. No man risked his life to become once again a slave to someone else's privilege. Most men took it for granted that there were none on the American continent who would seek to reintroduce privilege misery. Had not Diderot said that such a man "should be locked up as an enemy of humanity and a dangerous lunatic!"[3] This was to be a society resting on "honesty, self-government, justice and knowledge."[4]

Beyond the general aim of abolishing privilege and misery, the revolutionaries had little in common. Nor were they agreed on the precise nature of privilege or the cause of misery. However, none were so completely in the dark about the social effects of wealth and property as men of a later age were to become. Many had come to the new world because here was truly a "common treasury" to be shared by all the creatures who lived on it. Some, however, had come with British ideas of "ownership" and they claimed a right to collect debts and taxes from others. Shortly after the revolution, the antagonism between these two groups broke out in Shay's rebellion—a rebellion which shook the security of the new land's men of wealth and property, and brought into the open the conflict that was to divide into hostile camps "the good people of these colonies." Neither conservatives nor radicals were in the dark about the source of the conflict, nor did anyone try to deny that there was a conflict. Half a century ago, the historian Charles Beard showed, in his excellent and highly documented studies,[5] that eighteenth century Americans were lucidly aware that the success of the democratic experiment depended on the type of economic structure developed on the American continent. That property was a source of faction as well as the origin of the division of classes was well known to James Madison. "The most common and durable source of factions has been the various and unequal distribution of property. Those who hold and those who are without property have ever formed distinct interests in society. Those who are creditors, and those who are debtors, fall under a like discrimination. A landed interest, a manufacturing interest, a mercantile interest, a moneyed interest, with many lesser interests, grow up of necessity in civilized nations and divide them into different classes, actuated by different sentiments and views."[6] And the conserva-

tive John Adams knew that wherever property exists, there will be a struggle between the rich and the poor, because "The gentlemen are more intelligent and skilful, as well as generally richer and better connected, and therefore have more influence and power than an equal number of common people: there is a constant effort and energy in the minds of the former to increase the advantages they possess over the latter, and to augment their wealth and influence at their expense."[7] Adams, in fact, interpreted Roman history in terms of a theory of class struggle. "In Roman history we see a constant struggle between the rich and the poor from Romulus to Caesar. The great division was not so much between patricians and plebians, as between debtor and creditor. Speculation and usury kept the state in perpetual broils. The patricians usurped the lands and the plebians demanded agrarian laws. The patricians lent money at exorbitant interest and the plebians were sometimes unable and always unwilling to pay it. These were the causes of dividing the people into two parties, as distinct and jealous, and almost as hostile to each other, as two nations."[8] Nor did Adams have any doubt that such a division existed on the American continent. "We do possess one material which actually constitutes an aristocracy that governs the nation. That material is wealth."[9]

John Adams, second president of the United States and successor of George Washington as head of the conservative Federalist Party, did not have the illusion that the rich govern in the best interests of the nation. "It is not true, in fact, that any people ever existed who loved the public better than themselves, their private friends, neighbours, etc…" What is more, since the rich "have most address and capacity, they gain more and more continually, until they become exorbitantly rich and the others miserably poor."[10] The agrarian democrat John Taylor, outspoken opponent of Adams and his party, was painfully aware that the rich will govern in the interests of the rich. "If it is a moral truth, that mankind prefer themselves to others, then it is a moral certainty, that members, both of the government and of the corporation, will prefer the interest of the corporation to the interest of the nation."[11] Taylor argued that a virtue that had not been supplied by religion in the feudal era could hardly be supplied by wealth. "If responsibility to God cannot cure priests of the vices which infect legislative parties of interest, what security lies in a responsibility to man? If the love of souls cannot awaken integrity, laid to sleep by this species of legislative patronage, will it be awakened by a love of wealth and power?"[12] If the rich are permitted to augment their wealth and influence constantly, then, according to Adams, "This effort produces resentments and jealousies, contempt, hatred, and fear between the one sort and the other."[13] And according to Taylor, "Whatever destroys an unity of interest between a government and a nation, infallibly produces oppression and hatred."[14] In sum, eighteenth century Americans of different political persuasions were not unaware of the observation Thomas More had made almost three centuries earlier, that "wheresoever possessions be private, where money beareth all the stroke, it is hard and almost impossible that there the weal public may justly be governed and prosperously flourish."[15]

By and large, American revolutionaries were quite lucidly aware, and generally agreed, that the success of the democratic experiment depended on the nature and purpose of the social and economic structure developed on the American continent. Where they differed was on the emphasis one gave to property and another to democracy. Hamilton, for example, feared democracy as if it were a plague, precisely because he was aware that democracy entailed the abolition of the privileged class of "the rich and well born." Others, less committed to the old world's aristocracies than Hamilton, but not overly enthusiastic about democracy, accepted the institutions of wealth and property, but wanted the government to be a neutral mediator between the classes, uncommitted to the minority of the rich as well as the majority of the poor. James Madison, for example, accepted private property and the consequent division into classes as a "necessity," and urged a government that would "regulate" the different classes. "The most common and durable source of factions has been the various and unequal distribution of property…. interests grow up of necessity in civilized nations and divide them into different classes, actuated by different sentiments and views. The regulation of these various and interfering interests forms the principal task of modern legislation, and involves the spirit of party and faction in the necessary and ordinary operations of the government."[16] The more conservative John Adams also accepted the "necessity" of classes and class parties, but he was just as aware as Madison about the need for government to mediate between the classes. "Two such parties … always will exist, as they always have existed, in all nations, especially in such as have property, and most of all, in commercial countries. Each of these parties must be represented in the legislature, and the two must be checks on each other. But, without a mediator between them, they will oppose each other in all things and go to war till one subjugates the others."[17] Adams, however, was no revolutionary, and no democrat. In spite of the fact that wealth and property represented the greatest threat to the wellbeing of the nation, in spite of the fact that classes bred "resentments and jealousies, contempt, hatred, and fear," Adams was not willing to discard the institutions of wealth, property, and privilege. "The moment the idea is admitted into society, that property is not as sacred as the laws of God and that there is not a force of law and public justice to protect it, anarchy and tyranny commence." And Adams fearfully depicted some of the "catastrophes" which would accompany the abolition of private property. "The time would not be long before courage and enterprise would come, and pretexts be invented by degrees, to countenance the majority in dividing all the property among them, or at least in sharing it equally with its present possessors. Debts would be abolished first; taxes laid heavy on the rich, and not at all on the others; and at last a downright equal division of everything be demanded and voted. What would be the consequence of this?"[18]

The agrarian democrat John Taylor carried the logic of Madison and Adams to its conclusions, and he attacked Adams for assuming that the shortcomings of other social systems must necessarily be transported to the United States. "Mr. Adams's system promises nothing. It tells us that human nature is always the same: that the art of government can never change; that it is contracted into three simple principles; and that mankind must either suffer the evils of one of these simple principles; as at Athens, Venice, or Constantinople; or those same principles compounded, as at London, Rome or Lacedemon.... Such a computation is a spectre, calculated "to arrest our efforts, and appal our hopes, in pursuit of political good. If it be correct, what motives of preference between forms of government remain? On one hand, Mr. Adams calls our attention to hundreds of wise and virtuous patricians, mangled and bleeding victims of popular fury; on the other, he might have exhibited millions sacrificed to the pride, folly and ambition of monarchy and aristocracy; and, to complete the picture, he ought to have placed right before us, the effects of these three principles commixed, in the wars, rebellions, persecutions and oppressions of the English form, celebrated by Mr. Adams as the most perfect of the mixed class of governments. Is it possible to convince us, that we are compelled to elect one of these evils? ... But if the moral qualities of human nature are not always the same, but are different both in nations and individuals; and if government ought to be constructed in relation to these moral qualities, and not in relation to factitious orders; these authorities do not produce a conclusion so deplorable. The variety in the kinds and degrees of political misery, is alone conclusive evidence of distinct degrees of moral character, capable of unknown moral efforts."[19] Taylor concluded, if the monopoly of privilege and power begets faction and misery, then the function of government must be to prevent such a monopoly. And since vested military, religious, or monied interests inevitably acquire a monopoly of wealth and power, because "[s]uch interests are incapable ... of including the majority of a nation, or of a general division among its members," then such interests must be abolished, and the function of law must be the constant redistribution of land, which cannot be a "purely factitious" interest. "Land is not created by law; therefore it is under no apprehension of its death stroke from law. It does not subsist upon other interests; therefore it is not beset by an host of enemies, whose vengeance it is conscious of deserving. By the operation of laws adverse to its monopoly, it quickly adjusts itself to the interest of a majority of a nation; thenceforward it is incapable of the avarice and injustice of a factitious legal interest because no temptation to seduce it into either, exists. To this point of improvement, a landed interest will invariably be brought, by laws for dividing lands; nor can it be corrupted, except by laws which confine lands to a minority. Then it becomes in a degree a factitious legal monopoly, capable of being favoured by law, and infected with a portion of that malignity, which constitutes the entire essence of a minor separate interest purely factitious."[20]

Thus the "Fathers" of the American revolution were lucidly aware that the success, or failure, of the democratic experiment depended on how men lived and what men did. They were perfectly aware that democracy was incompatible with a social structure in which a monopoly of wealth, power, and privilege was lodged in one class of men. And their acceptance or rejection of democratic ideals cannot be understood except in that context. If wealth, power and influence were not equally distributed among all men, there could be no democratic institutions.

Once a democratic society is established, how does it remain democratic? It was this question that guided the search for "democratic institutions." Such institutions are democratic only if they maintain equality; clearly an institution that can serve as well for the maintenance of privilege and oppression is not, in itself, a democratic institution. American democrats were concerned with finding institutions that would function on a vast scale not only to maintain, but also to advance, the democratic experiment once established. One such institution was the New England Town Meeting, where all citizens participated, discussed important issues, and reached public decisions. But the Town Meeting could only be practiced effectively on a small scale. For all the citizens of the United States to gather in one place and discuss all public questions would have been impractical. American democrats rejected this type of "village democracy," perhaps without having explored its possibilities adequately. And if "village democracy" is abandoned, then "representatives" are apparently the only alternative. Whether or not a peaceful confederation of self-governing villages is possible has never been answered. It has never been tried on a significant scale. But be that as it may, in America the small self-governing villages were abandoned. "Representatives" were accepted as a substitute.

Yet whether "representatives" are, or can be, a democratic institution is still an open question. If a man truly "represents" the ideas and wishes of thousands of men, he thereby ceases to be an individual with ideas and wishes of his own; he becomes the embodiment of a Social Conscience, a General Will. This was Rousseau's version of Representative Democracy. In Rousseau's model, the Representative acts for thousands of men on the basis of their consent. But acquiescence often takes the appearance of consent, and in human society there are no impartial judges who can effectively distinguish between the two. Yet if a man is *not* the embodiment of the General Will, if he is merely one among thousands and has no special qualification except his desire to "represent" the rest, then what is his justification for "representing" thousands of men? Since he is not the embodiment of the wishes and ideals of other men, what is to keep him from using his position for the irresponsible fulfillment of purely personal desires? According to Jefferson, a representative can be made responsible if the people are educated and fully informed, if they exert control over and directly participate in the reaching of public decisions. "Every government degenerates when trusted to the rulers of the people alone. The people themselves are its only safe depositories. And to render even them safe, their minds must be improved to a certain degree.... The influence over government must be shared among all the people. If every individual ... participates of the ultimate authority, the government will be safe."[21] However, if ignorance is maintained and information suppressed, the government will inevitably degenerate into oppressive tyranny. "If a nation expects to be ignorant and free, in a state of civilization, it expects what never was and never will be. The functionaries of every government have propensities to command at will the liberty and property of their constituents. There is no safe deposit for these but with the people themselves; nor can they be safe with them without information."[22] Thus, there must be education that gives to all inhabitants an understanding of social problems and ideals, and there must be media of communication that are controlled by no interest and are responsible to inform, not defraud, the public. However, if "the weight of talents will follow leisure and wealth,"[23] if wealth acquires a monopoly of education as well as communication, then the public will be educated as well as informed by the very group whose interest it is to defraud them. "A government, a section of it, or a measure founded in an evil moral principle, such as fraud, ambition, avarice or superstition, must produce correspondent effects, and defeat the end of government."[24]

Thus the eighteenth century democratic ideal may be divided into four indispensable parts, without which it cannot be realized. The first is that all men have equal wealth, power, and influence, and that this equality be maintained by some form of agrarian reform law. Then, to ensure equality, and to develop the talents and minds of citizens, there must be universal education, there must be untrammeled communication, and there must be participation by every individual in the important affairs of society. Without these four requirements, equality, education, communication, and participation, applied in the spirit in which they were conceived, there can be no democratic society.

One must assume that the great majority of people who fought and killed in the American revolution did so to put a permanent end to oppression and exploitation. Members of a military society will murder merely because they've been trained to do so. But in the eighteenth century the United States was a civilian society, and non-military men will rarely risk their own or others' lives merely to exchange one form of oppression for another. Most Americans were then agreed that privilege must be abolished; that property generates a privileged class and thus brings faction and misery; that wealth cannot justly govern a nation because it will inevitably govern in its own interest. But they did not agree on the best means of ensuring that wealth should not again give birth to a tyrannical aristocracy, thus re-converting the United States into a nation of masters and servants. As we have seen, Madison wanted a modified aristocracy restrained by a government of detached men devoted to the best interests of the nation, presumably a government of Madisonian philosophers. Adams wanted a neutral government which would mediate between the interests of the rich and poor, would guard the rich from the poor and the poor from the rich, but especially it would protect the rich from the poor. (Adams apparently could not remember that the rich, with their wealth, could buy their own protection without state aid, whereas the poor could not.) From the democratic camp, John Taylor argued that a modified aristocracy would quickly degenerate into an unlimited and repressive aristocracy, and that a government seeking to mediate between those who possess a monopoly of wealth and power, and those who lack it, would quickly become an instrument used by wealth and power to subjugate the rest. And there were others, more numerous but less influential, who followed to the conclusion that private wealth and property should be altogether abolished, thus preventing once and for all the monopoly of power and privilege, and, as Winstanley had urged, converting the earth into a "common treasury" which is "free for every son and daughter of mankind to live free upon."

However divergent the solutions, however clashing the views, they were to be resolved experimentally; decisions were to be, above all, tentative. Many problems had been solved, many were in the process of solution, but the experimental search for a democratic society would be the work of generations. "We have chanced to live in an age which will probably be distinguished in history for its experiments in government on a larger scale than has yet taken place. But we shall not live to see the result. The grosser absurdities, such as hereditary magistracies, we shall see exploded in our day, long experience having already pronounced condemnation against them. But what is to be the substitute? This our children and grandchildren will answer. We may be satisfied with the certain knowledge that none can ever be tried, so stupid, so unrighteous, so oppressive, so destructive of every end for which honest men enter into government, as that which their forefathers had established, and their fathers alone venture to tumble headlong."[25] The experiment was to fulfill the needs and ideals of living men. The mistakes, the blunders, the institutions of one generation could not, in an experimental democracy, be binding on another generation. "The earth belongs to the living, not to the dead," wrote Jefferson. "We may consider each generation as a distinct nation, with a right, by the will of its majority, to bind themselves, but none to bind the succeeding generations, more than the inhabitants of another country."[26]

Thus despite the divergent views of the revolutionaries as to the division, control, or mediation of property, as to the responsibility of representatives, democratic solutions could endlessly be sought and tried so long as the experiment continued. But if the experiment was limited or curbed, oppression and bloodshed would return. "Each generation ... has a right to choose for itself the form of government it believes the most promotive of its own happiness," wrote Jefferson. "A solemn opportunity of doing this every 19 or 20 years should be provided by the constitution.... This corporeal globe, and everything upon it, belongs to its present corporeal inhabitants, during their generation. They alone have a right to direct what is the concern of themselves alone.... If this avenue be shut..., it will make itself heard through that of force, and we shall go on, as other nations are doing, in the endless circle of oppressions, rebellions, reformations; and oppression, rebellion, reformation, again; and so on forever."[27] This much was known to eighteenth century Americans, for they had written into their Declaration of Independence "that, whenever any form of government becomes destructive of these ends, it is the right of the people to alter or to abolish it, and to institute a new government, laying its formation on such principles, and organizing its powers in such form, as to them shall seem most likely to effect their safety and happiness."

However, for a small number of men, the revolution was not the beginning of a vast experiment in social organization; it did not promise the possibility for a better society; it represented nothing more than an opening for large-scale economic speculation. As in all wars, some men did not fight with their bodies but with their money, and not for ideals but for personal profit. The American revolution was not exempted from such men, and in a frightfully short time these men undermined the ideals for which the revolution had been fought.

When the colonies went to war with England, the American economy was disrupted, and the value of money deteriorated. The Revolutionary Government of the United States needed funds to carry on the war—especially to support and equip the revolutionary armies. When these funds were provided, the men who contributed received securities for the amount they loaned. The securities were made out in the nominal amount of money given, although the real value of the money had fallen to a fraction of the nominal amount. A large number of the contributors must have been poor, because most of them seem to have sold the securities, generally for an even smaller amount than they had paid for them—sometimes at one tenth their original value.[28] In any case, by 1787 a good part of the securities were in the hands, not of the men who had lent money to the revolutionary government, but of capitalist speculators who had not lent anything but had monopolized securities by buying them cheaply from original holders. These early capitalists were to become the gravediggers of every democatic ideal that had been brought to the American continent.

Professor Charles A. Beard brilliantly analyzed this most crucial chapter of American history in his *An Economic Interpretation of the Consitution of the United States*, and further elaborated his conclusions in *Economic Origins of Jeffersonian Democracy*.* Beard's study of the Constitution became a classic in American history, and, as often happens to classics, the book was revered, and its conclusions were conveniently forgotten.

In May 1787, a convention to draft a constitution for the United States assembled in Philadelphia. Fifty-five men representing twelve states attended the convention. "Forty of the members held public securities, fourteen were land speculators, eleven were intereted in mercantile, manufacturing and shipping activities, and fifteen were slaveholders. The small farmer and debtor classes were virtually without representation."[29] The men who participated in this convention were not "representatives" in Rousseau's sense. They did not embody a General Will. Nor were they "representatives" in Jefferson's sense of having been chosen, after careful consideration, by an educated and well informed public. "No popular vote was taken directly or indirectly on the proposition to call the Convention which drafted the constitution."[30] These men were not even representatives in the sense of Adams and Madison—in being disinterested mediators between different factions, concerned with the good of the nation as a whole. "The members of the Philadelphia Convention which drafted the Constitution were, with a few exceptions, immediately, directly, and personally interested in, and derived economic advantages from, the establishment of the new system."[31]

The chairman of this convention was George Washington, popular hero of the revolutionary war and Father of his Country. The chairman's qualifications especially suited him to head such a convention, for "Washington, of Virginia, was probably the richest man in the

---

*This chapter is heavily indebted to Professor Beard's monumental studies, published half a century ago, considered classics by scholars, yet shamefully ignored. Comparable studies of the American revolution's aftermath had not been made by an American since John Taylor's *Inquiry into the Principles and Policy of the Government of the United States*, which was contemporary to the events described. However, if my conclusions as to the far-reaching implications of the events are erroneous or overstated, Beard should not be blamed, since that careful scholar took infinite pain to understate the implications of his findings. Though Beard lucidly uncovered the nature of the period, which had been hidden for a century beneath a thick veil of pious apologetics, perhaps it was Taylor, though so close to events, who more truly grasped the historical importance as well as the tragic character of the period.

United States in his time, and his financial ability was not surpassed among his countrymen anywhere."[32] The unacknowledged leader of the convention, and the most eloquent defender of the document that emerged, was Alexander Hamilton, probably the cleverest man in the history of American politics. Hamilton did not share the democratic ideals of Thomas More, Cervantes, Gracchus Babeuf, or Thomas Jefferson. He did not even share the mild hopes expressed by Adams and Madison, that if an aristocracy of wealth was necessary, it should at least be curbed and made to serve the public good. According to Hamilton, "All communities divide themselves into the few and the many. The first are the rich and well born, the other the mass of the people. The voice of the people has been said to be the voice of God; and however generally this maxim has been quoted and believed, it is not true in fact. The people are turbulent and changing; they seldom judge or determine right. Give therefore to the first class a distinct, permanent share in the government. They will check the unsteadiness of the second, and as they cannot receive any advantage by a change, they therefore will ever maintain good government. Can a democratic assembly who annually revolve in the mass of the people, be supposed steadily to pursue the public good? Nothing but a permanent body can check the imprudence of democracy.... "It is admitted that you cannot have a good executive upon a democratic plan."[33] Hamilton, unlike his less candid descendants, did not deem it necessary to give lip-service to democracy while defending the rich and well born. He knew what democracy meant, and he devoted his life to the task of suppressing it. He was a brilliant man, and he accomplished his task with tremendous success. Hamilton's greatest fear, before, during, and after the revolution, was that the revolution would spread. He knew that the majority of his countrymen were not members of his own class, the class of "the rich and well born." He knew that the majority of his countrymen did not share his admiration for a government of "the rich and well born." In 1795 he wrote, "There are too many proofs that a considerable party among us is deeply proceed infected with those horrid principles of Jacobinism which, proceeding from one excess to another, have made France a theatre of blood."[34] He was also aware that the men who had participated in Shay's rebellion in New England shortly before the Constitutional Convention were not willing to be duped into believing that their hopes for a better life would be realized in the grave. They demanded that the world be shared among the living. "The consequences of this, even in imagination, are such as to make any virtuous man shudder."[35] Alexander Hamilton was, above all else, a virtuous man.

The other members of the Convention were as unrepresentative of America's democratic revolution as Hamilton. Most of them shared Hamilton's political philosophy. Some had no philosophy whatever: they attended the Convention merely for the financial promises and personal gain they could derive from it. Among them, the philosophic aristocrat Madison was a radical. And Madison did, in fact, join the opposition years later—but not before the Convention's and, especially Hamilton's, program had been fully carried out. A few Democrats did attend the Convention,[36] but they opposed its proceedings, as well as the document that emerged. Thomas Jefferson did not attend the Convention; he was in France.

As a result of their deliberations, the security-holding majority at the Convention, who constituted a fraction of the American population, drafted a document which gave a legal basis to their effort to put an end to the democratic experiment. As Beard pointed out, "The Constitution was essentially an economic document based upon the concept that fundamental private rights of property are anterior to government and morally beyond the reach of popular majorities."[37] But the drafting of the Constitution was only the first great step of the capitalist coup d'etat. The feast of the security-holders, this orgy of "paper and patronage," as John Taylor described capitalism, had only begun. The Constitution had yet to be made acceptable to the States, and then had to be put into practice, before the labor and ingenuity of the capitalists were rewarded. A Massachusetts newspaper published an eloquent enumeration of the virtues of the Constitution. The grounds on which the document is here defended have little to do with More's Utopia, Winstanley's "common treasury" or Babeuf's Society of Equals or Jefferson's democratic experiment. "It is in the interest of the merchants to encourage the new constitution, because commerce may then be a national object, and nations will form treaties with us…. It is the interest of all gentlemen and men of property, because they will see many low demagogues reduced to their tools, whose upstart dominion insults their feelings, and whose passions for popularity will dictate laws, which ruin the minority of creditors and please the majority of debtors. It is the interest of the American soldier as the military profession will then be respectable and Florida may be conquered in a campaign. The spoils of the West-Indies and South America may enrich the next generation of Cincinnati."[38]

When the Constitution was ratified, it was not by "The People." According to the first Chief Justice of the Supreme Court, John Marshall, a firm supporter of the document, "even after the subject had been discussed for a considerable time, the fate of the constitution could scarcely be conjectured; and so small in many instances, was the majority in its favor, as to afford strong ground for the opinion that, had the influence of character been removed, the intrinsic merits of the instrument would not have secured its adoption. Indeed it is scarcely to be doubted that in some of the adopting states a majority of the people were in the opposition. In of all of them, the numerous amendments which were proposed demonstrate the reluctance with which the new government was accepted; and that a dread of dismemberment, not an approbation of the particular system under consideration, had induced an acquiescence in it.... North Carolina and Rhode Island did not at first accept the constitution, and New York was apparently dragged into it by a repugnance of being excluded from the confederacy."[39] Beard concluded his carefully documented study of the Constitution with a denial that "we the people of the United States" had ever given their "unanimous consent" to the document which was henceforth to safeguard the rights of property from the intrusion of human life. "In the ratification of the Constitution, about three-fourths of the adult males failed to vote on the question, having abstained from the elections at which delegates to the state conventions were chosen, either on account of their indifference or their disfranchisement by property qualifications." There is even doubt that a majority of the few who voted were, in all states, in favor of the Constitution. "It is questionable whether a majority of the voters participating in the elections for the state conventions in New York, Massachusetts, New Hampshire, Virginia, and South Carolina, actually approved the ratification of the Constitution." But there's no doubt as to which interests gave their unwavering support to the document. "The leaders who supported the Constitution in the ratifying conventions represented the same economic groups as the members of the Philadelphia Convention; and in a large number of instances they were also directly and personally interested in the outcome of their efforts."[40]

So the Constitution of the United States was drafted and ratified. The third and last step of the Fathers of the American Way of Life was to adopt and put into effect Hamilton's economic plan. With the adoption of this program the democratic experiment would end, and not even Jefferson would be able, even if willing, to continue it.

In the first government under the Constitution, Washington was President and Alexander Hamilton was Secretary of the Treasury. The legislature was composed, by and large, of the same men who had drafted and supported the Constitution. From his post in the Treasury, Hamilton perpetrated the greatest sequence of frauds recorded in history. Hamilton's program consisted of nothing less than a capitalist *coup d'etat* which, at one blow, created a powerful capitalist class in America and insured its perpetual and uninterrupted growth short of a social upheaval. The class that was to take up the cry of *Laissez Faire* was created by the government, maintained by the government, and protected by the government.

Hamilton's first fiscal measure under the new government was to have the public debt funded at face value. The foreign debt amounted to $13 million, owed mostly to British capitalists, and the domestic debt amounted to $40 million, owed to the security-holders. The securities had been bought for less than face value because the dollar had deteriorated. When the dollar deteriorated even further, the men who had originally lent money to the government sold the securities for even less. Hamilton planned nothing short of paying the speculators for the face value of the securities they had bought for next to nothing. In the eighteenth century, $40 million was not the trifling sum expendable on military bungling it has since become in the United States. According to Beard, "The amount gained by public security holders through the adoption of the new system was roughly equivalent to the value of all the lands as listed for taxation in Connecticut. It was but little less than the value of the lands in New Hampshire, Vermont, and Rhode Island. It was about equivalent to one-half the value of the lands in New York and two-thirds the value of the lands in Massachusetts.

It amounted to at least ten dollars for every man, woman, and child in the whole United States from New Hampshire to Georgia."[41] The distribution of that much money among a small group of men meant the creation, at one stroke, of an aristocracy of great wealth which had not previously existed.

Many felt that the only just solution to the problem would have been to seek a discrimination between original holders and present holders of securities, and to pay the original holders at face value, but to pay the present holders (the speculators who had not originally lent money but had bought up securities) at the depreciated value, if at all. But the Congressmen voted against such a discrimination, and none was made; and it will probably never be known how many members of the First Administration were original holders, and how many speculators. In other words, the Hamiltonian funding bill was to commit the American government to pay the holders of public securities, the majority of whom had not lent anything to the revolutionary effort, a sum far greater than had been loaned by the more numerous original holders of the securities. As Beard pointed out, "It requires no very subtle analysis to discover that the immediate beneficiaries of these various proposals by the Secretary of the Treasury were the holders of public securities and capitalists generally. A study of the Treasury Books and the records of finance of the period indicates that the great capitalists were also large holders of public securities…. The immediate beneficiaries of Hamilton's plans were quite generally merchants, traders, shippers, and manufacturers."[42] In short, a tremendously wealthy and powerful class of capitalists would be created by government *fiat*.

Moreover, in the Congress which approved this measure, "Of the thirty-five, twenty-one were stockholders or dealers in the funds, and three of these latter bank directors and whose degree of zeal was obviously in the ratio above stated, as their relative profits; the bank directors being considerably more active and zealous than the other members of the corps."[43] Such a Congress could hardly take issue with so ambitious a program as this. Hamilton knew exactly which members of Congress held public securities, since the lists were kept in the Treasury Department. He was offering these security-holders a plan which, if they approved it, would make them and their kind extremely rich and powerful. Could they refuse? "Being on the great theatre of speculation and gain and possessed of more correct information, with the means of turning it to better account, will they abandon their occupation and slight the opportunity offered of becoming thrifty?"[44] As Beard pointed out, they thereby ceased to act as "representatives of the people" and became representatives of nothing but their own lust for gain. But could they be called dishonorable? Hardly. Hamilton was an extremely honorable man. They were all honorable men. Their honor left them no other course of action. They were all honorable men. Their honor left them no other course of action. They were all undoubtedly imbued with the "due sense of the sacred obligation of a just debt" which Hamilton described on a different occasion. Jackson, of Georgia, appealed to his fellow Congressmen. "Let us not rear a monument to mankind of the impossibility of preserving republican manners, by aping European nations and laying the foundation of our government in immense debts. Sir, our terms of service, happily I believe for the country, are near expiring. We shall return to the mass of the people, and participate in the burdens we impose. When the cool hour of investigation arrives, happy indeed will it be for us if, amidst the murmurs of an oppressed people, we have not to say, in self-condemnation, I too have been guilty of bringing this load of fetters on the people. America, sir, will not always think as is the fashion of the present day; and when the iron hand of tyranny is felt, denunciations will fall on those who, by imposing this enormous and iniquitous debt, will beggar the people and bind them in chains."[45] But the call went unheeded, the monument was reared, and the iron hand fell. The bill was passed, and with its passage the nation of men with approximately equal wealth, power, voice and control was extinguished from the American continent. "Alas! is it true, that ages are necessary to understand, whilst a moment will suffice to invent, an imposture?"[46]

Perhaps the greatest irony related to the funding bill was the role Jefferson played in its passage. Jefferson had been in France studying the makings of the French revolution. He was appointed Secretary of State of the first administration, partly because the extent and depth of his democratic leanings was not known, and partly because he had expressed no opinion of the Constitution. When he had returned to the United States, he was ignorant of the economic implications of the funding bill. When the Secretary of the Treasury told Jefferson that the funding bill was designed "for the national good," Jefferson believed it. When Hamilton told him that certain Southern Congressmen were opposed to the bill and thus threatened the unity of the nation, Jefferson was impressed. When Hamilton suggested that Jefferson's influence, if exerted in the proper manner, could change the votes of these Southern Congressmen, Jefferson listened. When Hamilton proposed that the Southerners would vote in favor of the funding bill if they were promised, in exchange, that the United States capital-city would be located in the South, on the Potomac, Jefferson agreed. Without Jefferson's influence, the funding bill might not have passed. But Jefferson talked to the Southerners, bargained with them, and the capital of the United States is still today situated on the Potomac.

Jefferson quickly became aware of the monstrous implications of Hamilton's program, but his revelation arrived too late. He resigned from his post as Secretary of State. He wrote an angry letter to President Washington. "I was duped ... by the Secretary of the Treasury, and made a tool for forwarding his schemes, not then sufficiently understood by me; and of all the errors of my political life, this has occasioned me the deepest regret."[47] Jefferson denounced Hamilton, and he denounced the capitalist economic program. "His system flowed from principles adverse to liberty, and was calculated to undermine and demolish the Republic, by creating an influence of his department over the members of the Legislature. I saw this influence actually produced, and its first fruits to be the establishment of the great outlines of his project by the votes of the very persons who, having swallowed his bait, were laying themselves out to profit by his plans; and that had these persons withdrawn, as those interested in a question ever should, the vote of the disinterested majority was clearly the reverse of what they made it. These were no longer the votes then of the representatives of the people, but of deserters from the rights and interests of the people; and it was impossible to consider their decisions, which had nothing in view but to enrich themselves, as the measures of the fair majority, which ought always to be respected."[48] But neither Jefferson's eloquence nor his indignation could abolish an entire class of newly created capitalists. Henceforth, nothing short of a social revolution would undo Hamilton's ingenious achievement.

The next great measure of Hamilton's scheme concerned the method of distributing the funds to the security-holding capitalists. For this purpose he proposed that Congress should authorize the establishment of a national bank. The bank would have the right to issue paper money in exchange for the public securities. All the funds of the United States government would go into the bank. The agrarian Congressman Jackson, of Georgia, who did not himself hold securities, probably did not know that he was addressing the bill's direct beneficiaries when he denounced the Bank Bill and told his fellow Congressmen that it was designed to tax the nation's poor in order to support the rich. The *Annals of Congress* reports Jackson's message to the "representatives of the people" in Congress assembled. "This plan of a National Bank is calculated to benefit a small part of the United States, the mercantile interest only; the farmers, the yeomanry, will derive no advantage from it; as the bank bills will not circulate to the extremities of the Union. He said, he had never seen a bank bill in the state of Georgia, nor will they ever benefit the farmers of that state, or of New Hampshire.... He urged the unconstitutionality of the plan; called it a monopoly, such a one as contravenes the spirit of the Constitution; a monopoly of a very extraordinary nature; a monopoly of the public moneys for the benefit of the corporation to be created."[49] James Madison, probably through a leak from the Treasury Department, had by this time become aware that the United States was being governed by a legislature of security-holders, and not by man interested in "the regulation of ... interfering interests." Consequently Madison was able to interpret the enthusiasm of his colleagues for the Bank Bill, and he opposed its adoption. Yet his main argument against the bill was the same as Jackson's: that it was unconstitutional. But surely Madison, whose Journal of the Constitutional Convention's proceedings is the fullest account extant, must have remembered that the same men had expressed the same vehemence during the Convention. Was Madison suggesting that the men at the Constitutional Convention had drafted a document which might be used against their interests?

The Bank Bill was passed. The security-holders who had voted themselves and the rest of their class such a large amount of wealth were not, at this point, to prevent themselves from collecting their prize. They had, after all, worked long and hard. But now that they had come this far, where was the United States government to get the money with which to pay the newly enriched capitalists? The amount, after all, was greater than all the lands in some states. At this point, the Constitution came to the aid of its authors. Under the Articles of the Confederation, the United States government did not have the power to collect taxes. This power had been reserved to the states. Each state, if the majority of its citizens desired, could cancel a debt incurred under difficult circumstances, especially if the original lenders had ceased to expect reimbursement and had sold or thrown away their security-notes. Such a cancellation would be injurious only to those speculators who had bought a monopoly of such notes, whereas the assumption of such a debt would mean hardship to a large sector of the population. The principle of such a cancellation is that the wellbeing of people is far more important than the inviolability of contractual obligations. The drafters of the Constitution, however, had a great deal of foresight. In the mists of all the Legislative, Executive and Judicial matter, they had written the following provisions into their document, provisions which became the law of the land.

> "All debts contracted and engagements entered into, before the adoption of this Constitution, shall be as valid against the United States under this Constitution, as under the Confederation." (Article VI, 1.)

> "The Congress shall have the power
>
>> To lay and collect taxes, duties, imposts, and excises, to pay the debts and provide for the common defense and general welfare of the United States; ...
>>
>> To coin money, regulate the value thereof ...
>>
>> To raise and support armies ...
>>
>> To provide and maintain a navy ...
>>
>> To provide for calling forth the militia to execute the laws of the Union, suppress insurrections..."
>
> (Article I, Sec. 8)

The debt had already been rendered "valid." The bank to "coin money, regulate the value thereof" had been created. The time had come to collect the money with which to pay the security-holders, and Hamilton suggested an excise tax on whiskey. Since whiskey was made and consumed predominantly by poor farmers, this tax meant that poor farmers would be taxed to support the speculators. "These taxes will bear heavily both on agriculture and commerce. It will be charging the active and industrious citizen, who pays his share of the taxes, to pay the indolent and idle creditor who receives them ... Thus the honest, hard working part of the community will promote the ease and luxury of men of wealth; such a system may benefit large cities, like Philadelphia and New York, but the remote parts of the continent will not feel the invigorating warmth of the American treasury; in the proportion that it benefits one, it will depress another."[50]

But now, after seven years of uninterrupted feast, the security-holding Federalists in Congress ran into their first serious difficulties. The trouble shocked many, but had long been anticipated by Hamilton. The indignation expressed by Jefferson's cry, "I was duped ... by the Secretary of the Treasury," spread to the hearts of his countrymen. But since they were not Secretaries of State, they could not resign; and since they had slowly become aware that George Washington was the living monument behind which Hamiltonian capitalism functioned, they did not think writing Washington a letter would be very effective. In 1794, a group of disaffected citizens met in Alleghany County, Pennsylvania. They passed a resolution, in which they declared: "We have observed with great pain, that our councils want the integrity or spirit of Republicans. This we attribute to the pernicious influence of the stock-holders or their subordinates; and our minds feel this with so much indignacy, that we are almost ready to wish for a state of revolution, and the guillotine of France for a short space, in order to inflict punishment on the miscreants that enervate and disgrace our Government."[51] A revolt broke out. And the Pennsylvanians found out, to their great amazement, that the highly praised Constitution had not been drafted "for the people." In fact, the Constitution's military provisions seemed to leave open the absurd possibility that the army of the United States could be turned against the people of the United States. A textbook on American history gives a brief description of the outcome of the "Whiskey Rebellion." "[Hamilton] was willing to see the tax collected by force so that the opponents of the government could be taught that they must obey the nation's laws whether they liked them or not.... The attempt to enforce the excise tax soon brought on the trouble that Hamilton had foreseen. The chief center of opposition lay in the Pittsburgh area, where bands of 'Whiskey Boys' raided stills that paid the tax, handled roughly the tax collectors, and successfully nullified the law in a number of western counties.... Washington now called out fifteen thousand state militia from the states of Virginia, Maryland, and Pennsylvania, and ordered them to march to the scene of the trouble. As the troops approached their destination, the enthusiasm of the rebels abated ... but the residents of western Pennsylvania and many other frontier areas were aghast at the power the Federalists in control of the central government had chosen to wield..."[52] Twenty years later, the agrarian philosopher John Taylor summarized the Hamiltonian sequence. "A legislature, in a nation where the system of paper and patronage prevails, will be governed by that interest, and legislate in its favour. It is impossible to do this, without legislating to the injury of the other interest, that is, the great mass of the nation. Such a legislature will create unnecessary offices, that themselves or their relations may be endowed with them. They will lavish the revenue, to enrich themselves. They will borrow for the nation, that they may lend. They will offer lenders great profits, that they may share in them. As grievances gradually excite national discontent, they will fix the yoke more securely, by making it gradually heavier. And they will finally avow and maintain their corruption, by establishing an irresistible standing army, not to defend the nation, but to defend a system for plundering the nation."[53]

> O, wonder!
> How many goodly creatures are there here!
> How beauteous mankind is! O brave new world,
> That has such people in't!

Charles Beard's study of this turning point in American history, which historians have tried so hard to forget, was published in 1913. A century before Beard, however, a much more immediate and painful analysis of the period was undertaken. This was *An Inquiry into the Principles and Policy of the Government of the United States* by John Taylor of Caroline County, Virginia. According to Beard, this book "deserves to rank among the two or three really historic contributions to political science which have been produced in the United States."[54] John Taylor had fought in the revolution and had shared its democratic ideals; he had served in the Virginia legislature as well as the United States Congress; and he had painfully watched Hamilton and his beneficiaries inscribe the revolution's ideal on a gravestone. Taylor was a personal friend of James Madison as well as Thomas Jefferson. The political, social and economic theories of Jefferson are known only from fragments and letters, since Jefferson never wrote a systematic treatise which expressed his views. However, Jefferson considered Taylor's work to be an expression of his own views, and said that "Taylor and he had never differed on any political principle of importance."[55] Thus Taylor has been called "the Philosopher of Jeffersonian Democracy."[56]

Though Taylor was a democrat in his theory, he was not one in his practice. He married into wealth and was, like Jefferson, one of the large plantation owners of Virginia. He did not, however, claim that his ideals described his own way of life. In the eighteenth century, Americans were much more reluctant than they are today to publish rationalizations of their privileges and fears. Taylor was well aware of the incompatibility between his habits and his beliefs. But the fact that he did not adjust the two should be held against his person and not against his theory. One should perhaps not judge Taylor too harshly for this incompatibility: if men commonly adjusted their worldly situations to their moral ideals, Buddha and Gandhi would not be as well known as they are. However, if a general writes a burning critique of military dictatorship, the fact that the author is a general should not deter one from reading the work, though one would be well-advised to be wary of a general's promise to prevent military dictatorship. And surely it could not be argued that because Engels was a capitalist, he therefore expressed the aspirations of capitalists. As Taylor himself said, "A despot may condemn tyranny; a soldier may condemn standing armies; and a stock-jobber may condemn paper systems. In reasoning boldly against the system of paper and patronage, no private reputation is attacked, more than that of Marcus Aurelius would be, by reasoning against despotism; or Washington's, by reasoning against standing armies.... Veracity in terms cannot be censurable, if veracity in matter is entitled to approbation. The discharge of a duty, cannot require an apology, and without making one, I will proceed."[57] Perhaps only an unprivileged, propertyless observer could write a truly sincere critique of privilege and property, but such a man would hardly write, and if he did write, his work could only too easily be dismissed as the rant of an envious lunatic. Taylor cannot be so easily dismissed; since he was himself a member of the privileged class, he is certainly well informed on the subject of privilege, and can hardly be called envious.

For Taylor, the greatest tragedy of the Constitutional Convention and its capitalist aftermath was that the Americans, who were so perceptive, so adept at unveiling the deceptions of the feudal aristocracy, should so meekly have submitted to the deceptions of the capitalist aristocracy. "We pity the ancients for their dullness in discovering oppressions, so clearly seen by ourselves now that they are exploded. We moderns; we enlightened Americans; we who have abolished hierarchy and title; and we who are submitting to be taxed and enslaved by patronage and paper, without being deluded or terrified by the promise of heaven, the denunciation of hell, the penalties of law, the brilliancy and generosity of nobility, or the pageantry and charity of superstition.

"A spell is put upon our understandings by the words 'publick faith and national credit,' which fascinates us into an opinion, that fraud, corruption and oppression, constitute national credit; and debt and slavery, publick faith. This delusion of the aristocracy of the present age, is not less apparent, than the ancient divinity of kings, and yet it required the labours of Locke and Sydney to detect that ridiculous imposture."[58]

Yet the Americans, with their widespread education, their knowledge of nature, their secular outlook, had far less ground to be deceived than the ancients. "Let us moderns cease to boast of our victory over superstition and the feudal system, and our advancement in knowledge. Let us neither pity, ridicule or despise the ancients, as dupes of frauds and tricks, which we can so easily discern; lest some ancient sage should rise from his grave, and answer. 'You moderns are duped by arts more obviously fraudulent, than those which deceived us. The agency of the Gods was less discernible, than the effects of paper and patronage. We could not see, that the temporal and eternal pains and pleasures, threatened and promised by our aristocracy, could not be inflicted or bestowed by it; you see throughout Europe the effects of your aristocracy. Without your light, oracles were necessary to deceive us; with the help of printing, and two detections, you are deceived by aristocracy in a third form, although it pretends neither to the divinity nor heroism claimed by its two first forms. And under these disadvantages, the impositions of our aristocracy were restrained within narrower bounds than those of yours. Did any aristocracy of the first age, extend its annual spoilation from one to thirty-five millions of pounds sterling, in less than a century?'"[59]

The Americans were not only better equipped than the ancients to unveil deception and recognize oppression. Only a few years before they submitted to the system of "paper and patronage," they had fought a war to abolish that very oppression when it was imposed on them at the hand of British capitalists. "It is strange, that it is so difficult to distinguish between honest and fraudulent taxes, imposed by a minor interest on the publick interest, and so easy to discern the real design of taxes imposed by one nation upon another. In the latter case, monopoly is clearly understood to be an indirect mode of taxation. The United States know, that the monopoly of their commerce by the English, was a tribute; but they refuse to know, that the monopoly of a circulating medium by banking, is also a tribute. Useless offices, established here by the English government, were clearly perceived to be a tribute; but useless offices established by our own government are denied to be so. Pretexts for taxation invented by England, were detected by dullness herself; but pretexts invented at home, seem to deceive the keenest penetration.

"And yet correct reasoning must conclude, that if one nation, by means of a monopoly, can impoverish another; a combination or corporate body, may also impoverish the rest of a nation, by the same means. That a monopoly which enriches, will correspondently impoverish, unless it produces or creates; that if Britain possessed the privilege of furnishing America with bank paper, at the annual profit of eight per centum, it would have constituted a tax, enriching Britain and impoverishing America—co-extensively with her former commercial monopoly; that if this privilege would have enriched the English at our expense, it must also equally enrich stockholders, at the expense of those who are not stockholders; that if national indigence is gradually produced by a subjection to a foreign monopoly, the indigence of the mass of the nation, will be produced by a domestick monopoly, profitable, but unproductive; and that if a nation has a moral right to liberate itself from an indirect tribute to another nation, it has also a moral right to liberate itself from a similar tribute to a domestick combination; unless it is a moral duty heroically to withstand evils imposed by foreigners, for the purpose of penitentially embracing them when imposed by natives."[60]

Perhaps the Americans would not have been so easily duped if the new aristocracy had avowed its true purpose from the very beginning, had admitted to the nation that it intended to consolidate into one class not only all the privileges heretofore enjoyed by kings and noblemen, priests and conquerors, but also an added flourish of never-ending accumulation of wealth. "Sincerity demanded ... the following confession: 'Our purpose is to settle wealth and power upon a minority. It will be accomplished by national debt, paper corporations, and offices, civil and military. These will condense king, lords and commons, a monied faction, and an armed faction, in one interest. This interest must subsist upon another, or perish. The other interest is national, to govern and pilfer which, is our object; and its accomplishment consists in getting the utmost a nation can pay. Such a state of success can only be maintained by armies, to be paid by the nation, and commanded by this minority; by corrupting talents and courage; by terrifying timidity; by inflicting penalties on the weak and friendless, and by distracting the majority with deceitful professions. That with which our project commences, is invariably a promise to get a nation out of debt; but the invariable effect of it is, to plunge it irretrievably into debt.'"[61] But such a confession was hardly to be expected. "All political oppressors deceive, in order to succeed. When did an aristocracy avow its purpose?"[62]

Men were overwhelmed by the unimagined wealth of the "undiscovered continent," and spent their time and energy accumulating it and killing the continent's previous inhabitants. And the institutions of "paper and patronage," of landlords and creditors and rich capitalists, were neither curbed nor outlawed; instead they were allowed to spread and to infest with a new master-slave arrangement the society in which democracy was to be created. A quickly shifting social context, coupled with the determined opposition of men who had privileges to lose and wealth to gain, was not such an ideal workshop for the Great Experiment after all. Harried theorists and ambitious politicians gave up the democratic ideal before it had even acquired a history. The Americans have always been a very busy people. In Taylor's time they were so busy concentrating their efforts on the abolition of real and imaginary tyrannies that they overlooked the one tyranny which was to enslave them and rob them of the one task whose fulfillment might have earned them a place of honor in human history. "The Americans devoted their effectual precautions to the obsolete modes of title and hierarchy, erected several barriers against the army mode, and utterly disregarded the mode of paper and patronage."[63] Such an utter disregard, wrote Taylor, was completely unwarranted. "This jealousy of armies, and confidence in paper systems, can only be justified if the following argument in its defense is correct.

"'An army of soldiers have a separate interest from the nation, because they draw their subsistence from it, and therefore they will combine for their own interest against the national interest; but an army of stockjobbers have no such separate interest, and will not combine. Soldiers admitted into the legislature, would legislate in favour of soldiers; but stockjobbers will not legislate in favour of stockjobbers. Soldiers may use our arms to take our money; but stockjobbers cannot use our money to take our arms. Soldiers may adhere to a chief in preference to the nation, as an instrument for gratifying their avarice and ambition upon the nation; but stockjobbers have no avarice nor ambition to be gratified, and will not therefore adhere to a chief for that purpose. Soldiers are dangerous, because they assail the liberty of a nation by open force; stockjobbers harmless, because they do it by secret fraud. All are jealous of soldiers, and therefore they will not be watched; few are jealous of stockjobbers, and therefore they will be watched. Many instances have occurred of the oppressions by the army system; one instance only of a perfect capacity in the paper system for oppression can be adduced; and as that has lasted only a single century, it would be precipitate to detect and destroy the aristocracy of paper and patronage, in less time than was requisite to detect and destroy those of superstition and the feudal system.'"[64]

If the "paper system" was a century old when Taylor wrote, it is now two and a half centuries old. Taylor would not be very happy if he knew that the Americans have still not destroyed the "aristocracy of paper and patronage"; he would be even less happy if he knew that their adherence to the "mode of paper and patronage" has caused Americans to destroy the "several barriers against the army mode and even to resurrect "the obsolete modes of title and hierarchy."

Another man whose theories repudiated the re-introduction of privilege to the American continent, whose position made him the symbol and spokesman of a widespread democratic social movement, whose name was synonymous with democracy among his countrymen, was elected third president of the United States. He believed that "No government can continue good, but under the control of the people."[65] He expressed great hopes for the American experiment. "We have chanced to live in an age which will probably be distinguished in history, for its experiments in government on a larger scale than has yet taken place."[66] He had observed and studied thirteen years of unbroken betrayal of the revolution's aims. Yet when he was elected by men who still took his ideals seriously, when he was charged with undoing the crime of self-seeking men, his goals became pitifully limited, his dreams diminished. "When this government was first established, it was possible to have kept it going on true principles, but the contracted, English, half-lettered ideas of Hamilton, destroyed that hope in the bud. We can pay off his debts in 15 years: but we can never get rid of his financial system. It mortifies me to be strengthening principles which I deem radically vicious, but this vice is entailed on us by the first error. In other parts of our government I hope we shall be able by degrees to introduce sound principles and make them habitual. What is practicable must often control what is pure theory."[67]

Thomas Jefferson was what has come to be known as a Liberal. He believed religiously in a nation of small farmers. "Those who labor in the earth are the chosen people of God, if ever He had a chosen people, whose breasts He has made His peculiar deposit for substantial and genuine virtue. It is the focus in which he keeps alive that sacred fire, which otherwise might escape from the face of the earth. Corruption of morals in the mass of cultivators is a phenomenon of which no age nor nation has furnished an example."[68] But he was himself a slaveholding plantation owner. He believed that each man should have as much power and control over his own affairs as other men, but his own wealth and power greatly exceeded that of his countrymen. He wrote for the poor and for democrats, but his own friends were the rich, and mostly aristocrats. He wrote that slavery was an aberration and a crime. "What a stupendous, what an incomprehensible machine is man! who can endure toil, famine, stripes, imprisonment, and death itself, in vindication of his own liberty, and, the next moment, be deaf to all those motives whose power supported him through his trial, and inflict on his fellow men a bondage, one hour of which is fraught with more misery, than ages of that which he rose in rebellion to oppose."[69] Yet he held slaves. Long before Jefferson's time, Quakers who had inherited or acquired slaves freed them and moved to states where slavery wasn't practiced. Jefferson wrote eloquent denunciations of slavery, but he did not follow the Quaker example, nor did he set an example of his own. His democratic professions were doubtless sincere, as they are more numerous in his private correspondence than in his public addresses. However, like his friend John Taylor, also a wealthy Virginia planter, Thomas Jefferson apparently did not experience the tension between his precept and his practice. His ideal was lofty, but alongside of his ideal his life was disappointingly ordinary.

During the Constitutional Convention, Jefferson was in France. His knowledge of the Convention's proceedings was supplied by his friend James Madison. At that time neither Madison nor Jefferson knew the economic interests of the Constitution's drafters, and neither the philosophic Madison nor the idealistic Jefferson could have suspected that economic interests were motivating men to gather for such a momentous occasion. When the document was finished, Jefferson not comforted by its similarity to English law, as he knew that England was no democracy, and that Americans had fled from England for that very reason. However, the document did embody many of the intellectually respectable eighteenth century theories of government, and Jefferson was duly impressed. In his correspondence with Madison, he limited his criticism to the lack of a bill of rights which would clearly delimit the powers of the rulers over the people. "I will now tell you what I do not like. First, the omission of a bill of rights, providing clearly, and without the aid of sophism, for freedom of religion, freedom of the press, protection against standing armies, restriction of monopolies, the eternal and unremitting force of the habeas corpus laws, and trials by jury..."[70] When such a bill was adopted in the form of the first ten amendments, Jefferson was apparently content with the document.

When Jefferson returned to the United States, he must have been completely ignorant of the Constitution's capitalistic implications or of Hamilton's enormous program for the creation of a privileged class, for otherwise he could not have been "duped ... by the Secretary of the Treasury." After his awakening, he became a bitter antagonist of those who had legislated with "nothing in view but to enrich themselves." Nevertheless through the years he apparently forgot that these same men had written their program into the Constitution, because while denouncing the restoration of privilege, he defended the Constitution. In fact, he even tried to level at the security-holders the same accusation Madison had aimed at them. He tried to argue that the program of the security-holders violated their own Constitution.

Jefferson's term of office was not extraordinarily impressive. It was not the revolution he prescribed for every generation. It was not even a palace revolt. John Taylor bitterly summarized the hopes and expectations his democratic friend left unfulfilled. "The history of man proves that all will often avail themselves of the precedents established by their predecessors, and reprobated by themselves. Every precedent, however clearly demonstrated to be unconstitutional and tending 'towards monarchy and an iron government' by a party out of power, will be held sacred by the same party in it; and those who clearly discerned the injustice and impolicy of enriching and strengthening federalists by bank or debt stock, at the publick expense, will seldom refuse to receive a similar sinecure. In short, a power in the individuals who compose legislatures, to fish up wealth from the people, by nets of their own weaving, whatever be the names of such nets, will corrupt legislative, executive and judicial publick servants, by whatever system constituted; and convert patriots from the best friends, into the most dangerous foes of free, equal and just principles of civil liberty."[71]

Like all liberals, Jefferson turned his energy and enthusiasm to smaller issues when the larger issues had become too unwieldy. He never abandoned his democratic ideals, he did not forget that democratic hopes had filled a nation of men with revolutionary ardor. He hoped that America would be a democratic beacon to oppressed men everywhere, but after "the contracted, English, half-lettered ideas of Hamilton, destroyed that hope in the bud,"[72] he turned his attention elsewhere. Certainly his role in repealing the Alien and Sedition Acts of the Adams Administration was nothing less than admirable; those Acts threatened to bury, so soon after its adoption, the entire Bill of Rights Jefferson had so greatly desired. But he made no attempt whatever to restore equality, justice, participation, he did not abolish privilege, he did not repeal the capitalists. Though his religion was an anti-theological humanism, he nevertheless accepted the Hamiltonian coup d'etat on the basis of the doctrine of original sin: "this vice is entailed on us by the first error." With such an explanation, there was nothing to do but make the best of a bad world. "In other parts of our government I hope we shall be able by degrees to introduce sound principles and make them habitual." While denouncing the capitalist economy superimposed on the United States by government *fiat* ("It mortifies me to be strengthening principles which I deem radically vicious…"), Jefferson nevertheless went on strengthening the "radically vicious" principles. "What is practicable must often control what is pure theory."

While Jeffersonian theory became the subject of scholarly admiration, Jeffersonian practice became the model for American politics. And as Beard pointed out, "Jeffersonian Democracy" as practiced was no more democratic than "Hamiltonian Democracy" or "Elizabethan Democracy" or "Napoleonic Democracy." Jeffersonian democracy did not imply any abandonment of the property, and particularly the landed, qualifications on the suffrage or office-holding; it did not involve any fundamental alterations in the national Constitution which the Federalists had designed as a foil to the levelling propensities of the masses; it did not propose any new devices for a more immediate and direct control of the voters over the instrumentalities of government. Jeffersonian Democracy simply meant the possession of the federal government by the agrarian masses led by an aristocracy of slave-owning planters, and the theoretical repudiation of the right to use the Government for the benefit of any capitalistic groups, fiscal, banking, or manufacturing."[73] What differentiates Jefferson from the successors is that he never claimed that his mediocre, un-democratic practice lived up to his lofty democratic ideals.

One of the strangest episodes at the origin of Jeffersonian Democracy was the role Hamilton played in Jefferson's election. In the election of 1800, Jefferson ran as the presidential and Aaron Burr as the vice-presidential candidate of the opposition Republican Party (a party which has no links with the later "Republican Party"). Jefferson and Burr both received the same number of votes, and the votes of each surpassed those of the Federalist candidate John Adams. The drafters of electoral procedure had not foreseen such a possibility, and had not specified that a vice-presidential candidate could not assume the presidency even if he received as many (or more) votes than the winning presidential candidate. Consequently, unless Burr withdrew, the outcome of the "tie" would have to be decided in the House of Representatives. Burr did not withdraw—a fact for which Jefferson was never to forgive him. Thus the House of Representatives was to decide between Jefferson and Burr. Since the House was stacked with Hamiltonian Federalists who feared they'd be undone by the outspoken democrat Jefferson, the absurd outcome of this "election" might have been that Aaron Burr would be the third president of the United States—the man who, instead, appears in the storybooks of American history as a Traitor. But the absurdity did not take place, for the balance was shifted in Jefferson's favor by Jefferson's bitterest opponent, Alexander Hamilton. Perhaps this was Hamilton's mode of repaying the debt he owed the one-time Secretary of State, for having "duped" him. The Father of American Capitalism did not suddenly become a champion of Jefferson. Far from it. "Perhaps myself the first, at some expense of popularity, to unfold the true character of Jefferson, it is too late for me to become his apologist; nor can I have any disposition to it. I admit that his politics are tinctured with fanaticism; that he is too much in earnest with his democracy...."[74] But Hamilton was a shrewd observer, and he knew that Burr might just as readily proclaim himself king as carry through a radical program of reform—and Hamilton feared the second possibility most. Burr's political and social views were not known, but it was known that he acted with ruthless determination. On the hand, Jefferson's democratic theories were widely known, and greatly feared by the capitalists. But Jefferson's practice was known too well by Hamilton. "I have more than once made the reflection that, viewing himself as the reversioner, he was solicitous to come into the possession of a good estate."[75] Hamilton, who had for so many years so effectively manipulated the security-holders in Congress, was above all a brilliant psychologist. He knew the precise relation between Jefferson's professed ideals and his actions. "Nor is it true that Jefferson is zealot enough to do anything in pursuance of his principles which will contravene his popularity or his interest. He is as likely as any man I know to temporize—to calculate what will he likely to promote his own reputation and advantage; and the probable result of such a temper is the preservation of systems, though originally opposed, which, being once established, could not be overturned without danger to the person who did it. To my mind a true estimate of Mr. Jefferson's character warrants the expectation of a temporizing rather than a violent system. That Jefferson has manifested a culpable predilection for France is certainly true; but I think it is a question whether it did not proceed quite as much from her popularity among us as from sentiment and, in proportion as that popularity is diminished, his zeal will cool."[76] The Congressmen, who by then owed their power, fame and fortune to Hamilton, could not help but follow their leader another time. And the leader proved right once more. The great theorist of Democracy made no great effort to revive the democratic experiment on American soil.[77]

Jefferson had expressed great hopes for the "experiments in government" which America was to offer humanity. But, he said, "the contracted, English, half-lettered ideas of Hamilton, destroyed that hope in the bud."[78] His friend John Taylor added, in the work Jefferson so heartily endorsed, that "A government, a section of it, or a measure, founded in an evil moral principle, such as fraud, ambition, avarice or superstition, must produce correspondent effects, and defeat the end of government..."[79] Jefferson, however, did not commit himself as definitely as Taylor. He claimed that "we shall not live to see the result" of the experiment. "The grosser absurdities, such as hereditary magistracies, we shall see exploded in our day, long experience having already pronounced condemnation against them. But what is to be the substitute? This our children grandchildren will answer."[80] He did not display the perception of his political opponent John Adams, who had warned "We do possess one material which actually constitutes an aristocracy that governs the nation. That material is wealth."[81] Perhaps, by saying that his "grandchildren will answer," Jefferson was suggesting that "it would be precipitate to detect and destroy the aristocracy of paper and patronage, in less time than was requisite to detect and destroy those of superstition and the feudal syetem."[82] In any case, it would have been difficult for Jefferson to take the position that America's democratic ideals had been betrayed, for then he would have had to confront his own statements in the Declaration of Independence, "that, whenever any form of government becomes destructive of these ends, it is the right of the people to alter or abolish it, and to institute a new government, laying its foundation on such principles, and organizing its powers in such form, as to them shall seem most likely to effect their safety and happiness."

3. GROWTH OF CAPITALISM

Perhaps the democratic dream was unrealizable. Perhaps it was inevitable that one or another group would turn the hopes of men into a new façade behind which the naked search for wealth and power would continue. Perhaps the faith in man's educability, in man's capacity to grasp and solve political problems intelligently in concert with other men, was unfounded. Perhaps democracy could only be practiced, as Aristotle had claimed so long ago, in small communities of a few thousand inhabitants at most. The eighteenth century revolutionaries did not know whether or not their dream was possible. That was the point of the "experiment." They asked for the indulgence and good will of spirited men for a grand collective effort to create Democracy. The task would be difficult and might take generations. Men everywhere waited anxiously for the results of the experiment. But the experiment never took place. The democratic dream became the rhetoric of a new aristocracy. The ideal which was to give suggestion and encouragement to men groping for a just society was housed in a glass cage and used by the Lawyers of an unjust society to defend injustice. The democratic experiment that was to be carried out through the concentrated effort of many generations was never even started, and in time it was forgotten by men who claimed "democracy" had been fully established in 1776, before it had ever begun. The blueprint of the palace was housed in a slum, and the slum-builders pointed proudly to the blueprint they had not made, nor even studied, while their hovel continued to deteriorate.

The system that emerged after the American revolution was not democracy, but capitalism. The privileged may wish to speak of America as a "Hamiltonian Democracy," as a "democracy of the rich and well born." Such a usage of language is one of the many privileges they derive from the American system. For the "rich and well born," "freedom" is always synonymous with privilege. But since the "freedom" of the rich involves the abuse of the majority of men, the majority of men cannot long be content to accept the definitions of the rich; they cannot forever call their abuse "freedom." Nor can the rich depend eternally on the poor to "check the imprudence of democracy."

Yet the Hamiltonian community of "the few and the many" where "the first are the rich and well born, the other the mass of the people," has maintained itself with tremendous success on the American continent. On the basis of the staying power of American capitalism, it could almost be argued that capitalism was the "progressive" force in the eighteenth century, whereas the democratic ideals were "reactionary." And it has, in fact, been argued that the democrats were looking towards the Golden Age of the past, whereas capitalists were moving towards the future. It has, in fact, even been argued that capitalism has not yet been overthrown because it is "consistent" with "human nature." If such an argument means that capitalism in any way fulfills the potentialities of human beings, it is absurd, since the capitalist society converts a minority of human beings into counting machines and the majority into mindless work animals. But if the argument means that "human nature" is able to put up with capitalism, it is obviously true. In some parts of the world, notably in Western Europe, human beings have put up with capitalism for centuries. But for this there's no need to invoke "human nature"; "human endurance" would serve as well.

The argument that capitalism was more "progressive" than any other social movement in post-feudal Western Europe has been endlessly repeated by writers on the Left, Right, and Center, ever since Karl Marx expounded it with all but irrefutable logic. Marx obviously meant something radically different than did the apologists for capitalism, but he did hold that, under the conditions of the time, capitalism was the only system consistent with the new means of production. It will be contended here, although by no means "scientifically," that the social and legal relations of capitalism preceded the technological means of production; that capitalist institutions were nothing more than streamlined versions of feudal privilege; that capitalist institutions were neither suited nor unsuited to the technological economy, but were imposed on it by force and fraud. It has also been held that every major change in knowledge, technology, or social organization constitutes "progress." But surely if such a change does not lead to the ennoblement and completion of human beings, it cannot constitute "progress." Something that leads to human degradation cannot be called "progressive." (It would be absurd to speak of atomic physics or Freudian psychology as "progressive," or as in any way constituting "progress." The outstanding effects of both have been to annihilate human beings, the one physically, the other psychologically. The notion of "progress toward human degradation and annihilation" serves the purposes of nihilism, not of human life.)

When Don Quixote de la Mancha described the age when "No man, to gain his common sustenance, needed to make any greater effort than to reach up his hand and pluck it from the strong oaks, which literally invited him to taste their sweet and savoury fruit," he was no doubt making idyllic an age long past, and he was neglecting to mention that the men who ate the food of oak trees were at the mercy of storms and cold, and spent their time fleeing from animals. But the socially conscious Don Quixote did not invoke the Golden Age merely because he wanted to review his historical scholarship. He invoked the picture of paradise because his own age was befouled with "fraud, deceit ... malice"; because in his own time "those two words *thine* and *mine*" defined the potentialities of a person's life; because in the feudal society all things were not "held in common." Don Quixote's invocation of the Golden Age is not a reminiscence about mankind's childhood; it is a sharp critique of the two props of feudalism: privilege and property.

Nor did Thomas More design his Utopia as a picture of the Christian afterlife. More was quite explicit about his frame of reference: "wheresoever possessions be private, where money beareth all the stroke, it is hard and almost impossible that there the weal public may justly be governed and prosperously flourish." Don Quixote and Thomas More did draw their model from a mythological past. But they did not draw it merely for its esthetic quality. They showed men glowing pictures of Utopia thereby to undermine a system which gave a monopoly of wealth and power to the few, and made the rest of mankind servants. The feudal aristocracy and the Church maintained their positions because they had a monopoly of the means of violence, education, and communication, not because they were especially "suited" to the agrarian economy. The researches of anthropologists have turned up many agrarian societies where the institutions of privilege and property, knight and serf, are unknown.

Gerrard Winstanley and the Diggers did not confine their activities to writing books about Utopia, and consequently cannot be accused of addressing themselves to a literary mirage. The Diggers actually tried to carry out their experiment by cultivating common land, and giving the produce to the poor. They were going to demonstrate through action that "the earth is free for every son and daughter of mankind to live free upon." And it was not the new means of production that put an end to their experiment. If technology had been available to them—if they'd had tractors and chemical plants and all the other means made available to man in succeeding centuries—their experiment would have been so much more effective, especially if other men had followed their fine example. England would then truly have become a "common treasury" instead of the hothouse of factories and slums it became in the nineteenth century. It was not the means of production that put an end to the Diggers' experiment. The historian Sabine has described what happened when a few men in seventeenth century England tilled some land in common. "This action caused a flurry among the landlords concerned but it had no lasting effects. The Diggers, who probably numbered only a few score, kept their experiment going for a year but they were finally dispersed by legal harassment and mob-violence."[1] The Diggers' spokesman Winstanley was lucidly aware that it was not the means of production, but the social institutions and legal structure of England that transformed this pioneering venture into a historical oddity, for he later wrote: "The poor people whom thou oppress shall be the saviours of the land.... If thou wilt find mercy ... disown this oppressing ... thievery of buying and selling of land, owning of landlords, and paying of rents, and give your free consent to make the earth a common treasury."[2] It was not the unprogressive character of their experiment, but the "thievery of buying and selling," that put an end to the Diggers.

When German peasants demanded a more humane dispensation than the misery entailed in supporting feudal privilege, Martin Luther was quite explicit about the agents and institutions that made short shrift of the peasants' attempts to create a humane and just society. According to Luther:

> The princes of this world are gods, the common people are Satan, through whom God sometimes does what at other times he does directly through Satan, that is, makes rebellion as a punishment for the people's sins.
> I would rather suffer a prince doing wrong than a people doing right.
> There are no better works than to obey and serve all those who are set over us as superiors. For this reason also disobedience is a greater sin than murder, unchastity, theft, and dishonesty, and all that these may include.[3]

In 1776, an entire nation, not just a small group of "diggers," broke out in revolt against privilege and proclaimed that "all men are created equal" and that all men are endowed with the "unalienable rights" of "life, liberty, and the pursuit of happiness." And the workshop for this unprecedented experiment was to be, not a plot of unenclosed common land, but an entire continent. The democratic experiment failed. Capitalism developed in America. And for its failure, apologists for capitalism have claimed that the democratic ideal could not have succeeded, because it was incompatible with the technological economy developing at that time. Those who gloat over the betrayal of democracy level at this untried experiment the same nasty epitaph: "unprogressive" and "unsuited" to the age of machines. I will try briefly to argue that it was not the machines, but the institutions of private property and privilege, institutions far older than technology, that betrayed the democratic experiment.

According to Jefferson, "An industrious farmer occupies a more dignified place in the scale of beings ... than a lazy lounger, valuing himself on his family, too proud to work, and drawing out a miserable existence by eating on that surplus of other men's labor, which is the sacred fund of the helpless poor."[4] And in America, he said, "We have now lands enough to employ an infinite number of people in their cultivation. Cultivators of the earth are the most valuable citizens." John Taylor wrote, "The laws ... for dividing lands diminish the evils of a landed monopoly,"[5] and Jefferson added that one of the central functions of democratic government would be the "restriction of monopolies."[6] Both Jefferson and Taylor were highly ambiguous in their pronouncements about the division of property among the men who work it, since neither was very eager to see his own estate divided among his laborers—at least not in his own lifetime. But whatever their personal misgivings, both of these spokesmen for the democratic wing of the American revolution envisaged the United States as a society of ongoing agrarian reform. And they were lucidly unambiguous in their condemnation of monopoly in the form of a monied aristocracy: "... money is a vehicle for ... conveying the most oppressive usurpations, and possesses a complete capacity for re-enslaving nations indirectly, after an accession of knowledge or a division of property, has liberated them from the direct feudal slavery.... An artificial currency is subject to no ... check, and possesses an unlimited power of enslaving nations, if slavery consists an binding a great number to labour for a few. Employed, not for the useful purpose of exchanging, but for the fraudulent purpose of transferring property, currency is converted into a thief and a traitor, and begets, like an abuse of many other good things, misery instead of happiness."[7]

Jefferson was opposed to manufacturing of the type he saw spreading in England: he was disgusted by the sweat shops, the mindlessness of the work, the unemployment, the degradation of human beings converted into "hands," the slums in which the people who did the work were forced to live. But was Jefferson "unprogressive" for being disgusted? Was it not rather capitalism, which so degraded human beings and served no human purpose but to enlarge the wealth of wealthy men, that was "unprogressive"?

The American revolutionary program of maintaining a nation of small farmers, of giving land to the tillers, of abolishing the system of creditors and debtors, and thus of making it possible for every human being to have consideration, voice, and control in the affairs of society—such a program was no more "unprogressive" in the eighteenth than it is in the twentieth century. Even today, feudal and capitalist landlords fear democratic agrarian reform, not because it harks to the past, but precisely because it is still today a radical program.

The means of production were no less favorable to such a program in the eighteenth century than today. If Americans had not betrayed the origins of their rebellion, if they had truly created an equalitarian society by expropriating landlords and abolishing the system of creditors and debtors, they a would have undertaken a social experiment that was not to be tried again on such a scale until the twentieth century. The rise and growth of technology would have facilitated, not obstructed, the further development of this program. Machines are indifferent instruments. Their use depends on human beings. There's nothing about a machine that makes it particularly "suited" to private ownership. In a region where the land is divided among the tillers, machinery would surely have been used in a humane manner. The farmers would have pooled their resources to acquire machinery which none could afford individually. They would, perhaps, have formed farmers' cooperatives and taken turns in the use of machinery which is most useful over large areas and useless on small plots. Their concern would surely have been to make the machinery serve their own needs, rather than enslaving themselves to fulfill a landlord's greed. They would surely have sought to decrease drudgery and increase their own development as human beings. Within such a context, marvelous uses might have been made of all the technological and scientific discoveries, all the land and resources, which became available to Americans in succeeding decades. Science and technology would then have been truly "progressive" forces, as they would have served to ennoble, not to debase, human beings.

Technology need not have served the greed of capitalists; it could just as well have served the ends of all human beings from its very beginnings. It was not technology that demanded the continuation of privilege and property: rather the institutions of privilege and property made the technological means of production serve their own inhuman ends. As Babeuf argued, "In a society which was really sound, there would be neither poor nor rich. There would be no such systems of property as ours. Our laws of heredity and inalienability are 'humanicide' institutions. The monopoly of the land by individuals, their possession of its produce in excess of their wants, is nothing more nor less than theft; and all our civil institutions, our ordinary business transactions, are the deeds of a perpetual brigandage, authorized by barbarous laws."[8] It was not the shortcomings of the democratic ideal, but the coup d'etat of security-holding capitalists, that put an end to the possibility of cooperative, democratic, self governing communities on the American continent.

▲▲▲

Capitalism did not develop because it was more "progressive" than other methods of social organization; its success is due largely to its very adept use of fraud and deception. Its use of fraud was similar to the deceptions of previous aristocracies, and its shrieks have not substantially changed since John Taylor described them in 1803, after Capitalism's victory in America: "Whenever the intricate structure of the system of paper and patronage is attempted to be dissected, we moderns surrender our intellects to the yells uttered by the living monster, similar to those with which its predecessors astonished, deluded, and oppressed the world for three thousand years. The aristocracy of superstition defended itself by claiming, the Gods! the temples! the sacred oracles! divine vengeance! And Elysian fields!—and that of paper and patronage exclaims, national faith! sacred charters! disorganization! and security of property!"[9] Once capitalism is in power, it quickly consolidates to itself a monopoly of the means of violence, and henceforth maintains itself as the government through the use and the threat of violence. "If wealth is accumulated in the hands of a few, either by a feudal or a stock monopoly, it carries the power also; and a government becomes as certainly aristocratical, by a monopoly of wealth, as by monopoly of arms. A minority, obtaining a majority of wealth or arms in any mode, becomes the government."[10] In the Constitution, the capitalists drew themselves an instrument which would be used for the protection and augmentation of the property of the rich, as well as for the creation and maintenance of an army, navy, and militia subservient to the central government. Taylor said, "The only two modes extant of enslaving nations, are those of armies and the system of paper and patronage."[11] Availing themselves of both, the capitalists ruled out all opposition; it was then that all other possibilities of social organization became far more difficult than they had been before. Once capitalism became "the way of life" of a region, it not only consolidated the means of violence, of communication, and of production; it also converted the rest of humanity in that region into means for the maintenance and growth of private wealth. The institutions and principles of the old aristocracy were turned into more efficient means of lodging society's wealth into the hands of the few. The morality of the old order was modified to suit the unprecedented accumulation of private wealth; parts of the old morality were even discarded or reversed if they clashed too obviously with the practices of the acquisitive society. "Observe what happened to the seven deadly sins of Christian theology," wrote Lewis Mumford. "All but one of these sins, sloth, were transformed into positive virtues. Greed, avarice, envy, gluttony, luxury and pride were the driving forces of the new economy: if once they were mainly vices of the rich, they now under the doctrine of expanding wants embraced every class in society. Thus unbounded power was harnessed to equally unbounded appetites."[12] Not Don Quixote or St. Thomas More, but Malvolio and Benjamin Franklin became the heroes of the age. The transvaluation of values followed close on the heels of the transplantation of dominant human types. Greed was seen as Industry, avarice as Thrift, and envy as Competition. Gluttony was called Ambition and luxury Consumption. Pride was named Respectability—and even Dignity.

Eventually, when philosophy, law and police were recruited to run the race of the new Bourgeoisie, the taking of land from those who work it became an "inviolable natural right." The new machines and factories, the regimentation and standardization, enabled men to produce increasing amounts of food and other material goods. But the majority of men, those who produced ever more, never saw an increase. The new wealth "circulated" back to the wealthy, those who owned the machines and factories. This arrangement came to be called "free enterprise." In time the rich no longer worked; they created an institution where their money "worked." This bizarre institution became "Finance."

Originally, money had been merely a convenient means of exchange. It was easier to "buy" butter in exchange for a standardized metal than it was to trade pigs for chickens and then agree on the number of chickens that would fetch the butter. The metal made a set price possible and also simplified the bookkeeping of bureaucrats. But capitalism revealed a new trait of money—it revealed that money could be abstracted from the exchange of goods, could be treated as a separate entity, and could be accumulated with no reference to the needs of the accumulator. It was found that a man can buy food cheaply from a farmer and sell it expensively to a rich man. He can repeat the process and put the difference in his pocket. In this way, the man who neither produces nor consumes the food becomes quickly rich from it. He can soon buy out the farmer's other customers and become the only buyer, and in this not-very-subtle manner can convert an independent farmer into a hired servant, a "tenant." After Hamilton's introduction of the Bank into the United States, John Taylor had clearly seen the potentialities of money in the hands of capitalists. "An artificial currency is subject to no ... check, and possesses an unlimited power of enslaving nations, if slavery consists in binding a great number to labour for a few. Employed, not for the exchanging, but for the fraudulent one of transferring property, currency is converted into a thief and a traitor, and begets, like an abuse of many other good things, misery instead of happiness.

"Mankind soon discovered that money was easily converted into a medium for oppression as well as for commerce, and hence arose nearly as strong a dislike to heavy taxes in money as in kind; it being clearly seen that labour and property were transferred by money. This plain truth, awakened the exertions of avarice and ambition, to deceive the vigilance of labour and industry: the objects of pillage. The first intricacy with which they endeavoured to hide their design, was woven of indirect taxes travelling in mazes; the second, of loaning obscured by the mist of futurity; and the third, of an artificial currency or banking, complicated by the crookedness of its operation, flattering to industry, and restrained by no natural check, as a medium of fraud and tyranny."[13] Even a few medieval churchmen had seen this process taking place and had wanted to stop it. But the Organized Church needed the rich men to support its plunder and extravagance, and so the process grew like a cancer until the Church itself was thrown off the land.

When machinery came into existence, the process of producing money was highly refined. A man with money built a factory. He hired many men to produce "goods." He then sold the goods, not on the basis of how much they cost to produce, but on the basis of how much people would pay for them. And then he paid his workers, not according to the price the goods fetched on the market, but the bare minimum which would keep the workers alive. Thus there was a large surplus at both ends: from overcharging the customers and underpaying the workers, so to speak. The surplus was used to increase and improve the machinery, so that a worker could produce, in the same period of time, three or fifteen times as much as he produced before. But the worker wasn't paid three or fifteen times as much. His share was still no more than the minimum that kept him alive and chained to "his" factory. The increasing wealth kept returning to the same men. Men who did not produce became wealthier from production than men had ever been before. This was only possible in a society where money had become the most important characteristic of human beings, a society where money "talks" and money "works."

The cycle of capitalist production is so outlandish that future historians will undoubtedly be hard-put to explain how men could have been made to accept it for such a long time. The whole process consists of society's permitting a few men to gather for themselves what belongs to all mankind. This gathering is the only point of all the bother, all the seriousness, all the Bourgeois Morality. The factory owner accumulates profits. He puts the profits into the expansion of his factory. The factory then produces more. The capitalist sells more. Then he has even more profits. So he again expands his factory. Production is for profit, and profit for more production. This cycle, meaningless in the middle and at both ends, is not only taken seriously by the man engaged in it: he takes this to be the meaning and essence of life. The counting of money is life's reward, the accumulation of money is life's main task. According to Benjamin Franklin, inventor, politician, and Philosopher of Avarice, "The more there is of it, the more it produces at every turn, and profits rise quicker and quicker." Franklin's poetry of money suggests that he derived greater spiritual and sensual satisfaction from profit-making than from love or adventure or any other human pursuit.

Benjamin Franklin was the direct descendant of Malvolio, in real life. When Malvolio was asked, "Dost thou think, because thou art virtuous, there shall be no more cakes and ale?" he was unable to answer. Ben Franklin answered unequivocally a century and a half later: "there shall be no more cakes and ale." The only Virtue is the constant accumulation of money. The primary goal of life is to make the "profits rise quicker and quicker." Everything else is secondary. A rich man not engaged in raising profits comes to be called a "diletante." A poor man not engaged in raising the profits of the rich becomes a "vagrant" and later on a "bohemian." Quantity, Calculation and Measurement become the only legitimate aspects of life. The new men of money soon came to dislike philosophy and hate metaphysics, because philosophers kept asking for the human purpose of all the quantity, calculation, and measurement, and metaphysicians kept suggesting that human life had other qualities and potentialities besides these. Since capitalism had neither aim nor life, capitalists were very uneasy in the presence of men who discussed the aim of life. Since they did not themselves discuss, they solved the problem in the only way that businessmen ever solve problems: with money. They subsidized the universities. This gesture accomplished many purposes with one stroke: it gave capitalists the illusion that they were humanitarian patrons of learning; it quickly put philosophers on the "right" track; and it put an abrupt end to metaphysics. The gesture worked most effectively in England. There a School of philosophers who called themselves "empiricists" developed. This School invented and embellished a doctrine whereby only that which can be measured and calculated is "real"; everything else is "secondary." The doctrine attained its clearest exposition in the writings of David Hume. In the restrictive boundaries of this doctrine, ideals and goals, feelings and colors, became the "secondary qualities" of human experience. Since businessmen have a monopoly on measurement and calculation, that being their only concern, then businessmen become the most important members of the human community. And since measureable and calculative activity is the "primary quality" of life, then everything businessmen do is good. Although Hume did himself develop these implications of his doctrine, his followers, Jeremy Bentham and James Mill, did. These two prophets of production, even more humorless than their fictional ancestor Malvolio, held that business is not only society's most important activity, but that all business activity is done for "the greatest good of the greatest number." The proof of this "empirical" claim was derived, not from consulting the greatest number, but from consulting the assumptions of Hume's doctrine.

When the breeding of money became the main preoccupation of an entire society, all other human activities were forced into the same narrow channel, and in time the practitioners and professors of other activities fell in line. Literature, which until the advent of capitalism had been man's primary means of communicating intellectual and emotional experience, became for the businessmen a trivial pastime. The only function of literature was to provide "entertainment" for tired men of business after they were done with the day's counting. Although literacy rose, the books of great writers had diminishing audiences until they were read exclusively by the "bohemians" and the "misfits" of capitalism. Meanwhile, a new crop of "writers" appeared on the literary scene, a group of men who would "produce" literature to fill the businessmen's needs. These literary capitalists "produced" novels, poems, and plays, the same way businessmen produced commodities. And the purpose of the entertainment-commodities was the same as the purpose of all business activity: to fetch profit. Where businessmen thoroughly infiltrated the educational field, as in the United States and Nazi Germany, children were pushed through an "educational system" on a fare made up almost exclusively of entertainment-commodities and propaganda-goods. Art, which before capitalism had been an exploration of the dimensions of reality in visual terms, became so thoroughly degraded by the men blinded by profits, that even serious artists lost their vitality. When the instruments of painters came to be used for the advertisement of commodities, an irreparable death-blow was dealt to Western art. The history of European art since the Renaissance is the tragic story of a brilliant beginning followed by a ruthlessly unbroken deterioration. The painters' open or tacit protest against the capitalist debauchery of visual reality has been carried so far that the twentieth century American painters splashing grotesque footnotes on to the nihilistic DADA have attained creative freedom only by passing into lunacy.

Along with the degradation of creative activity came the glorification of business activity. The very impersonality of the process of production gave the men of money an illusion of its spirituality. In order to produce ever increasing amounts of profit, the early businessman had to be frugal in his spending habits: "the more there is of it, the more it produces at every turn…" Comparing his own miserliness and self-repression with the debauchery and extravagance of the aristocracy, the businessman thought of himself as almost a saint, and his later admirers called him "ascetic." However, asceticism refers to a concern with intellectual or spiritual as opposed to material interests, whereas the businessman's exclusive concern with wealth and its accumulation is the epitome of self-indulgence. The mistaken notion of a businessman's "asceticism" grew up because there was a purely external similarity between the habits of early profit-makers and those of some ascetics, although the content of the habits had no similarity whatever. The businessman was thought "ascetic" because he devoted the same single-mindedness to the pursuit of wealth as an artist devoted to the creation of a work of art. He was thought "ascetic" because he disciplined and regimented himself as much as a monk whose life was "as regular as clockwork." He was even thought "ascetic" because his boundless greed enabled him to visualize a great accumulation of wealth as enthusiastically as a prophet visualizes an ideal. The illusion of a businessman's "asceticism" can only be maintained if one omits mentioning that all these admirable virtues of devotion, self-discipline, and vision, were put at the service of a very crude and sensual goal: the accumulation of wealth and privilege.

Between Malvolio and Rockefeller stands Daniel Defoe, author of *Robinson Crusoe* and prophet of the Profitable Life. A favorite theme of Defoe's "practical" writings was The Great Law of Subordination. Everyone in society must know his "place" in relation to the society's masters, the men of business. Conjugal Harmony, the prime requisite of a businessman's ordered life, defines the master-slave relationship as it applies to husband and wife: the husband commands, the wife obeys. The wife must know that she is no more than her husband's private property. In the early days of capitalism, when there were still "women of blood" in Western society, businessmen often paid generous sums for wives with impressive pedigrees. The Great Law of Subordination also decrees that the son's activity shall consist exclusively of obedience, until his apprenticeship is over and he, in turn, exacts obedience. And, needless to say, obedience constitutes the morality of servants, tenants, workers.... Obedience and subordination, the morality of slaves, became the virtues of the entire working population. The feudal relations of noble over serf, Church over Sheep, became even further rigidified. Father-son, husband-wife, employer-worker, master-servant: these are the relations of the new society. Since the same man, the father-husband-employer-master, is the top half of every relation, this arrangement is for him the New Freedom. As President John Adams had said, "wealth is the great machine for governing the world."[14] However, from the late eighteenth century on, revolutionary democrats challenged this relationship, and the businessmen became deathly afraid. They heard Gracchus Babuef's cry, "Our butchers have taught us bad manners," and they trembled. They had so thoroughly inculcated a whole society with the master-slave morality that they feared a social uprising would turn the tables and new masters would practice the Great Law of Subordination with former businessmen as servants.

Defoe's Robinson Crusoe was stranded on an island. He was a very practical man. He converted the island into a world made up exclusively of economic activity—a world mastered and managed by one Complete English Tradesman. He converted a "wild man" into a servant, into His Man Friday, into a subordinate who understood obedience. Robinson Crusoe converted nature's order, which to him meant chaos, into the drab economic order of the English Tradesman. Robinson Crusoe had a big desire to dominate and a small imagination. He became the hero of the business class.

Each capitalist wants his own island—his own closed world where he has a monopoly of wealth and power. Direct intellectual domination did not, until very recently, interest capitalists, because the realm of ideas does not yield economic profits. It was the desire for a monopoly of economic activity that provided the "drive" of capitalism. C. Wright Mills has described the manner in which the Robinson Crusoes of America, the Exemplars of Our Way of Life, consolidated their economic empires. "The robber barons, as the tycoons of the post-Civil-War era came to be called, descended upon the investing public much as a swarm of women might descend into a bargain basement on Saturday morning. They exploited national resources, waged economic wars among themselves, entered into combinations, made private capital out of the public domain, and used any and every method to achieve their ends. They made agreements with railroads for rebates; they purchased newspapers and bought editors; they killed off competing and independent businesses, and employed lawyers of skill and statesmen of repute to sustain their rights and secure their privileges. There *is* something demonic about these lords of creation; it is not merely rhetoric to call them robber barons. Perhaps there is no straightforward economic way to accumulate $100 million for private use; although, of course, along the way the unstraightforward ways can be delegated and the appropriator's hands kept clean. If all the big money is not easy money, all the easy money that is safe is big. It is better, so the image runs, to take one dime from each of ten million people at the point of a corporation than $100,000 from each of ten banks at the point of a gun. It is also safer."[15] This was called "Free Competition." Big fish eat little fish, except that in the sea the big fish die while little fish multiply very rapidly, whereas in America the big fish become consolidated into immortal corporations while the little fish are forever exterminated.

In the late nineteenth century, the English philosopher Herbert Spencer erroneously read into Darwin's biological theories a justification of tycoons. Besides his theory of evolution, Darwin had also developed a theory of natural selection which tried to explain the survival and extinction of species on the basis of their ability to cope with their environment, that is, their "fitness." Since proof is hard to come by in these matters, the theory remains till today a metaphysical assertion, a plausible guess. As a guess, it is one among many. Darwin's contemporary, Prince Peter Kropotkin, argued that species survive because they cooperate, and more recently Immanuel Velikovsky has argued that "fit" as well as "unfit" species are extinguished by natural catastrophe, not natural selection. In any case, Herbert Spencer constructed an erudite Moral Science out of Darwin's biological guess. For Spencer, Darwin had "proved" that the struggle for existence, natural selection, and the survival of the fittest, were the very essence of life. The most bloodthirsty animals, the most ruthless thieves and murderers, the Rockefellers, Carnegies, Rhodeses and Leopolds, win the struggle for existence. The role of creative intellect and imagination in the building of human culture was easily forgotten in an age when big capitalists were despoiling every countryside with ugly monuments of their ruthless lust for power. Men filled with the light of Spencer's doctrine failed to observe that dogs rarely eat dogs, or monkeys, monkeys; they failed to notice that not one animal destroys members of its own species the way capitalists destroyed other men.

As competition fulfills its purpose, the "fittest" do away with all competitors and attain a monopoly on one activity after another. As each corporation consolidates all phases of a certain activity, it ceases to waste its profits ruining its peers and turns its competitive machinery against the rest of society. When the capitalist attains his dream and becomes the master and sole supplier of his "island," he starts to "compete" against his own workers and against the consumers of his products. The vast mechanical and psychological machinery of the commercial society is then turned to the dehumanization of workers and the manipulation of consumers.

The capitalist corporation is a private corporation. Its only function is to increase the wealth of the rich men who own it. It is run by managers who are hired to see to it that the rich profit. The things produced are irrelevant so long as they are profitable. That is, things are not produced to benefit the people who buy them, but to profit the corporation owners. Useful things are produced if, and only if, they are profitable. Since the manager is hired to maximize the profits of his employers, he is not interested in the quality or human value of a product, but only in its profitability. He often finds that useless products of poor quality can be much more profitable, if properly advertised, than useful products of high quality. It is not that the manager is a "bad man;" it just is not his "job" to make useful products of high quality—not so long as the system of private profit survives among men. If profitability is the measure of men and things, then the vast resources and energy that could be used for human growth and development will be "invested" in advertising-men, salesmen, public relations men, and weapon making men.

The capitalist who doesn't catch on to the fact that advertisements bring bigger profits than quality, who remains under the illusion that people will buy things so long as they are well made—if such a capitalist goes on "investing" in quality instead of public relations, he will quickly fall down the tube of Failure, he will lose the struggle for survival and become extinct.

Those who "survive" are those who can buy the best systems of advertisement, public relations, and salesmanship—those who can effectively peddle the Big Lies, pressure customers into buying what they do not want, and manipulate human beings into desiring what they do not need. The vast system of organized manipulation of human beings, where all means justify the end of big profits, is the "natural selection" by which the holders of the capitalist society maintain their dominion.

———

The squid ... was considered the rightful prey of the lobster; and the latter had no other food offered him. The lobster lay at the bottom of the clear glass tank on the yellow sand, apparently seeing nothing—you could not tell in which way his beady, black buttons of eyes were looking—but apparently they were never off the body of the squid.... The [lobster], as young Cowperwood was one day a witness, would leap like a catapult to where the squid was apparently idly dreaming, and the squid, very alert, would dart away, shooting out at the same time a cloud of ink, behind which it would disappear. It was not always completely successful, however. Some small portions of its body or its tail were frequently left in the claws of the monster below. Days passed, and, now fascinated by the drama, young Cowperwood came daily....

He returned one night, and lo! to his grief and astonishment, his wish was granted. There was a little crowd around the tank. The lobster was in the corner. Before him was the squid cut in two and partially devoured.

"That's the way it has to be, I guess," he commented to himself. "That squid wasn't quick enough. He didn't have anything to feed on." He figured it out. The squid couldn't kill the lobster—he had no weapon. The lobster could kill the squid—he was heavily armed. There was nothing for the squid to feed on; the lobster had the squid as prey. What was the result to be? What else could it be?[16]

Watching the lobster destroy the squid was the central experience of Theodore Dreiser's Financier, Frank Cowperwood. Edward Hyams has rendered such an experience as an epigram: "Capitalism turns men into economic cannibals and, having done so, mistakes economic cannibalism for human nature."[17] And J. R. Walsh has given a historical summary of the same event. "By 1905, the Morgans had organized U.S. Steel, General Electric, International Harvester, and other giants. The Rockefellers had assembled Standard Oil. The Mellons had built aluminum, the DuPonts chemicals. Centralized control of insurance and banks had been achieved. By the panic of 1907, the competitive market of the nineteenth century had gone in finance and in many sectors of industry. World War I accelerated this trend....

"Under Mellon, Hoover, Harding, Coolidge, the broad regulatory powers of the federal government became in effect police powers of private monopoly."[18]

Dreiser's episode treated bankers as lobsters. We may consider corporations as octopi. After the squid is "cut in two and partially devoured," the octopus, a larger relative of the squid, enters the tank and starts to tease and train the lobster. Before long, the powerful tentacles of the octopus gain mastery of the fish tank, and the humiliated lobster functions as nothing more than a trouble-shooter for Octoporate interests.* Since Dreiser's fish tank is one among many, and since each fish tank represents a region of the North American continent, the spread of the octopus and the elongation and strengthening of its tentacles is an ominous event for all other forms of life in the region. In the single area of manufacturing, for example, William A. William has described the speed with which the tentacles spread. "By 1899 ... two thirds of all manufactured goods were produced by corporations, and by 1929 the figure was more than nine-tenths. In 1904 the corporations employed seven-tenths of all wage earners in manufacturing, and by 1929 they employed nine-tenths."[19] The vastness of the corporate spread and consolidation has been vividly described from "inside" the tank by the Corporate Lawyer A.A. Berle, Jr. "...in a considerable and growing number of industries (covering at a rough estimate 70 percent of all American industry) a pattern has emerged.... Two or three, or at most, five, corporations will have more than half the business, the remainder being divided among a greater or less number of smaller concerns who must necessarily live within the conditions made for them by the "Big Two" or "Big Three" or "Big Five" as the case may be.... Slightly more than half [of American Industry] is owned outright by not more than 200 corporations."[20]

The Great Depression of 1929 seemed to put an end to the spread of the grasping tentacles. It looked, for a while, as if the Age of Man would replace the Era of the Octopus. Revolution became a respectable word for the second time in American history. In every city of the "world's wealthiest country," grumbling men who had worked all their

---

*"...even at the height of finance capitalism the bankers functioned more as troubleshooters for the corporate system than as outsiders who moved in and took over—or changed—the economic system. It remained a corporate system ...

From the time of the Panic of 1873, which signaled the death of the old individualistic entrepreneur, the corporation was the key institution of the American economic system." William A. Williams, *The Tragedy of American Diplomacy*, p. 105.

lives stood on breadlines. They waited to receive, as "welfare handouts," a minute fraction of the vast material wealth they had created. Humiliated men, who received as a gift what was really their own, quickly lost faith in the American Way. In a brief moment of lucidity they realized they were still at the "far side of Paradise."

In 1932, one year before Hitler started his transformation of Germany into one vast weapon-manufacturing corporation, Franklin Delano Roosevelt was elected President of the United States. Owing his fortune and his fame to the American institutions of private wealth and hereditary privilege, Roosevelt did not look with favor at the prospect of a social revolution which would abolish private wealth and privilege. Being a humanitarian, he did not admire the Nazi or Fascist "solutions" to capitalist economic instability by means of brutal repression and a permanent war economy. Being a politician, he chose a middle course: to improve the condition of the working population on mildly socialist lines, and to revive the corporations on mildly fascist lines. In this way be kept away the social revolution and postponed the arrival of an indigenous fascism. Roosevelt stood at a crucial crossroads in American history. Conditions were favorable, the time was ripe, and people were willing, for a sweeping economic change. The system of unrestrained corporate capitalism could no longer function. Roosevelt stood at a watershed—he could have let the corporate system roll on down the road of destruction and demolish itself on a desolate crag without ruining any more human lives; he chose instead to patch the corporate system along familiar lines with a vast scheme of governmental machinery. And to carry on his reconstruction of corporate capitalism, he recruited precisely the bitterest left-wing critics of capitalism. Roosevelt knew that the people who best understood the flaws and absurdities of capitalism were not the rich men who ran and managed it from the inside, but the socialists and communists who watched and recorded its every move from the outside. Thus he knew that the men who could patch and restore the capitalist system as a whole were not the Corporate Boards of Directors who could not see beyond the profit, loss, and their own take, but precisely the radicals who wanted to overthrow the system. And "radicals" were eager recruits to Roosevelt's program of reconstruction. The New Deal was designed to give a new start to a slightly more humanitarian and less blatantly brutal version of the Old Deal. Reforms and welfare measures were institutionalized and labor unions were legalized—which, within the confines of American capitalism, were tremendous achievements. However, Roosevelt's administrations also consolidated and coordinated the vast structure of monopoly capitalism, and encouraged the corporation-men to administrate their own affairs by means of government agencies. When the United States became involved in the Nazi War, and the consequent war economy put a final Nazi-type "patch" on America's still-ailing economy, the corporations recruited unwillingly into Roosevelt's Recovery Program gained wealth and power they could never have reached without Roosevelt's "reforms." It was during the war, while Roosevelt was still alive, that the American economy took the shape of the economies of its Axis enemies, Italy, Germany and Japan. "During the New Deal the corporate chieftains joined the political directorate; as of World War II they have come to dominate it. Long interlocked with government, now they have moved into quite full direction of the economy of the war effort and of the postwar era."[21] Roosevelt had started his presidential career as a prophet of the socialist left. When he died, he left behind an America governed by a corporate directorate and sustained by a permanent war economy—two institutions that define the fascist state. The strangest irony of all, however, is the story of some of Roosevelt's "radicals": they identified intensely with the program of capitalist "recovery"; they grew old and conservative carrying out the program; after the war, they emerged enamoured with America's Capitalist System, even in its semi-fascist form; and, during the great postwar Purge of the 1950s, they viciously turned on, betrayed, and denounced as many of their former comrades as they could still remember. The New Deal not only strengthened the American Right; it almost completely abolished the American Left. And probably the greatest factor in debilitating the Left was the spectacular persecution of radicals by their former friends. This display of the Informers, an exhibition of gross brutality, betrayal and inhumaneness, could not but disillusion one about the moral quality of the men in the American Left. The maliciousness of the betrayers was itself the worst blow dealt against the Left.

The economy that emerged from the New Deal was not a "Welfare State." If workers were paid more wages, it was not because anyone felt that men were entitled to the fruits of their own labor, but because business psychologists found out that workers do more work if they're well-fed and if the factories are clean. The post-New Deal economy was a corporate economy: its function was to "maximize the profits" of the wealthiest men. Even squids—independent small businessmen—were disappearing. In the land with the myth that every "little man" can be a millionaire, there were a million "little men" to every millionaire. Trusts, monopolies, cartels, had been "against the law" and "unconstitutional" for over half a century. But the Justices of the Supreme Court, the land's highest Guardians of Law and Constitution, wore special glasses when reading Anti-Trust legislation. According to Justice Douglas, frequent dissenter from the Court's rulings, "the economic theories which the court has read into the anti-trust laws have favored rather than discouraged monopoly. As a result of the big business philosophy underlying [cases cited], big business has become bigger and bigger. Monopoly has flourished. Cartels have increased their hold on the nation. The trusts are strong. There is less and less place for the independent."[22] Justice Douglas' charge is oddly reminiscent of similar charges made by Madison and Jefferson—charges which assume that the capitalists who drafted the Constitution and the Laws had intended to create, within their own documents, obstacles to their acquisition of wealth. It seems probable that the interpretation Justice Douglas criticises is more historically accurate than his own, and that the American Constitution will legally justify and protect wealth, privilege, and monopoly, until such a time as the American People "abolish it, and, ... institute a new government, laying its foundation on such principles, and organizing its powers in such form, as to them shall seem most likely to effect their safety arid happiness."[23] But if Americans believe in Free Competition, in the Law that the "fittest survive," should they be surprised if only the "fittest" survive? Monopoly was only recently achieved, but monopoly was always the goal of the "Free Competition." Capitalists didn't "compete" to help each other out, but to do away with each other. In a society where men were allowed to compete for the control over human life and destiny, the fact that some men would win overwhelming control was built-in at the very beginning.

Among corporations, the "fittest" are the oil companies. According to Leo Huberman and Paul Sweezy, "there are ten billion-dollar oil companies with assets of $21.1 billion compared to nine billion-dollar companies with assets of $18.7 billion *in all other fields of industry combined.*"[24] Harvey O'Connor has described, in vivid detail, the workings of the Empire of Oil.[25] These gigantic oil companies, known in the industry as "the majors," control every facet that has to do with oil, from drilling it in Arabia to refining it in Texas and selling it at the corner Esso station. Such a monopoly is tremendously profitable to the holders of these corporations. According to O'Connor, "A good bit of argument has raged around the exact source of the industry's profitability. Is it in the production of crude, in the control over pipe lines, in the refineries, or at the gas station? For the integrated company, all four sections seem to be needed to assure over-all profitability. Marketing may be run at a loss but the majors feel that without control over the retail market, profitability will be affected further back in the line. Pipe line profits, while imposing, are merely a bookkeeping affair, for the companies can charge themselves as much or as little as they choose for transporting their own product. Refining is an essential bottleneck of the industry kept out of reach of overweening independents. But the real money, most oil people agree, is in the production of crude, and the rest of the apparatus merely protects that vital source from which all blessings flow. Standard of California, for example, says it costs 88 cents to produce and market a barrel of crude, sold for $2.90.... the industry is in truth monolithic and not merely an assembly of parts and divisions. The fact that consumers can be charged prices far in excess of total costs of production, refining, transport, and marketing is the real source of profit. For those companies with access to cheap foreign crude, the profits become colossal."[26] If the Independent Enterprise, hero of American elementary-school text books, wants to refine oil, he must have a patent. And, "Standard of Jersey is affiliated with no less than ten patent companies; some of the majors team together to control a patent. Most of these are available to the independent refiner, but at a fee which represents another toll he must pay to his competitor for the right to exist."[27] If an Independent Enterprise wants to drill his own oil, he must be able to transport it to a refinery; he must have access to pipe lines. But here again, "Only the majors can build such arteries for the lifeblood of the industry. Even they sometimes pool their interests in construction and operation of lines which cost as much as $50,000 to $100,000 a mile....

"The majors control the great arteries—89 percent by land and 87 percent by sea. By law, the pipe lines are "common carriers" open presumably to anyone who has oil to transport from hither to yon, but little "independent" oil moves in the big lines. In the first place, it is rather pointless, for the price at the other end of the pipe line is just as controlled as the price at the beginning. The independent, if he uses the line, does so at the major's convenience, and it may not be convenient if the capacity is all taken. Or the minimum consignment acceptable may be so large as to exceed the independent's capacity....

"All but a negligible amount of oil, whether crude or refined, must enter the line at some time; as the majors do most of the buying, oil in excess of "market demand" cannot reach the consumer in appreciable quantity."[28]

Nor do the big corporations compete with each other. C. Wright Mills has described their relationship, which is not the relationship of the "free competitive market" but that of the cartelized economy. "The top corporations are not a set of splendidly isolated giants. They have been knit together by explicit associations, within their respective industries and regions and in supra-associations such as the NAM. These associations organize a unity among the managerial elite and other members of the corporate rich. They translate narrow economic powers into industry wide and class-wide powers; and they use these powers, first, on the economic front, for example with reference to labor and its organizations; and, second, on the political front, for example in their large role in the political sphere. And they infuse into the ranks of smaller businessmen the views of big business."[29] If, for example, the oil corporations competed with each other, gasoline would be very cheap in the United States, because the Free Market would be literally flooded with it. But the market isn't flooded. Under the guise of "free competition," there are in fact commissars who control and plan and limit the production of oil. The function of these indigenous American commissars is actually very similar to that of economic planners in the USSR, with the main difference that the theory of Soviet planning is to benefit society as a whole whereas the theory of American planning is to maximize the profits of the corporations. According to O'Connor, "The key position in the edifice of production control is held by the Texas Railroad Commission whose state accounts for nearly half the entire domestic productions This Commission's action on the magic market demand figures, flashed from the Bureau of Mines in Washington each month, sets the pattern for the other oil state commissions ...

"The Commission meets monthly in Austin, its main mission being to set allowables for the ensuing month. Before the Commission are the U.S. Bureau of Mines figures. Around the Commissioners are the representatives of the major corporations who announce their "nominations" for crude for the following month. Company A says it needs so many thousands or hundreds of thousands of barrels of oil, Company B adds its figure, and so on down the line. These figures are totaled and compared with the Bureau of Mines figures. Government agencies, such as the Petroleum Administration for Defense, may also offer their suggestions, particularly in regard to the needs of the military.

"The Commission thereupon decrees the allowables. Fields generally may be put on a 19-day production basis, with east Texas, the major field, cut several days under."[30]

In 1940, the Department of Justice almost took action against the oil corporations. "The Department said that the American Petroleum Institute and the majors were a combination with monopolistic power, dominating each branch of the industry through size, integration, tying clauses, price-fixing, and restriction of production."[31] However, when the United States became involved in the War, the case was postponed, since, as O'Connor points out, "there could not have been a war, much less a victory, if the indicated firms would not cooperate with the government which had indicted them. So the suit was put on the shelf for the duration. In 1946, it was dusted off, but neither Attorney General Tom C. Clark, of Texas, nor his successor, J. Howard McGrath, pressed it, and it died a lackadaisical death in 1951 under circumstances which on other times and other lands might well have excited more curiosity than was shown here."[32] In actual fact, there is not as much government control *of* the corporations as government control *for* the corporations. For example, a field as unprofitable as the development of power from nuclear energy is left for the government to explore with public money. As soon as the sale of nuclear energy becomes a profitable affair, it must be given to "private enterprise," that is, to the corporations. The United States Government, especially after the New Deal, has been a corporate convenience. Compared to the present shape of the American economy, Hamilton's aristocratic regime was almost democratic. Hamilton's program for "the rich and well born" had been designed to benefit all capitalists at the expense of the rest of the nation. But even Hamilton might gasp at the sight of the corporate regime of today, which enriches the wealthiest capitalists at the expense, not only of the entire working population, but of the majority of smaller capitalists as well.

Some of the marvels of distribution resulting from the corporate arrangement of the American "democracy" are truly striking. "At the very top of the mid-century American economy, there are some 120 people who each year receive a million dollars or more. Just below them, another 379 people appropriate between a half a million and a million. Some 1,383 people get from $250,000 to $499,999. And below all these, there is the broader base of 11,490 people who receive from $100,000 to $249,999."[33] And below these, there is the yet broader base of millions of people who receive less than $10,000 a year, sometimes less than $1000. And below even these, there are the people in the colonies, the Good Neighbors, who receive between $300 a year and $50 a year. The bizarre nature of this distribution is hard to grasp. To understand a phenomenon, one must be familiar with it in some way, and in these matters the familiarity of millions of people extends only to the weekly payroll which covers rent, food, gadget-expenses, and little else. Yet as O'Connor points out, Standard Oil of "Jersey's annual revenue of nearly $6 billion is greater than that of the Canadian government, and six times that of its affluent Latin American dependency, Venezuela. Its annual profit of half a billion is greater than the tax revenues of all but handful of states."[34] And "the Temporary National Economic Committee's figures in 1939 showed that 47 percent of the shares were held by the 100 largest shareholders, and that most of these were the descendants of the original Rockefeller and his associates."[35] A vivid passage in C. Wright Mills' *The Power Elite* captures some of the flavor of living under a social system which uses human beings as instruments for the maintenance of privilege.

"The economy of America has been largely incorporated, and within their incorporation the corporate chiefs have captured the technological innovations, accumulated the existing great fortunes as well as much lesser, scattered wealth, and capitalized the future. Within the financial and political boundaries of the corporation, the industrial revolution itself has been concentrated. Corporations command raw materials, and the patents on inventions with which to turn them into finished products. They command the most expensive, and therefore what must be the finest, legal minds in the world, to invent and to refine their defenses and their strategies. They employ man as producer and they make that which he buys as consumer. They clothe him and feed him and invest his money. They make that with which he fights the wars and they finance the ballyhoo of advertisement and the obscurantist bunk of public relations that surround him during the wars and between then.

"Their private decisions, responsibly made in the interests of the feudal-like world of private property and income, determine the size and shape of the national economy, the level of employment, the purchasing power of the consumer, the prices that are advertised, the investments that are channeled. Not 'Wall Street financiers' or bankers, but large owners and executives in their self-financing corporations hold the keys of economic power. Not the politicians of the visible government, but the chief executives who sit in the political directorate, by fact and by proxy, hold the power and the means of defending the privileges of their corporate world. If they do not reign, they do govern at many of the vital points of everyday life in America, and no powers effectively and consistently countervail against them, nor have they as corporate-made men developed any effectively restraining conscience."[36]

Yet never were Free Enterprise, Competition, and Individual Success so greatly celebrated as in the age of corporate capitalism. Men who have never known hardship or struggle sponsor elaborate propaganda about the virtues of competitive enterprise. Images of an automatically adjusting economy made up of small competing capitalists are held up for public admiration by corporation holders who have a monopoly and never compete. Images of the isolated individual abound in the society where even Beats cannot successfully isolate themselves from the corporate world. "The image of success and its individuated psychology are the most lively aspects of popular culture and the greatest diversion from politics. Virtually all the images of popular culture are concerned with individuals, and more, with particular kinds of individuals succeeding by individual ways to individual goals. Fiction and non-fiction, movies and radio—indeed almost every aspect of contemporary mass communication—accentuate individual *success*. Whatever is done is done by individual effort, and if a group is involved, it strings along after the extraordinary leader. There is displayed no upward climb of and by collective action to political goals, but individuals succeeding, by strictly personal efforts in a hostile environment, to personal economic and erotic goals."[37]

But the Individual Enterpriser, the hero of American propaganda, does not in fact exist. The picture of an economy of enterprising businessmen struggling to replace each other to supply the public with the best goods, is a "far-fetched fiction," in the words of the economist Galbraith. "In fact, the present generation of Americans, if it survives, will buy its steel, copper, brass, automobiles, tires, soap, shortening, breakfast food, bacon, cigarettes, whiskey, cash registers and caskets from one or another of the handful of firms that now supply these staples. As a moment's reflection will establish, there hasn't been much change in the firms supplying these products for several decades."[38] Competitive Free Enterprise is the ideology under which monopolies consolidated. The capitalist "competes" only to do away with his competitors: he is interested in maximizing his own profits, not in maintaining competitors. For the corporate rich, "competition" is the useful cover under which a monopoly carries on its activities away from public scrutiny. And the Little Man who has not reached the Top defends "competition" because it is the ideology of his heroes, the corporate rich. But the Little Man does not believe in competition. Mills has recorded an enlightening dialogue with the prototype of free enterprise. "When small businessmen are asked whether they think free competition is, by and large, a good thing, they answer, with authority and vehemence, 'Yes, of course—what do you mean?' If they are then asked, 'Here in this, your town?' still they say, 'Yes,' but now they hesitate a little. Finally: 'How about here in this town in furniture?'—or groceries, whatever the man's line is. Their answers are ... 'Yes, if it's fair competition,' which turns out to mean: 'if it doesn't make me compete.'"[39]

In the society where a handful of billionaires and some hundred millionaires own most of what there is to be owned, the favorite myth says that every poor man can, through his own efforts, become a millionaire. If the myth were true, at least one hundred million hard-working Americans would be millionaires. Yet the myth is believed. Every farmer, worker and bureaucrat cherishes the dream that someday he, too, will populate the upper reaches of the American economy. And Hollywood supplies the furniture and the women that enliven the dream. If their dreams were fulfilled, there would be no upper reaches. If every man shared the facilities and the privileges of the rich, there would be no privileges, and there would be no rich. Yet every farmer, worker and bureaucrat tenaciously defends the myth, finding compensation in the dream for a drab, unprivileged reality.

The institutions within which millions of Americans spend their lives, and the institutions through which a few Americans maintain their wealth and privilege, do not correspond. One exaggerated illustration should make this clear. A wage worker who earns as much as

$100 a day seven days a week will earn a maximum of $36,500 a year. If such a worker had no expenses, saved every single penny, and paid no taxes whatever, it would take him 30 years, seven days a week with no vacations, to accumulate one million dollars. Clearly it is not by "honest labor" nor by "thrift" that a man becomes a millionaire. If such a thing were really possible, the myth that every worker can become a millionaire would not be such a popular American tale. The fact that every farmer's son can become a farmer excites no one. This myth was not born in America. It was known to every society that sanctioned inequality and privilege. In the Middle Ages, farmers loved to hear stories about a Prince who married a farmer's daughter, or about a serf who became Pope. It was precisely the exotic rarity of such an event that accounted for the popularity of the tale. The few instances when such an event took place became folklore: they were held up for public awe, though never for public scrutiny. When Stendhal described the fraud and deceit by which a poor boy "climbed" to the upper reaches of the feudal society, his books were not read. This aspect of the myth did not become popular until after the feudal society had collapsed.

Benjamin Franklin's injunction to work hard and save every penny will not take one very far in the corporate society. Industry and thrift were "virtuous" methods at a time when there were not too many capitalists, nor too much wealth, nor too great a discrepancy between rich and poor, nor too elaborate a legal structure which facilitated a hothouse breeding of wealth. In the world of the corporation, as in the old aristocracy, it is Fortune that pushes one up to the top. Machiavelli's "provision against [Fortune] by dykes and banks" is still erected and maintained only for the rich. Once a man reaches the top, the post is hereditary. The richest oil men are the sons and grandsons of rich oil men. But when a rancher does make a leap into the millions, it is not by thrift, work, talent, or imagination. It is literally by Fortune, by a Gift of the Gods: "If you have oil under your land, you are lucky. You may also be rich. If the deposit is lush and you are a west Texas cattle baron, you will quickly advance to front rating among the parvenus. Hollywood will be your oyster and Cannes your resort.

"So far as you are concerned, the whole thing is quite accidental. You didn't put the oil there, you didn't discover it there, and neither will you take it out. You will merely sign a document, sometimes a lease 88, and manna will fall from the heavens."[40] The wealthiest investment bankers are the sons and grandsons of the wealthiest investment bankers. Yet occasionally an outsider, provided he has a small fortune to begin with, can rise to the top in one lifetime. But not through thrift or labor, "... if you had bought only $9,900 worth of General Motors stock in 1913, and, rather than use your judgment, had gone into a coma—allowing the proceeds to pile up in General Motors—then, in 1953, you would have about $7 million....

"Once you have the million, advantages would accumulate—even for a man in a coma."[41]

The exceptions, the men who reach the top from below, are becoming increasingly rare. The list of names of the very rich is much the same from one decade to the next, and most of the names are followed by Jr. or III, as were formerly the names of kings. But the exceptions do still happen, and the corporate rich see to it that the exceptions continue happening because without them the myth would lose its pretext. As soon as an exception takes place, the public relations and advertising men go to work on it. For it is the men on whom Fortune happened to shed her grace that are held up as the justification of the American Way of Life. The rare men who in one lifetime rose from drudgery to privilege provide a public relations "proof" that every Texan can, by ranching conscientiously, become an oil magnate, that every Lower East Side soap peddler can, by peddling soap imaginatively, become an investment banker. The rancher who may have been on vacation when oil was discovered on his land, the peddler who may have gone into a coma for forty years, suddenly finds that he is a national celebrity. Every aspect of his career is exploited For Immediate Release and public consumption. The very event which demonstrates the near-impossibility for "the backwoods boy" ever to become a corporation owner, the very illustration of the rigid stratification of the American economy and of the gulf which separates those who have from those who don't, is used to justify precisely the reverse.

The myth serves many purposes. It informs the impatient climber that he does, in fact, have a chance, but he must wait for its arrival. It tells millions of workers that they must apply themselves in their work if they, too, want to share the big wealth. And it "proves" that men only rise "on their own efforts" and that organized social "interference" would curb every man's "freedom" to rise. Since no man wants to curb his own freedom to rise, organized social action from the bottom is avoided like a disease, whereas organized action at the top is accepted as necessary to protect every man's "freedom."

Once a man is on top, he is there forever. Privilege, in America, is hereditary. If a man invests a million he gets ten, if he invests 10 million he gets billions. For those already rich, the multiplication of wealth is a never ending process. But the myth of "free enterprise" effectively hides this process from public view. Once the rich are on top and have no competition, they hire the ad men to celebrate "free competition" to make it appear that the rich rose that way. Once Heredity or Chance provide a man with never-ending privileges, he cries that every man must rise through his own efforts. In the American mythology, Private Enterprise is used to justify a state of affairs where only the rich can undertake enterprises; Individuality is made synonymous with privilege and used to condone one individual's thriving at the expense of millions; Laissez Faire is used to ensure that a government controlled by the very rich shall have no external interference or control. Underneath the labels there's a corporate society that thrives on fraud and plunder, maintains itself on war, and promises the final annihilation of mankind.

"…the soldier pampered and petted, the democrat crushed: *Voila la Republique!*"[42]

4. IDEOLOGY AND MANIPULATION

In April, 1961, the State Department told the people of the United States and Ambassador Adlai Stevenson told the United Nations that the Cuban government had "betrayed" the Cuban revolution. This is bizarre. Cuba had carried out a democratic revolution for the first time in the history of the Americas.

Cuba had not only proclaimed, but substantially realized, a program almost identical to the one betrayed in the United States in the 1790s by Hamilton and the security-holding capitalists.[1] One must assume that Ambassador Stevenson, who is widely known as an intellectual, is familiar with history—or at least with American history. Yet in his outburst to the United Nations, he not only displayed ignorance of the rules of the United Nations, which do not allow the type of meddling in the internal affairs of another state that Mr. Stevenson indulged in; he also displayed incredible ignorance (for an "intellectual") of his own country's 170-year old betrayal of its own revolution. Before his Ambassadorial mission, Mr. Stevenson had earned great fame and popularity among American liberals for professing to hold and cherish the equalitarian democratic ideals betrayed in the United States in the 1790s. And yet he called "betrayal" the success of those very ideals; he termed "betrayal" the Cuban victory over the very system that had betrayed the democratic ideal in the United States. Stevenson told the United Nations that "there was great sympathy in the United States for the proclaimed goals of the Cuban revolution when it took place."[2] This is a paradoxical claim. The last time there was official sympathy in the United States for the *realization* of democratic goals was in 1776—and the Cuban revolution had not then taken place. Yet Mr. Stevenson's statement is not an outright lie. Mr. Stevenson is an honorable man. His statement does not say there was sympathy in the United States for the *realization* of the goals of the Cuban revolution; it says there was sympathy for the "proclaimed goals." In this sense, Mr. Stevenson's statement was unchallengably true and is in the best tradition of American rhetoric, which consists of the proclamation of democratic ideals alongside the realization, consolidation, and undisturbed growth of capitalist property, privilege, and power. Democracy is the ideological cover beneath which the aristocracy of the "rich and well born" extends its dominion. And this is what the Cuban revolution betrayed. Cuba did not merely proclaim a democratic ideal, as had been done over and over again everywhere in the Americas; Cuba also proceeded to carry out the democratic goals, and by taking this unprecedented step the Cuban revolution dealt an irreparable blow to the "inter-American system" and the capitalist facade.

The Cuban people understood, from painful experience, that "wheresoever possessions be private, where money beareth all the stroke, it is hard and almost impossible that there the weal public may justly be governed and prosperously flourish."[3] But this understanding was not enough to carry through a revolution; with understanding alone, they would have confined their political activity to the writing of Utopias. They also needed Thomas Münzer's "courage and strength to realize the impossible," because the obstacles arrayed against their success were extraordinary. The handful of United States corporations with vested interests in Cuban land, resources, and men had greater wealth and power than all Cuba. Any one of the corporations could have bought a puppet leader, supplied an army, and invaded Cuba—and a combination of corporations did in fact invade Cuba under the auspices of the United States Central Intelligence Agency. Yet the Cuban people successfully repelled the invaders who tried to accomplish by violence what had been accomplished by fraud after the American revolution. And Cuba went on expropriating the corporate landlords in spite of terrific pressure and violent opposition far greater and bloodier than that which had provoked an earlier French revolution's frantic self-defense by means of a Reign of Terror. Cubans continued to give reality to the "proclaimed goals" of democracy and continued to betray the brutally undemocratic practice of their complacent accusers.

Thus Cuba's betrayal was very serious. Cuba had betrayed every major prop of the capitalist edifice. After United States capitalism had succeeded in consolidating the means of production, education, communication, and violence, it had claimed to possess a monopoly of the democratic ideals as well. Cuba's betrayal consisted, not only of disrupting the monopoly of United States capitalists over Cuban land, food, and human life, but also of disrupting the monopoly United States capitalists claimed over the democratic ideal. By depriving the corporate rich of their profits, their ideology, as well as their ability to regain their lost property and privilege by means of violence, and by exposing in unmistakable terms the relationship between the democratic proclamations and the barbarous practice of the Northern Goliath, the Cuban revolution dealt what is probably the most painful blow felt by American capitalism since its Hamiltonian establishment. The complacency and smugness of American capitalism momentarily wore thin, and the wild beast, feeling caged for the first time, raged with a brutal determination to destroy every living creature on earth before departing.

Perhaps the most ingenious achievement of American capitalists was the manner in which they laid claim over the democratic ideal they had betrayed. The indignant accusations of democrats against the capitalist betrayal of the American people had not yet died down before the capitalists took up the claim that they were themselves "the people." Yet, before the coup d'etat of 1787, the division between democrats and anti-democrats had been quite clear. The aristocratic Hamilton did not think himself a democrat, nor did he claim to be one. Hamilton made no attempt to hide his sympathy for the rich and well born or his contempt for "the mass of the people." Nor did Hamilton consider it necessary to conceal from public scrutiny his view that "Nothing but a permanent body can check the imprudence of democracy." And Jefferson, though he was, as Hamilton said, "as likely as any man I know to temporize … and the probable result of such a temper is the preservation of systems,"[4] nevertheless did not surrender his democratic theory to the system with which he "temporized" in practice. Even as late as 1823, after United States capitalists had enjoyed thirty lucrative years as the New World's ruling class, Jefferson still held that capitalists constituted an aristocracy of privilege, that the new aristocracy, as the old, would govern by means of force, fraud, and the maintenance of ignorance, and that aristocracy was not synonymous with democracy: "…at the formation of our government, many had formed their political opinions on European writings and practices, believing the experience of old countries, and especially of England, abusive as it was, to be a safer guide than mere theory. The doctrines of Europe were, that men in numerous associations cannot be restrained within the limits of order and justice, but by forces physical and moral, wielded over them by authorities independent of their will. Hence their organization of kings, hereditary nobles, and priests. Still further to constrain the brute force of the people, they deem it necessary to keep them down by herd labor, poverty and ignorance, and to take from them, as from bees, so much of their earnings, as that unremitting labor shall be necessary to obtain a sufficient surplus barely to sustain a scanty and miserable life. And these earnings they apply to maintain their privileged orders in splendor and idleness, to fascinate the eyes of the people, and excite in them an humble adoration and submission, as to an order of superior beings."[5] Jefferson's own party, on the other hand, "believed that men, enjoying in ease and security the full fruits of their own industry, enlisted by all their interests on the side of law and order, habituated to think for themselves, and to follow their reason as their guide, would be more easily and safely governed than with minds nourished in error, and vitiated and debased, as in Europe, by ignorance, indigence and oppression. The cherishment of the people then was our principle, the fear and distrust of them, that of the other party."[6]

Nor was there great misunderstanding, in post-revolutionary America, either about the democratic nature of the Constitution or about its popular approval. An opponent of the Constitution's ratification wrote in 1788 a satirical analysis of the type of regime America could expect if the document was ratified: "The legislature have no right to interfere with *private* contracts, and debtors might safely trust to the humanity and clemency of their creditors who will not keep them in gaol all their lives, unless they deserve it ... Men of great property are deeply interested in the welfare of the state; and they are the most competent judges of the form of government, best calculated to preserve their property, and such liberties as it is proper for the common and inferior class of people to enjoy. Men of wealth possess natural and acquired understanding, as they manifest by amassing riches, or by keeping and increasing those they derive from their ancestors, and they are best acquainted with the wants, the wishes, and desires of the people, and they are always ready to relieve them in their private and public stations."[7] Such a popular revolutionary hero as Patrick Henry denounced the Constitution. "I believe it to be a fact that the great body of yeomanry are in decided opposition to it.... You have not solid reality —the hearts and hands of the men who are to be governed;"[8] and he devoted great energy to oppose the Constitution's ratification in Virginia. Henry later acquired an estate, became conservative, and smugly shared the privileges he had earlier denounced. (Ironically, Patrick Henry has lately become the hero of American reactionary groups who employ Henry's revolutionary denunciations of privilege and oppression to justify privilege and oppression. But perhaps the latter-day admirers of Patrick Henry are unfamiliar with their hero's revolutionary youth and admire rather his conservative retirement. It is puzzling that the "patriotic societies" should worship the conservative estate owner, however, since as a smug rich man, Henry made no fiery pronouncements.)

Many were well aware that the Constitution, and the government founded on it, was not a "government of all." Many knew it was untrue that "its powers are delegated by all; it represents all, and acts for all."[9] Even the great John Marshall, the first Chief Justice of the Supreme Court, the first real "expert" on the Constitution, as well as an ardent supporter of the document and its purpose, was well aware that the Constitution had not been universally applauded, supported, or adopted by the American people. He wrote in his *Life of*

Washington "that even after the subject had been discussed for a considerable time, the fate of the constitution could scarcely be conjectured; and so small in many instances, was the majority in its favor, as to afford strong ground for the opinion that, had the influence of character been removed, the intrinsic merits of the instrument would not have secured its adoption…. a dread of dismemberment, not an approbation of the particular system under consideration, had induced an acquiescence in it."[10] Nor was Marshall confused about the interests that were served by the Constitution, or about the interests that were suppressed. Being one of those who, in Jefferson's description, "deem it necessary to keep [the people] down by hard labor, poverty and ignorance," Justice Marshall wrote with unconcealed admiration about the creditors who acquired immense fortunes, not by industry, but by legislation. Marshall wrote that they "struggled with unabated zeal for the exact observance of public and private engagements…. They were consequently the uniform friends of a regular administration of justice, and of a vigorous course of taxation which would enable the state to comply with its engagements. By a natural association of ideas, they were also, with very few exceptions, in favor of enlarging the powers of the federal government."[11]

Thus, up to the time of the ratification there was no ideological confusion about the "democratic" nature of capitalism nor about the "democratic" intentions of the Constitution. The document was recognized as a blatant piece of class legislation. Nor was there confusion about the "democratic election" by which the Constitution was ratified. The people who were to be affected by the document received no education on the issues involved; the voters were not informed that the majority of the drafters were security-holders and capitalists; and the group that was to be affected most adversely by the document: the debtors, poor farmers, and laborers—the majority of the population—did not vote. Beard summarized the process by which the Constitution was ratified: "…the disfranchisement of the masses through property qualifications and ignorance and apathy contributed largely to the facility with which the personalty*-interest representatives carried the day. The latter were alert everywhere, for they knew, not as a matter of theory, but as a practical matter of dollars and cents, the value of the

*Personal property. (F.P.)

new Constitution. They were well informed. They were conscious of the identity of their interests. They were well organized. They knew for weeks in advance, even before the Constitution was sent to the states for ratification, what the real nature of the contest was. They resided for the most part in the towns, or the more thickly populated areas, and they could marshall their forces quickly and effectively. They had also the advantage of appealing to all discontented persons who exist in large numbers in every society and are ever anxious for betterment through some change in political machinery....

"The opposition on the other hand suffered from the difficulties connected with getting a backwoods vote out to the town and county elections. This involved sometimes long journeys in bad weather, for it will be remembered that the elections were held in the late fall and winter. There were no such immediate personal gains to be made through the defeat of the Constitution, as were to be made by the security holders on the other side. It was true the debtors knew that they would probably have to settle their accounts in full and the small farmers were aware that taxes would have to be paid to discharge the national debt if the Constitution was adopted; and the debtors everywhere waged war against the Constitution—of this there is plenty of evidence. But they had no money to carry on their campaign; they were poor and uninfluential—the strongest batallions were not on their side. The wonder is that they came so near defeating the Constitution at the polls."[12]

During the conflict over ratification, a momentous event took place. Many of the democrats who had initially opposed ratification switched sides when the capitalists promised that, *after* the Constitution was adopted, a bill of rights would immediately be appended to it. Perhaps the greatest tragedy of the American revolution was that the American people, so recently emerged from a successful anti-colonial revolution with no historical precedents, did not foresee that their victory would be followed by a counter-revolution. Farmers left the revolutionary army and returned to their lands, confident that the abhorrent British system would surely not be restored by Americans who had fought against it. They returned to their farms content with the hope that their lot would improve now that their labor no longer supported wealthy landowners in England. When the Constitutional conflict raged in the towns, the farmers received little accurate information of it, they heard a few reports that sounded preposterous, and they did not attach too much importance to the issue. As time passed, their lot did not improve—but time also dulled their expectations. Many years later they, or their children, were confronted by capitalists to whom they had mortgaged their land. They were given the choice of becoming the capitalists' tenants or of going to the growing cities and becoming wage laborers. But by then the revolution was only vaguely remembered: it had become a part of History.

The liberals, the intellectuals, those democrats who stayed in the towns, had, unlike the capitalists, no program, no organization, and no plan of action. The revolution had succeeded. A great democratic experiment was to take place on the American continent, an experiment which would show to all mankind "that all men are created equal" and are endowed with "unalienable rights" to "life, liberty, and the pursuit of happiness." These goals were inspiring; they crystallized with great brevity and conciseness the finest ideals of the Western European "enlightenment," but they were very vague about the course of action to be followed for their attainment. And, as Jefferson said, "we shall not live to see the result." Consequently, when ardent capitalists, whose vision of the great debt they'd pay themselves animated their tongues, told the liberals about the marvelous document that would give a new birth to America, the liberals listened, and they temporized. They were theoretically opposed to the document, for they could not but notice that the "inviolability of property" had been written into it too many times and in too many forms, and that such a principle could only lead to the violability of human life, liberty, and happiness. But liberals, in whom the American revolutionaries had unfortunately placed their trust, are men who in theory believe in the possibility of a better society, but in practice accept the institutions of a worse society. And as the cunning Hamilton so well knew, "the probable result of such a temperament is the preservation of systems, though originally opposed..." So, when the liberals were harrassed by so many wealthy and powerful men, they re-examined the document. The Constitution did, after all, provide for elections as well as for a parliament. Eighteenth century democrats were not under the illusion that elections and parliament constituted democracy; they were familiar enough with history to know that elections and parliaments had long existed in undemocratic England, in ancient Rome, and even in the feudal middle ages; they were quite enlightened about the undemocratic use to which tyrannies, aristocracies, and oligarchies had put elections and parliaments. It was not the provision for elections and parliament that changed the minds of the democratic liberals, but the promise of a bill of rights, "providing clearly, and without the aid of sophism, for freedom of religion, freedom of the press, protection against standing armies, restriction of monopolies, the eternal and unremitting force of the habeas corpus laws, and trials by jury..."[13] They must have thought that surely a bill of rights, supplemented by elections and a parliament, would prove too much of an obstacle for the avaricious "stock-jobbers." They must have hoped that surely the capitalist interlude would be only temporary, the democratic experiment would continue with undiminished zeal, that "as new discoveries are made, new truths disclosed, and manners and opinions change with the change of circumstances, institutions must advance also, and keep pace with the times."[14] Consequently, with "a dread of dismemberment, not an approbation of the particular system under consideration," the liberal democrats and the capitalists reached a compromise on the bill of rights. The liberals changed their votes. If they had not changed their votes so quickly, there might have been time to inform the population about the momentous issues involved. But so many men of great wealth, power and influence were in such a hurry. And liberals are above all expedient and practical men. Since it is never expedient or practical to oppose or delay wealth, power, and influence, the liberals changed their votes quickly. As Jefferson said, "What is practicable must often control what is pure theory."

So the Constitution was ratified; it was amended by a bill of rights; it became the law of the land. And thereupon a strange, unexpected, barely perceptible event took place. Before its adoption, the Constitution had been merely a document written by a few capitalists, a document whose flaws and tendencies every liberal and radical democrat could recognize and denounce. But after its adoption this document of dubious value and questionable quality became The Law. Before the Constitution's adoption, the democrats had known that the capitalists constituted a small but dangerous anti-democratic element.

But after the adoption, the surprised democrats were confronted by a Leviathan: the small, anti-democratic element had suddenly acquired Authority and Power: the capitalists now constituted The State. Even the conservative Adams, Federalist successor of George Washington, was well aware of what had taken place. Adams wrote in 1808: "We do possess one material which actually constitutes an aristocracy that governs the nation. That material is wealth." The liberals had miscalculated; they had not expected a mere document composed by a handful of capitalists to become transformed into a way of life for generations of men; they had not known that they were inscribing their names on the gravestone of American democracy.

Eighteenth century democrats knew a great deal about the natural rights of men and about the brutal abuses of tyrants. But they too lightly dismissed the psychological effects of vested authority. They were familiar with the fraud and violence by which medieval feudalism had maintained its Earthly City. But they'd forgotten the repulsive phenomenon of men destroying, murdering, and dying because the Authority of the Church had decreed that Christians must destroy Mohammedans in the name of Jesus Christ. And they'd forgotten how many times aristocracies and monarchies, acting "in the name of the people," had used Authority to gain their ends by using one portion of the people to rob and massacre another portion of the people. What the liberals underestimated was the extent to which Authority absolves crime.

If one man robs another on the street, he is a thief. But if a group of thieves robs an entire nation from a legislature, they are not considered criminals. They have Authority. They are the Legislators of the Land. Their robbery is always "in the national interest" and they speak "in the name of the people." And anyone who should try to prosecute the criminals in power is guilty of high treason. The capitalist or the banker need no longer feel ashamed of his "calling," for in a capitalist state with a capitalist Constitution, a usurer is no longer despised; he has become "a man who has a due sense of the sacred obligation of a just debt;[15] he has become a Respectable Man.

Draped with Authority, the Constitution ceased to appear a blatant piece of class legislation drafted by self-seeking security-holders. It was strangely transformed, not only into the law of the land, but also into an "expression of the will of the people." Chief Justice of the

Supreme Court John Marshall had written that "the fate of the constitution could scarcely be conjectured; and so small in many instances, was the majority in its favor, as to afford strong ground for the opinion that, had the influence of character been removed, the intrinsic merits of the instrument would not have secured its adoption...." Yet only twelve years later, the very same Chief Justice John Marshall wrote the following: "The government [of the United States] proceeds directly from the people; it is 'ordained and established' in the name of the people, and it is declared to be ordained in 'order to form a more perfect union, establish justice, insure domestic tranquility, and secure the blessings of liberty' to themselves and to their posterity.... The government of the Union then ... is emphatically and truly, a government of the people. In form and substance it emanates from them. Its powers are granted by them and are to be exercised directly on them and for their benefit.... It is the government of all; its powers are delegated by all; it represents all, and acts for all."[16]

Thus, by 1819, the capitalists who had once constituted a small but dangerous anti-democratic force, had become "emphatically and truly, a government of the people." The aristocracy of wealth now calls itself a democracy. The government of "paper and patronage," of what John Taylor called "a sly thief, who empties your pockets under a pretense of paying your debts," whose rule is "a climate deadly to liberty,"[17] had now been launched on its career of plunder, oppression and crime, all committed in the name of Freedom, Liberty, and National Defense.

As Taylor observed, "The aristocracy of superstition defended itself by exclaiming, the Gods! the temples! the sacred oracles! divine vengeance! and Elysian fields!—and that of paper and patronage exclaims, national faith! sacred charters! disorganization! and security of property!"[18] And many years after Taylor's death, the aristocracy of paper and patronage did not hesitate to borrow from the aristocracy of superstition, and add to its own armory, the exclamations, the Gods! the temples! and the Elysian fields of Our Way of Life!

When the ideals of revolutionaries became the ideology of counter-revolutionaries, the democrats were disarmed. When capitalists in power called themselves democrats, the democrats out of power had little ground to stand on. It had been difficult enough for democrats to oppose an aristocracy that claimed to be superior to other men.

But it was virtually impossible for democrats to oppose an aristocracy that claimed to rule in the name of the people, that claimed its wealth enriched the people, that claimed its wars of conquest and plunder were for the defense of the people. By appropriating the democratic ideal, the capitalists emasculated the democrats. From here on, the vast literature in defense of democracy was used by capitalists to defend capitalism. From here on, every man who still spoke favorably of democratic ideals was seen as a defender of capitalism. If usury was Freedom and theft Democracy, then radical democrats had no choice but to cut out their tongues and paint their intentions to their fellow men. Capitalist as well as older aristocracies all over Europe followed the lead of their American bretheren, and before long every form of tyranny and oppression, without undergoing a revolution, without any change whatever, called itself a democracy. And it took radical democrats almost half a century to abandon the name of their cherished ideal, and to realize that if oppression was called Democracy, then democracy would have to be called communism, or socialism, or even anarchy. Radical democrats lost their unity and coherence until the brilliant historian and scholar Karl Marx recast and crystallized the fragmented pieces of the democratic ideal into a powerful new mould. However, while gaining unity and coherence from the newly formulated program and the untainted name, the democrats confirmed and greatly strengthened the capitalist claim to a monopoly on the democratic ideal. Whatever the virtues of the new name, the Communist Manifesto wrote the democratic goals of Liberty, Equality and Fraternity on the banners of men who could no longer call themselves democrats.

Historians who do not write to enlighten their readers, but to endear themselves with those in power, quickly caught on to the nature of their important task within the capitalist regime. When the American revolution was still within the memory of living men, books that told of the security-holders' *coup d'etat* were entitled "The Birth and Growth of Democracy." Before long men spoke of the history of American capitalism as the "History of American Democracy," and exotic new topics like Hamiltonian Democracy, Jacksonian Democracy, Southern Democracy, Midwestern Democracy, and Grass Roots Democracy, filled scholarly monographs. In Britain there appeared a Victorian Democracy, and elsewhere there were Constitutional Monarchies, Equalitarian Oligarchies, and even a few Democratic Kingdoms. And in the middle of the twentieth century, an alliance of capitalist, feudal, and fascist military states called itself The Free World. American children were indoctrinated to believe that the unscrupulous brutality of Rockefeller, the cunning thievery of Carnegie, the criminal usury of Morgan, were ideal models of the Democratic Way of Life and living proof "that all men are created equal." And on the world scene, American capitalists harrassed the unfed, unprivileged millions in the colonies to choose between Socialism, which, they said, gives "only bread," and The American Way, which, they said, gives "freedom." But by the middle of the twentieth century, too many miserable men knew that the "freedom" given by capitalists was the freedom of slaves to work for their masters or die. Too many knew that the freedom of capitalists was restricted to the capitalists, and that other men received only its obverse side: misery and oppression. And yet when men rejected The American Way and chose the possibility for both "bread" as well as their land was invaded by the "arsenal of democracy;" they were subjected to terrorist reprisals, sabotage, and massacre that did not and would not end; and during the campaign of utterly inhuman rationally manufactured horror, they were told, by Hamilton's and Rockefeller's heirs, that they had "betrayed" their revolution.

The democratic ideal required that all men have equal power, voice and influence in all the important matters of the human community. For this to be possible, land and wealth had to be equalized, since "If wealth is accumulated in the hands of a few, either by a feudal or a stock monopoly, it carries the power also; and a government becomes as certainly aristocratical, by a monopoly of wealth, as by a monopoly of arms."[19] The equalization of land and wealth was to take place either in the form suggested by More, Winstanley, Babeuf, and their followers by making the earth a "common treasury" and for every son and daughter of mankind to live free upon;" or in the form suggested by Taylor, Jefferson, and most of the early American liberal democrats: by dividing the land among its tillers, by government "restriction of monopolies," by agrarian reform. In either case "cutthroat competition" would have been a crime, and the enslavement and employment of some men by other man would not have been tolerated. Every advancement in knowledge and in technology would have benefitted all men; and even those men who were otherwise inclined would have had to seek personal advancement by cooperation and not war. For such a society to survive and maintain itself, all men would have to be educated, not in the mystifications of a ruling class, but in the relations of each to his fellows, his society, and his age, as well as in the ideals and potentialities of human life. Without such education, the experiment would surely fail, "if a nation expects to be ignorant and free, in a state of civilization, it expects what never was and never will be."[20] To supplement the general education, there must be concrete and full information on all important issues. For example, if a constitution is proposed, citizens cannot exert intelligent control over this most important affair of the nation unless they are informed of the exact number of drafters who attended the Convention in order to benefit their fellow men, and the exact number who attended in order to defraud and plunder their fellow men. Since information is always colored by the man who transmits it, there must be untrammeled freedom of speech—which means that every man has access to the ears of all; and there mast be unlimited freedom of the press—which means that one man's written thoughts are as prominently distributed and as widely available as any other's. Since concrete and complete information would play such a crucial role in a democracy, publicly disseminated lies and deceptions would not be permitted any more than they are in science, and men would be encouraged to express important and imaginative ideas and discouraged from publishing unoriginal or familiar ones. Freedom of speech and of the press obviously did not mean that a few men would be "free" to address and inform the rest, while most men were "free" to speak to and write for their own friends. There's nothing democratic about such an arrangement—and nothing new. Every form of government in human history, whether monarchy or tyranny, aristocracy or oligarchy, has provided unrestricted freedom of expression to a few, and has given to the rest the "freedom" to express themselves to their friends—but this is not democracy, nor is it an achievement, since only a total police state composed of illiterate, tongueless and mindless men could prevent such "freedom" from taking place. And lastly, the democratic ideal required the participation of every man in the important affairs of society. Participation in trivialities was nothing new: even in the repressive tyranny of the Russian Czars, the poorest men could "participate" in the services of the Russian Orthodox Church and in the celebrations of cheering the Czar; in every slave society, the slaves could "participate" in their masters' affairs by doing their masters' work. Democratic participation was to open a new era in man's relation to man: each human being was to be master of his fate, insofar as his fate did not depend on natural obstacles; each man was to control the direction and content of his life.

Thus there were four main principles for a democratic government. They have been given many names by many men. John Taylor called them justice, knowledge, honesty, and self-government.[21] These four principles can be examined within a social context in terms of the distribution of land, wealth, and privilege; the quality of education; the facility of communication; the degree of participation in the important affairs of society. All other social institutions can then be evaluated in terms of these four principles, and their democratic or undemocratic character can thus be ascertained.*

The first requirement of the democratic society is that all men have equal power and influence—it is what John Taylor called Justice. The perennial symbol of Justice is a scale in balance. In order to have equal power and influence, men must have equal control over the means of exerting power and influence, and every augmentation of society's means of power must pass to all men. Obviously this state of affairs cannot exist in a society where a few men have a monopoly over the

---

*In the rest of this chapter, I will confine myself to an analysis of equality, education, and communication. The degree of participation in the affairs of the corporate society will be analyzed in the following chapter, on the "Corporate Dispensation."

means of power. This power will enable the few to appropriate any new means of power which become available to society. With their augmented power, the few will have yet greater access to more power. Once this process is allowed to start, it clearly will not end until very few men have an unchallengeable monopoly over all available means of power, influence and control.

The history of the United States is not a history of Justice, of a scale in balance. It is not the history of a Society of Equals. American history is a history of capitalism. If there was once hope that wealth and privilege would be equalized by the peaceful means of agrarian reform, cancellation of debts, and division of unoccupied land among its tillers, that hope was killed by the Constitutional Convention. The Constitution hallowed the property of the rich and condoned the enrichment of some by means of the impoverishment of those less able to defend themselves. Hamilton's fiscal program enlarged on the Constitution by giving public money to the unsavory group who had speculated on the revolutionary war. The Hamiltonian program encouraged these men to employ the wealth and labor of the nation to enrich themselves yet further, created a bank to help their acquisitive projects, and as if this weren't enough, increased the taxes and used violence to collect them, in order to enlarge the bank's funds. Alexander Hamilton, who saw, feared, and despised the democratic leanings and hopes of the American people, delineated clearly the type of society he wanted established on the American continent. Hamilton's ideal was not a commonwealth of freedom, equality and brotherhood. It was a society of "the few and the many. The first are the rich and well born, the other the mass of the people.... Give therefore to the first class a distinct, permanent share in the government."[22]

Hamilton was undoubtedly pleased by the New World that emerged from the Constitutional Convention and its aftermath. It was a society where part of the nation were negro slaves whose entire lives were the private property of plantation owners, where another part of the nation were tenant farmers and workers whose time and labor were the private property of capitalists. The wealth of the nation was safely lodged in the hands of "the few," the "rich and well born," and "If wealth is accumulated in the hands of a few, either by a feudal or a stock monopoly, it carries the power also..."[23] With wealth and power, and with a legal system designed to protect wealth and power, the "rich and well born" quickly appropriated to themselves the land as well as the labor of "the many." The previous chapter, on the Growth of Capitalism, reviewed the historical process by which "the few" appropriated the land, wealth and power of the nation. With the invention and development of technological means of production, a tremendous new source of power became available to society. But in capitalist America, technology was not used for the collective enrichment and creative development of all human beings but to enlarge the power of the rich and well born. During the 1860's, a fabulously mushrooming enrichment of the rich took place. The Hamiltonian dream passed into frenzy as delirious capitalists "exploited national resources, waged economic wars among themselves, entered into combinations, made private capital out of the public domain, and used any and every method to achieve their ends. They made agreements with railroads for rebates; they purchased newspapers and bought editors; they killed off competing and independent businesses, and employed lawyers of skill and statesmen of repute to sustain their rights and secure their privileges."[24] The United States became a hot house for the growth of fortunes. Ambitious, mindless and determined men abandoned their lives and homes in other parts of the world and frantically hurried to gamble for the big take in the gold rush. The overwhelming majority of gamblers lost, and they spent their lives in the New World as immigrant laborers whose slums and working conditions were in many cases worse than those they'd left. As in all gold rushes, however, the gold was not long available to all comers. The gold rush was institutionalized, and all the gold was carefully channeled into the hands of the mine owners, the hands of those who had the wealth and power to buy the "rights." As one observer summarized, "From the time of the Panic of 1873, which signaled the death of the old individualistic entrepreneur, the corporation was the key institution of the American economic system."[25]

A social system which lodges an excess of power in the hands of "the few" and condones the further augmentation of that power, will in time lodge a monopoly of wealth and power into the hands of very few men. And this is in fact the central characteristic of twentieth century America. I have already quoted the authoritative corporation lawyer who estimated that "Slightly more than half [of American industry] is owned outright by not more than 200 corporations."[26] I have also quoted the sociologist who translated this fact into its social meaning: "Within the financial and political boundaries of the corporation, the industrial revolution itself has been concentrated. Corporations command raw materials, and the patents on inventions with which to turn them into finished products. They command the most expensive, and therefore what must be the finest, legal minds in the world, to invent and to refine their defenses and their strategies. They employ man as producer and they make that which he buys as consumer. They clothe him and feed him and invest his money. They make that with which he fights the wars and they finance the ballyhoo of advertisement and the obscurantist bunk of public relations that surround him during the wars and between them."[27]

Thus the United States is not a society where all men have equal wealth, power and influence. It is a society where Justice is monopolized by the "rich and well born." The scale is out of balance: on the lower half the weight of "the mass of mankind" supports "the few" on the upper half. A few men have a monopoly of wealth, power and influence, as well as a monopoly over the means of augmenting wealth, power and influence. "The mass of mankind" are instruments of the rich; they are tools, they are employed as "hands;" their labor and time are *not* their own, they are *not* their own masters, they do *not* exert control over the important matters of their lives. The influence and voice of the majority of Americans is symbolized by an Intercommunication System in a capitalist factory or industrial plant—what workers call a "bitch-box." The "boss" has a centralized "box" in his office from which he can call and direct all the workers; the workers, in turn, have the power and voice, they have the "freedom," to answer the boss's call. The United States is a society of masters and servants, euphemized as "employers" and "employees," or "management and labor." It differs slightly, but significantly, from a slave or serf society. In a slave society, the master has absolute power over the entire lives and fortunes of "his" slaves. He is their "father," they are his "children," and thus he is "responsible" for them. Capitalism decreases the power over the entire life of human beings to a power over their time and labor, and at the same time abolishes the paternal "responsibility" with which slave-masters were charged. Since time and labor are the two qualities with which a human being shapes his destiny, the servitude of a man who has alienated these qualities to another is just as real as that of a slave or a serf. However, the capitalist does not view his employees as "children" but as "hands," and by thus degrading men from sub-humans into things, he does not feel in any way "responsible" for them: he can break, fire, and replace them at will. Thus the existence of a large number of "unemployed," of men who are outside the boundaries of the economy, is of no concern to capitalists. Unlike the slave society, the capitalist society gives men a choice of masters whom they can serve. The choice is obviously limited to the "openings" available at any given time. But if a man should choose not to serve any master, nor to be a master himself, he is free to starve.

For those who refuse servitude, and for those who cannot find it, capitalism provides a vicious institution, unknown in any slave society: the institution of Unemployment. In the capitalist economy, there must always be a surplus of labor, since a shortage of labor would make workers too powerful in a strike, too insistent in their demands for a greater share of the wealth, and too curious about the necessity of retaining unproductive capitalists whose only function is to suck up the fruit of other men's labor. Thus there are always some who are unemployed—who do not want or cannot find capitalists to serve. Since the capitalist society inculcates in all men the desire to serve, the great majority of the "unemployed" are men who crave for employment and are deprived of it by a shortage of "openings." And for this they are criminals. Perhaps the most instructive short course on capitalism is that which is given very day in the courts of big cities where men are tried for petty crimes and "disorderly conduct." In such a court, one miserable wretch after another is dragged in—one for vagrancy, another for drinking to forget his hunger and misery, another for sleeping on a park bench. The first count against the man who slept on the bench is that he has no address, no home to which to return; the second count, that he has no job, no "gainful employment;" and the third count against him is that, due to his lack of means, he slept on the park bench. If he is a "repeated offender" he is sent to the "work house" for a period of forced labor. He is then released as poor and miserable as before, and in time picked up again for "disorderly conduct." "Therefore, that one covetous and unsatiable cormorant and very plague of his native country may compass about and enclose many thousand acres of ground together within one pale or hedge, the husbandmen be thrust out of their own ... they must needs depart away, poor, silly, wretched souls, men, women, husbands, wives, fatherless children, widows, woeful mothers and young babes. And yet then also they be cast in prison as vagabonds, because they go about and work not; whom no man will set a-work, though they never so willingly offer themselves thereto."[28] The misfits of capitalism are criminals; they are condemned for being unemployed; the victims are themselves charged for the misery the capitalist society inflicts on them. The "unemployed" of the capitalist society are not slaves; they are stray animals.

The "restriction of monopolies" Jefferson had advocated is still given lip-service in the United States, in the form of anti-trust legislation and "free enterprise" propaganda, but in practice it is utterly discarded. If the salesmen of corporations are taught to claim they are "individual free enterprisers," their status as servants is not thereby changed. Government does not restrict but magnifies monopolies. Both Law and the Officers of the Law are charged with the maintenance and protection of corporate property, not the maintenance and protection of human life and wellbeing. Law, which means institutionalized violence, protects the fortunate from the deprived. "They will borrow for the nation, that they may lend. They will offer lenders great profits, that they may share in them. As grievances gradually excite national discontent, they will fix the yoke more securely, by making it gradually heavier. And they will finally avow and maintain their corruption, by establishing an irresistible standing army, not to defend the nation, but to defend a system for plundering the nation."[29] Those who gain from the plunder acquire a monopoly over the means of violence and the threat of violence embodied in Law, and they henceforth employ violence and law to defend their plunder. In the New World, as in the old, men are again instruments of the law, not law the instrument of men. The practitioners of the law, the magistrates of capitalism, must believe, as a requisite for acceptance in their profession, that a state of affairs there law is the instrument of all men constitutes "chaos" and "anarchy."

Thus the first and foremost requirement for a democratic society does not exist in the land that calls itself the world's defender of Democracy, Freedom and Justice. It is a society of privilege, where law condones the enrichment of some at the expense of others, and then protects the riches thus acquired. It is a society of masters and servants that does not greatly differ from previous forms of such an arrangement, except that the degree of inequality is greater and the "responsibility" of masters toward servants smaller. The far-sighted John Taylor had clearly perceived that the aristocracy of wealth is no mild successor to the aristocracy of title and superstition. The new system is a far more efficient and far deadlier method of enslaving men than any previous aristocracy. "A nation exposed to a paroxysm of conquering rage, has infinitely the advantage of one, subjected to this aristocratical system. One is local and temporary; the other is spread by law and perpetual. One is an open robber, who warns you to defend yourself; the other a sly thief, who empties your pockets under a pretence of paying your debts. One is a pestilence, which will end of itself; the other a climate deadly to liberty.

"After an invasion, suspended rights may be resumed, ruined cities rebuilt, and past cruelties forgotten; but in the oppressions of the aristocracy of paper and patronage, there can be no respite; so long as there is any thing to get, it cannot be glutted with wealth; so long as there is any thing to fear, it cannot be glutted with power; other tyrants die; this is immortal.

"A conqueror may have clemency; he may be generous; at least he is vain, and may be softened by flattery. But a system founded in evil moral qualities, is insensible to human virtues and passions, incapable of remorse, guided constantly by the principles which created it, and acts by the iron instruments, law, armies and tax gatherers. With what prospect of success, reader, could you address the clemency, generosity or vanity of the system of paper and patronage? Wherefore has no one tried this hopeless experiment? Because clemency, generosity and vanity, are not among the moral qualities which constitute the character of an evil moral system.

"The only two modes extant of enslaving nations, are those of armies and the system of paper and patronage."[30]

The respectable eighteenth century plantation owner from Caroline County, Virginia, as well as his famous friend Thomas Jefferson, would doubtless be "investigated," maligned and ruined as "atheistic Marxist communist conspirators" by present day American Congressmen. Taylor's book was published four years before the birth of Karl Marx. And over four centuries ago, a man who was sanctified in 1935 but beheaded in 1535 had written, "wheresoever possessions be private, where money beareth all the stroke, it is hard and almost impossible that there the weal public may justly be govemed and prosperously flourish."[31]

⚖ ⚖ ⚖

Jefferson and the early American liberals had hoped that, with a parliament, a bill of rights, elections, and universal education, the capitalist interlude would be temporary, the American people would gradually unseat the aristocracy of wealth, and the democratic experiment would continue. But Jefferson and the liberals didn't show as much discernment as was shown by Thomas More three centuries earlier. Among the liberal democrats, only John Taylor had seen clearly that neither parliament, nor bill of rights, nor elections, nor universal education, could function for democratic ends once they fell to an aristocracy of paper and patronage. "A government, a section of it, or a measure, founded in an evil moral principle, such as fraud, ambition, avarice or superstition, must produce correspondent effects, and defeat the end of government ... It is the same thing to a nation whether it is subjected to the will of a minority, by superstition, conquest, or patronage and paper. Whether this end is generated by errour, by force, or by fraud, the interest of the nation is invariably sacrificed to the interest of the minority."[32] As soon as "the few" acquire a monopoly of wealth, power and privilege, then education, communication, and participation, the three instruments by which men were to maintain democratic justice once established, became converted into instruments by which "the mass of mankind" are enthralled to wealth, power, and privilege.

Ignorant men are the instruments of those who have the power and will to manipulate ignorance. Democrats once dreamed of preventing such manipulation in America by means of a program of education which would give each man a broad understanding of his relations to his fellow men, his society and his age, as well as an insight into the possibilities of human development. C. Wright Mills has lucidly summarized the goals and content of democratic education: "...to assist in the birth among a group of people of those cultural and political and technical sensibilities which would make them genuine members of a genuinely liberal public, this is at once a training in skills and an education of values. It includes a sort of therapy in the ancient sense of clarifying one's knowledge of self; it includes the imparting of all those skills of controversy with one's self, which we call thinking and with others, which we call debate. And the end product of such liberal education of sensibilities is simply the self-educating, self-cultivating man or woman.

"The knowledgeable man in the genuine public is able to turn his personal troubles into social issues, to see their relevance for his community and his community's relevance for them. He understands that what he thinks and feels as personal troubles are very often not only that but problems shared by others and indeed not subject to solution by any one individual but only by modifications of the structure of the groups in which he lives and sometimes the structure of the entire society....

"It is the task of the liberal institution, as of the liberally educated man, continually to translate troubles into issues and issues into the terms of their human meaning for the individual.... In a community of publics the task of liberal education would be: to keep the public from being overwhelmed; to help produce the disciplined and informed mind that cannot be overwhelmed..."[33] Without such a program, men will be overwhelmed. "If a nation expects to be ignorant and free, in a state of civilization, it expects what never was and never will be."[34]

The most common type of ignorance is trained ignorance. And in the society ruled by the aristocracy of paper and patronage, education, the prime instrument for human enlightenment and liberation, becomes a highly refined method of inculcating delusions. The intelligent public is replaced by the ignorant mass. Instead of being taught to understand their relations to their situation, men are nurtured on far fetched delusions and disciplined in minute techniques. The result is a society where men have infinite knowledge about an infinitesimal task which other men cannot understand, and vague, meaningless platitudes about the problems and concerns men have in common. The result is a mass society where each silently fulfills his appointed task with utmost precision, but cannot understand his task, cannot control it, and cannot communicate this fact to other men. The result is a rationally created society in which reason and thought are superfluous and irrelevant—as superfluous as would be ideas and thought in animals who could not communicate them or in any way indicate they had them. In this process of "massification" men become something less than human: they become objects: their only specifically human possession becomes the mass thought, the mass delusion. "Right you are if you think you are," wrote the playwright Luigi Pirandello. This doctrine has become the central principle of American pedagogy. Each person is brought up on a false image of the American society, an image in which political activity is in the hands of independent and responsible elected officials, and the economy is in the hands of small enterprising businessmen. The image does not describe anything with which people are familiar, yet the image cannot be challenged. For an oil worker whose machines and tools are so immediate and real, the corporations and the profits are hard to grasp and best forgotten; surely if multi-billion dollar corporations and rich men whose profits come in millions really existed, this fact would have been mentioned in the schoolbooks, it would appear in the newspapers. For a student of economics who confronts books that consistently draw the same finely-detailed picture and professors who consistently expound the same reality there can only be one image; could sections of libraries and faculties of teachers all be devoted to describing what has never existed? The inhabitants of the corporate society could neither justify nor defend the corporate society because they do not know they live in it. The image does not correspond to any society, and has nothing to do with corporate capitalism. The image is based on what Marx called a false consciousness.

Within Pirandello's moral framework, a false consciousness is everyone's privilege, provided the delusion is one's own. However, in the corporate mass society, a private false consciousness is still as unrespectable as it was in Pirandello's day. Psychotics are still taken to institutions, and efforts are still made to "correct" their mental image so it will correspond with a popularly accepted "reality." Unlike Pirandellian delusions, the ideology of the corporate society is not a self-induced private delusion. It is a socially induced mass delusion. The consciousness of the American Masses is a systematically manipulated consciousness. The manipulation of the human mind is a technique that Hitler learned from the United States—he was an avid student of American "education" by means of Advertising and Public Relations. It is this manipulation of consciousness, the training of the human mind and spirit into one system of ideas and desires, that converts people into "masses."

The corporate society is again a society of aristocrats who waste other men's labor on elaborate, tasteless monuments to their wealth, on vast hierarchies of filing experts and servile parasites, on the biggest and ugliest arsenal of death-weapons in human history. It is again a society of soldiers whose sole function is to murder and destroy what other men build. It is again a society of priests. Winstanley had once urged that priests be turned to schoolmasters, that they teach men about the world they live in, about human history, about the laws and diversity of nature. But in the corporate society, the schoolmasters are priests again, and they again "make sermons to please the sickly minds of ignorant peoples, to preserve their own riches and esteem among a charmed, befooled, and besotted people."[35] Men's relations to their fellows, their society, their age, are again covered by impenetrable mist, and men are drilled in blind faith, political incompetence, and vocational expertise. The program that was to "produce the disciplined and informed mind that cannot be overwhelmed" is replaced by a systematic rape of the human mind designed to yield pliant, obedient "employees" who are "good citizens" when they know their "place." The liberating education envisaged by democrats was not given a chance in the United States. As C. Wright Mills points out, "the function of education shifted from the political to the economic: to train people for better-paying jobs and thus to get ahead. This is especially true of the high school movement, which has met the business demands for white-collar skills at the public's expense. In large part education has become merely vocational; in so far as its political task is concerned, that has been reduced to a routine training of nationalist loyalties."[36]

The democratic liberals who hoped that education might in time liberate men from the aristocracy of paper and patronage were not very discerning. If an educational program is implemented and paid for by capitalists, it will reflect the interests of capitalists. It is *not* to the interest of an aristocracy of wealth to let men be taught independence of mind, for such teaching would undermine men's adherence to a system which treats the earth and its inhabitants as the "private property" of a few; such teaching might lead men to realize that "private property" is not a law of nature but a human convention, and as a convention it can be overthrown. Capitalists are not interested in a nation of men who "cannot be overwhelmed;" they are interested in "employing," in using materials and men in order to accumulate private wealth. An educational system supported by "employers" will be designed to yield employable men. The content of such a program will be loyalty, obedience, and vocational training. Men who are disciplined in political incompetence and vocational proficiency can hardly be expected to reject their masters and continue a long forgotten democratic experiment.

Perhaps the greatest triumph of American "education" is the incredible success with which it has equated vocational servility, political ignorance and nationalist loyalty. The "finished product" of this educational factory is a man who ardently believes that servility is freedom, ignorance is strength, war is peace, and capitalism is democracy. As an article in *Monthly Review* remarked, "all these blubbering protestations of love for democracy, and all this trembling solicitude for her safety and happiness, would seem to be the perfect strategy for those who are determined to perpetuate capitalism but who presently prefer to perpetuate it under cover of a ready-made national delusion that Free Enterprise, the American Way, Our Way of Life, Democracy are *all* one and the same thing—inseparable, indistinguishable, and indissoluble.

"It's amusing how most apologists for capitalism shy around the use of the word in public; almost invariably they draw on their stock of shopworn and phony euphemisms. The stock itself has become a glutinous nationalistic complex in which the phrase, "Our Way of Life," is designed to carry tender undertones suggesting memories of Home, Mother, Santa Claus, the Family Bible, Thanksgiving Turkey, the Ol' Smimmin' Hole, and those fondly-remembered freedoms of barefoot boyhood. [Thus the] wide-spread delusion among the masses of the people that we already have democracy in this country—even a surplus for export to the backward nations."[37]

The systematic inculcation of the grand nationalistic delusion which hides the corporate reality is not confined to the "ordinary man" nor to the "lower schools." The Ivory Towers of American "higher education" have become as divorced from the western humanist tradition as the "lower schools." Harvey O'Connor has described some of the Savants who rule over American Higher Education. "While Columbia's loss of its president, Dwight D. Eisenhower, was the oil industry's gain when he campaigned against federal ownership of the offshore oil land, the great university lost little in its understanding of the industry's problems. Eisenhower was succeeded by Dr. Grayson Kirk, a director of Socony-Vacuum. Dr. Kirk announced, after his elevation, that he saw no incompatibility in holding the two posts. Soon thereafter Courtney C. Brown, in charge of Standard of New Jersey's higher public relations, was named dean of Columbia's Graduate School of Business."[38] And to make doubly sure that students don't become too curious about the details of capitalist production, distribution, and consumption, the corporations support about a fourth of university research, most of the rest being supported by the military. That is, the corporations get the credit for supporting university research. Actually almost all of the funds they "give" are tax deductible.[39] The effect is that tax-payers support the research, while corporations get the power to dictate, overtly or subtly, the purpose and direction of the research. Academic Freedom Week is yearly celebrated on American campuses. Whatever may have been the noble or ignoble purposes of universities in other times and places, American universities are for the training of corporation managers, military experts, mind manipulators. And when literature professors train the attention of their students away from the content of a literary work to its form, and philosophy professors teach that the analysis of man's world must be replaced by the analysis of man's words, they too join the Americanist bandwagon and effectively prevent any message from entering the student's consciousness which will conflict with the corporate message.

The consequence is that clarity of thought and power of imagination are not among the strong points of a United States-educated man. The intellect-technicians, the so-called "intellectuals" of America, experts of a minute fragment of a "field," are ignorant of all other "fields" as well as of the interrelations and values of the "fields"; yet at the same time these intellect-technicians are condescendingly cynical of thought which relates man to a larger structure than the fragment of a "field." With a cynicism grounded on ignorance and barely masking a desire to conform to the prevalent ideology, the intellect-technicians can guard their positions only with contempt and defend their positions only with stereotypes. The "literary men" derive superiority by dismissing with contempt the engineers and manual workers who do not know the date of Marlowe's death, and they dismiss socially relevant art by stereotyping it "sociology"—and "sociology," to these latter day "literary experts," has the same connotations that "diabolism" had for a medieval priest. "Sociologists" react in kind, by dismissing any studies which go beyond the statistical tabulation of the reactions of 5723 farmers to a manure pile in Northern Michigan as "art, not science." The "political scientist" is expert in converting political problems into administrative problems and adept at treating human beings as material for corporate management. The "architect" is an expert in the maximization of returns and the minimization of costs, and to him the proposition that buildings are for human beings to live and work in is as exotic and irrelevant as the claim that there are cows on the moon. Each is an expert in his field and an ignoramus in the human consequences of his "field." American physicists who pliantly let themselves be used for the manufacture of weapons of genocide have shamelessly advertised the inhuman logic of expertise: 'Since we are experts in the arts of annihilation, and baboons in the arts of life, we will devote ourselves to the creation of genocidal weapons, and will leave the consequences to those who are in the fields that have to do with the preservation of life.' Unfortunately, there are no "fields" that have to do with human life, because such activity would have to transcend all "fields," and in the corporate society the only activity that transcends all "fields" is the accumulation of profits by the corporate masters. Life is not the goal but the victim of capitalism. A satirical portrait of experts, which H. G. Wells, half a century ago, located on the moon, is unfortunately no longer satirical, nor is it on the moon. The Selenites differ little, and then mainly in appearance, from the all-too-familiar present day "men" below the moon. "In the Moon, every citizen knows his place. He is born to that place, and the elaborate discipline of training and education and surgery he undergoes fits him at last so completely to it that he has neither ideas nor organs for any purpose behind it. If, for example, a Selenite is destined to be a mathematician, his teachers and trainers set out at once to that end. They check any incipient disposition to other pursuits, they encourage his mathematical bias with a perfect psychological skill. His brain grows, or at least the mathematical faculties of his brain grow, and the rest of him only so much as is necessary to sustain the essential part of him.... His brain grows continually larger, at least so far as the portions engaging in mathematics are concerned; they bulge ever larger and seem to suck all life and vigour from the rest of his frame. His limbs shrivel, his heart and digestive organs diminish, his insect face is hidden under its bulging contours. His voice becomes a mere stridulation for the stating of formulae; he seems deaf to all but properly enunciated problems. The faculty of laughter, save for the sudden discovery of some paradox, is lost to him; his deepest emotion is the evolution of a novel computation....

"Or, again, a Selenite appointed to be a minder of mooncalves is from his earliest years induced to think and live mooncalf, to find his pleasure in mooncalf lore, his exercise in their tending and pursuit.... And so it is with all sorts and conditions of Selenites—each a perfect unity in a world machine....

"They differed in shape, they differed in size, they rang all the horrible changes on the theme of Selenite form. Some bulged and overhung, some ran about among the feet of their fellows. All of them had a grotesque and disquieting suggestion of an insect that has somehow contrived to mock humanity; but all seemed to present an incredible exaggeration of some particular feature..."[40]

If radicals once dreamed that education would liberate men by giving them an insight into the potentialities of human development and social organization, this is once more the dream of radicals. Education is used to train men to serve a society that does not serve human ends. For men indoctrinated into Our Way of Life, there are no potentialities beyond the obedient compliance to corporation demands. For men who surrender their minds, time and labor to the genocidal arsenal that calls itself the Guardian of Human Dignity, there can be neither ideals nor potentialities; the metaphysical outer boundaries of their world are profit, production, and marketing. Human ideals cannot be served by the pursuit of an inhuman end that leaves a train of distorted sub-human victims behind lofty proclamations.

The New World did not become known either for its equality or its education, either for its Justice or its Knowledge. The democratic program of ongoing agrarian reform which was to bring all men equality, power and influence, was replaced by a monied aristocracy with a greater concentration of wealth, power and influence than had been held by any previous aristocracy. The democratic program of education was to give men insight and understanding of the society into which they are born and did not make, and thus to give men knowledge of the means by which they can change their society and, if they find it unacceptable, "to abolish it, and to institute a new government, laying its foundation on such principles, and organizing its powers in such form, as to them shall seem most likely to effect their safety and happiness."[41] But instead, education was fitted to the needs, not of society, but of the aristocracy, and men were "educated" to be loyal and diligent servants of capitalist "bosses."

The liberal democrats of 1788 had swallowed their objections to the Constitution when they were promised a bill of rights. The Bill of Rights was appended to the Constitution, and is still there. On this Bill, which was added as an afterthought by security-holders anxious to collect their fortunes, rests the entire case of American "civil liberties." And yet, if there is no social justice, if men are neither taught the meaning of human equality nor educated in the means of instituting it, such a bill of rights can never be more than an afterthought.

The first amendment says, "Congress shall make no law respecting an establishment of religion, or prohibiting the free exercise thereof; or abridging the freedom of speech, or of the press; or the right of the people peaceably to assemble, and to petition the government for a redress of grievances."[42] But Congress need make no law respecting or prohibiting any of these things if the aristocracy of paper and patronage exerts a prohibitive control over them. Thus only one part of the first Amendment was realized, and that was the provision for the "free exercise" of religion or irreligion. And this is undoubtedly a great achievement—for the eighteenth century. There have been no religious wars in the United States, nor mass persecutions of religious minorities. However, the nineteenth century saw no more religious wars were in Europe either, for by that time the type of religious intolerance for which Europe will forever be remembered had, by and large, declined (until the twentieth century revival of religious persecution in Nazi Germany). American achievements in official religious tolerance should not be underestimated, but the unofficial survival of American religious bigotry should not be forgotten. What is more, the hatred was not removed but transferred: the racial bigotry of Americans, legalized in many states, has been surpassed only by the barbarians of Nazi Germany and the European marauders of Africa.

It was the provision for untrammeled communication, written into the Bill of Rights as freedom of speech and of the press, that gave hope to the democrats and promise to America. Even if security-holders constituted the government, even if education was controlled by the rich, could not an atmosphere of free discussion unseat the aristocrats in power and enable the democratic experiment to continue? Jefferson expressed such a hope. "No experiment can be more interesting than that we are now trying, which we trust will end in establishing the fact that man may be governed by reason and truth. Our first object should therefore be to leave open to him all the avenues of truth. The most effectual hitherto found is the freedom of the press."[43] However, if "the avenues of truth" are clogged, if the public is uneducated, or rather dis-educated into ignorance, mediocrity and servility, as well as uninformed or misinformed by the press, then the democratic experiment cannot continue, for there will be no democratic public to effect it. "If a nation expects to be ignorant and free, in a state of civilization, it expects what never was and never will be."[44]

To eighteenth century democrats, freedom of speech and of the press meant that all the "avenues of truth," the media of communication, would be free—open and available—to all men; not "free" for some and closed to others. Clearly, a press that is "free" only for those who have the power to control it is not a free press. The kings and tyrants of Europe, the wealthy noblemen of England, the Czars of Russia, had always been "free" to express themselves as they saw fit. But if the press is open only to the apologists for Czarist oppression, and closed to those who want to abolish Czarist oppression, it is not a free press—it is precisely the clogged type of press the democratic experiment was to abolish from the American continent.

Democrats rejected the species of communication where a few men speak and the rest merely listen. Democracy meant that each would have access to the ears of all. Each man's written thoughts would be as prominently distributed and as widely available as any other man's. The press would be open to every man who could express himself truthfully and coherently. To be available to all, the press must be supported by all. And if the press is socially supported, this means that no man and no group of men can have monopoly over it. If the press is socially supported and freely available to all, it obviously cannot be bought. If the press can be bought, it will be bought by those who can best afford to buy it, and will be most readily available to those who have a lot of money; such a press will not be equally available to all men.

Where there's freedom of speech and freedom of the press, there cannot be "dangerous ideas." There can be imaginative and unimaginative, original and trite ideas, but no "dangerous" ones. The advocacy of public sabotage, misery and oppression for the sake of private aggrandisement and power is dangerous, but it is not an idea. In a democratic society, the man who advocates personal gain at public expense would be greeted as a lunatic, since he expresses, not reasoned conclusions, but an irrational will to dominate over and enslave other men—such a man expresses the type of irrationalism which twentieth century Freudian Psychoanalysts are frantically trying to justify. Fraud, slander and deception are not ideas, and a well-informed, well-educated democratic society had best greet them with indifference. Excessive punishment of the perpetrators of fraud and deception invariably does more harm than good, since punishment is next of kin to oppression, and once the spreading circle of oppression is given a foothold, it swells like a cancer and overruns all of a society's institutions. Fraud and deception thrive on ignorance; to cope with them, a democratic society would seek, not to repress fraud and deception, but to abolish ignorance. Clearly the maintenance of a healthy body, not the endless consumption of medicines, is the best way to prevent disease. In a democratic society, a truthful and original idea well expressed cannot be "dangerous." At the outer limit, it can be unpopular. But an unpopular idea, if it has value, will quickly gain popularity, and when it gains popularity and approval, a democratic public will experiment with it and enact it. Democrats envisioned a society where men would continually experiment with social arrangements and institutions in order to fulfill the needs of the human being and enlarge his intellect, imagination and understanding. The limits beyond which the experiment could not trespass were "certain unalienable rights" among which are "life, liberty, and the pursuit of happiness."[45] In an undemocratic society, the problems of a democratic society seem insurmountable, and the ideals unattainable. To a blind man, it is hard to grasp that others can see. In an undeveloped society beridden with poverty and hunger, the elimination of disease appears to be an insurmountable problem; there are difficulties at every turn; each solution reveals new problems; each victory is accompanied by countless defeats. Yet in a society where poverty and hunger are on the way to being abolished, many of the "insurmountable problems" disappear; men suddenly find that the maintenance of cleanliness is not impossible; the elimination of disease suddenly seems a reasonable expectation. To shed ideals because they seem "unattainable" is cowardly; to condemn the abolition of disease because its problems seem "insurmountable" is to offer apologies for those interested in maintaining disease. Perhaps perfect physical and social health of human beings will never be attained, but perfection is merely a guide, not a state of affairs; perfection is a standard, a measure by which directions and tendencies can be judged. One who gives up a problem because of its difficulties, instead of seeking the causes of the difficulties, is a coward. Human physical health will not be approached, and the abolition of disease will seem "insurmountable," so long as poverty and hunger exist. Social justice, honesty and knowledge will seem "unattainable," so long as privilege and inequality exist.

A press cannot at the same time be a Business; a free press would be a social function socially supported, as free as air to every individual. If wealthy and powerful men control the press, and if wealth is required for access to it, then a free press cannot exist. Whatever their personal virtues, the members of a group will judge ideas in terms of their own interests. They will judge "good" those ideas which are favorable to their interest, and "bad" those ideas which are antagonistic to their interest. What's more, if ideas threaten to abolish their interest on the ground that it is oppressive to other men, the men in control will always judge such ideas "uninteresting" and often "dangerous." If thieves supported and ran a press, they would not encourage writings that exposed theft; they would lack interest in writings that condemned theft; they would suppress as "dangerous" writings that urged the abolition of theft. If the press is owned and controlled by one class of men, it cannot be a free press. The virtues of the men who control it are irrelevant. If one group of men acquired a monopoly over the world's air, bottled it, and sold it to the world's inhabitants, air would not be free, no matter how "good" or how "evil" the men who controlled it. A press that is not socially supported and as easily available to all men as air, is not a free press.

Yet the phenomenon that calls itself a "free press" in the United States is neither supported nor run by society, nor is it available to all men. Newspapers, publishing houses, printing establishments are not social functions in the United States; they are all "privately owned." In other words, the press is the "private property" of businessmen, and it is run for financial profit. The bulk of support of American newspapers comes from advertising. Poor men don't advertise. Only the rich advertise. The biggest and wealthiest corporations have the greatest wealth and power to advertise. Advertisement supports the newspaper. If the newspaper publishes ideas unfavorable to corporations, the corporations will not support it. Such papers will die. The only papers that survive will be those that are favorable to the rich men who support them. But this is not a free press. The rich constitute only a fragment of the population. A press supported by an aristocracy of wealth is no more "free" than a press supported by a king, a czar, or an aristocracy of title and superstition. Nor is the United States press equally available to all men. The rich man who owns a newspaper has the power to hire his own staff. Only a very unusual rich man will pick men whose important ideas differ from his own; only a very unusual hired man will dare to disagree significantly with his employer's ideas. The outcome will be that the owner and his staff will provide readers with the same system of ideas. Such a newspaper is a corporation; and the interests of the newspaper owners are the same as the interests of the owners of other corporations. The rich men who own the newspapers express themselves through the editorial columns; they set the policy, the "line"; they limit the range of ideas expressed in their newspapers; they define the purposes, the goals, of the press. The readers of such newspapers will get an undiluted view of how the rich interpret the world; ideas antagonistic to the corporate aristocracy of wealth will be suppressed: they will be relegated to the "little magazines" which are not widely distributed, are not prominently displayed, are not readily available to all men, are at times totally unavailable to most men. The United States press is the press of the rich, and though the rich differ from each other on many topics, from grasshoppers to plays, there are many things they all hold in common, among which are the sanctity of private property, the obligation of debts, the inviolability of wealth and privilege, the necessity to suppress insurrections, and "the imprudence of democracy…"[46]

An excellent illustration of the workings of the American "free press" is an article written by Leo Huberman in the New York *Daily Compass* on May 5, 1952. In the article, Huberman quoted a renowned nineteenth century newspaperman, John Swinton, who "had been managing editor of the New York *Times* and assistant editor of the New York *Sun* under Charles A. Dana; from 1883 to 1887 he published his own paper."[47] Huberman quoted a statement Swinton made to a group of editors at a banquet in his honor. The nineteenth century editor and publisher told his fellow editors: "There is no such thing in America as an Independent press, unless it is in the country towns.

"You know and I know it. There is not one of you who dares to write his honest opinions, and if you did you know beforehand that it would never appear in print.

"I am paid $150 a week for keeping my honest opinions out of the paper I am connected with—others of you are paid similar salaries for similar things—and any of you who would be so foolish as to write his honest opinions would be out on the streets looking for another job.

"The business of the New York journalist is to destroy the truth, to lie outright, to pervert, to villify, to fawn at the feet of Mammon, and to sell his race and his country for his daily bread.

"You know this and I know it, and what folly is this to be toasting an 'Independent Press.'

"We are the tools and vassals of rich men behind the scenes. We are jumping-jacks; they pull the strings and we dance. Our talents, our possibilities, and our lives are all the property of other men. We are intellectual prostitutes."

The *Daily Compass*, the newspaper in which Huberman's article was published in 1952, no longer exists. It "died" shortly after Huberman's article appeared in it. The *Daily Compass* had hired radical democrats, socialists, liberals, and other independent-minded writers, many of them antagonistic to the society of corporate wealth, and it had allowed the men to express themselves. But the *Daily Compass* did not get support from the corporate rich whose plunder many of its writers attacked; it did not get the required Advertisements. Huberman wrote a sad prediction of the *Daily Compass*' collapse in the same article. "Our highly-praised freedom of the press ... means freedom for very rich men to own newspapers and give the public a picture of the world through their eyes, the eyes of Big Business. No law makes the press unfree in the United States. None is needed. Working men haven't the money to buy and run daily newspapers. Rich people have. Therefore the news we get is slanted, distorted, suppressed—against the poor and for the rich."

A newspaper with a staff that runs against the grain of the corporate aristocracy must seek support from that very aristocracy in order to survive. To express themselves in the United States, men who are opposed to wealth and privilege must seek aid from a wealthy man who betrays the interests of his own class. Poor men—workers, students, intellectuals, artists—cannot possibly support a newspaper as well equipped and staffed, as widely circulated, as prominently displayed, as the New York *Times*, the New York *Herald Tribune*, the *Daily News*, the *Daily Mirror*, etc. The fact that there have often been rich men in the United States who supported newspapers that analyzed and exposed wealth, privilege and property, does not mean that the United States press is free: it merely means that men whose ideas differ from the official line must, in order to express themselves, seek the patronage of rich men who betray the interests of their class. In the France of Louis XV, Voltaire and Rousseau had to seek the patronage of noblemen in order to have the leisure to write and the wealth to publish. But Louis XV's France is not known for its free press. The American revolution of 1776 could hardly have taken place if, to acquaint their fellow countrymen with their views, the American revolutionaries had needed to seek King George's permission to publish their views, King George's support to print them, and King George's influence to distribute them.

In a democratic society, concrete and complete information would be so important that the dissemination of frauds, lies and deceptions would not be permitted. Scientists recognize such a principle in their own "field," and they become justifiably indignant when someone "fakes" an experiment and sabotages years of study and research by supplying his fellow scientists with false and deceptive data. Yet outside their "fields," American scientists are creatures of the corporate society: the wellbeing of physics, or chemistry, is far more important to them than the wellbeing of human life. The principle which scientists value so highly in their "fields" is flaunted in their society. Swinton told the editors, "I am paid $150 a week for keeping my honest opinions out of the paper I am connected with—others of you are paid similar salaries for similar things—and any of you who would be so foolish as to write his honest opinions would be out on the streets looking for another job." Not only does the newspaperman in the corporate society suppress his own views. "The business of the New York journalist is to destroy the truth, to lie outright, to pervert, to villify, to fawn at the feet of Mammon..."[48]

In order to "lie outright, to pervert, to vilify" most effectively, a unique institution has been invented and highly refined in the United States: the institution of Advertising, supplemented by the so-called "Public Relations Field." In advertising, self expression plays no role whatever, concrete information is withheld, complete information is suppressed. Advertising is a vast system of organized lying, perversion, villification, whose sole purpose is to sell the products of corporations by any means whatever. Corporations hire the advertisers to create in people the desire to buy the products the corporations make. In other words, the corporations themselves create the "needs" they fill. This type of plunder is unique in human history. The advertising man lies, deceives and defrauds in order to sell the products of his employer to a public that does not need them. The ad man and the public relations man do this for money; they are hired to deceive men for the financial gain of their employers. The ad man sells his imagination to the task of inventing slogans and his intellect to the task of defrauding men.

In the United States, the expenditure for advertising greatly exceeds the expenditure for education, for cultural and artistic ennoblement, for intellectual growth. According to an observer, "by 1951 the American people were spending $6,548 million a year on ads, a billion and a half more than on education. By 1956 the advertising expenditure reached about ten billion, and it now seems to he growing at the rate of around a billion a year."[49] The obvious result is that "the good people of these colonies"[50] are thoroughly ignorant of the workings of the corporate world in which they live, but vastly informed on the "brand names" of the corporate products and gadgets. Some vivid illustrations are cited by Harvey O'Connor in *The Empire of Oil*. The book's frontispiece quotes the New York *Herald Tribune*'s description of American economic ignorance, with specific reference to oil ignorance. "There is no country in the world which has the body of technical doctrine regarding petroleum in all its aspects which is possessed in the United States. There is no country which is so thoroughly geared to the power supplied by petroleum. Yet, thanks to the mixture of unsupported argument, official reticence and sheer hypocrisy which befog the subject, there can be few peoples so poorly informed of the global implications of oil production and distribution as the Americans."[51] This world-renowned American ignorance does not depict a low level of intelligence; it illustrates who owns and runs the instruments of communication, education, manipulation. Big corporations, like the oil companies, can buy the ideas and opinions of millions of men. As O'Connor points out, "Radio and TV are admirably attuned to the needs of such corporations. For one thing, there is no back talk from the listeners, and, at the moment of the broadcast, no competition for the listener's ear or eye. As only those with millions can sponsor such programs, there is little likelihood of radio and TV listeners absorbing incorrect ideas. In the American way, the corporations foot the bill for the nation's entertainment and information and can properly call the piper's tune. Here there is little need to bow before the shibboleths of objectivity for it is frankly a commercial proposition, even if draped in terms of public service."[52] The outcome is that, while "there can be few peoples so poorly informed of the global implications of oil production and distribution as the Americans," there can be few peoples so well informed in the deceptions inculcated into them by the corporations' advertisers. A small but significant illustration with reference to oil shows that though Americans may not believe their advertisers, they nevertheless follow like docile sheep the paths laid out for them. According to a Readers Digest article cited by O'Connor, Americans spend $200 million a year on "premium" and "Ethyl" gasolines which are advertised as "the best" on the ugly billboards that line the nation's highways and despoil what is surely one of the world's most varied and beautiful natural landscapes. Each citizen dutifully internalizes the message on the billboards; each can tell his neighbor many technical and philosophical reasons why "Ethyl" is "best." And yet, "President Reese H. Taylor of Union Oil summarized the situation for his cohorts: we are steering clear of the rash of gasoline additives described everywhere in newspapers and on billboards. Our research boys gave all of these so-called wonder chemicals a thorough going-over. They find that the wear and tear on motors, the deterioration of valves, and so on, resulting from the use of such additive-fortified gasolines more than discounted the benefits, if any. We found there was no substitute for good gasoline." Car owners obey the billboards and pay a great deal extra for the gas in the tank with the "tetraethyl lead."And yet, "...According to the continuing survey of the DuPont company, main supplier of tetraethyl lead ... a third of the regular gasoline sampled had as much or more lead than the premium, and two samples of premium had no lead whatsoever!"[53]

This abysmal ignorance of human potentialities and social institutions, wedded to a fictitious knowledge of things, is clearly a revival of superstition on a grand scale—a superstition far deadlier than feudal religious superstition precisely because of its non-religious content and its inhuman purpose. The ad men create the "image" through which Americans see the world. The content of the "image" inculcates fear, hatred, envy, and a never-ending desire to buy the products peddled by the corporations.

The result is an ignorant, superstitious, manipulated population of docile men and women who spend their working hours making gadgets they have not chosen to make and do not control, and spend their leisure hours buying the gadgets and returning to their corporate masters the incomes they got for making the gadgets. This cycle of purposelessness and human irrelevance has its toll, for apparently the creative intellect, the human imagination, the sense for truth, cannot be completely obliterated. The population of men whose humanity is suppressed is a population of anxiety-ridden men constantly seeking outlets for repressed passion, repressed imagination, repressed hatred. The advertisers are aware of this objectless anxiety of the American people—and the advertisers have learned to manipulate the very fear and anxiety they have themselves so largely created for the purpose of serving their corporate employers yet more effectively. A typical report of an advertisers' "Council" outlines a campaign in which the disease created and maintained by corporate advertising will be manipulated by corporate advertising. The Report reads:

> "The rationale for the campaign was along the following lines. More people than ever seem to be suffering from an outraged sense of justice, a feeling of inadequacy, a delusion that the world is down on them and that they are trapped by their jobs, their marriage problems, their financial situation, etc. These emotional conflicts and frustrations are leading to both a conscious and an unconscious search for peace of mind.
>
> "Some of the manifestations of this are evident in increased church attendance, in an unprecedented demand on professional psychiatrists, psychoanalysts, clergymen, marriage counsellors and even in the sale of tranquilizer drugs.
>
> "…people who go to psychiatrists for help, in most cases are not seeking any change in themselves, but rather are looking for comfort, reassurance and advice.
>
> "That is one side of the climate in which [the product] must be sold.

"The other side, of course, is that a mass audience is more apt to be moved by cheerful promises than by pointing a finger, no matter how truthfully, at its problems, conflicts and sore spots.

"The human animal is basically happy. People acquire tensions. They learn fears—it isn't part of their basic makeup. The prophets of doom complain that no one will listen to them. Why? Because no one wants to listen to them.

"Now, these two conflicting points of view in the average American's makeup can be reconciled. The catalyst is humor—humor combined with a completely new promise about the benefits of [the product] in the idiom of today.

"Pursuing this total concept led naturally into an examination of the various conditions of tenseness to which all are subject from time to time...

"The list of such frustrations in the vernacular of everyday American living is practically inexhaustible...."[54]

The report also says that "nothing short of boldness could hope to penetrate the consciousness of the American public."[55] And all this is for the sale of the almighty Product. To sell the products from which the corporate rich reap their fortunes, all the means that money can buy are used: psychologists, sociologists, educators, theologians, writers, philosophers. The appeal is made, not to understanding, but to emotions and fears; the advertiser's aim is not to resolve, but to exploit for their maximum profit, the problems and tensions of human beings. Millennia of human thought, study, classification, analysis and discovery are here put to the service of multiplying the wealth of the rich. The drastic effect of advertising on intellectual and artistic activity has been pointed out by Leo Marx: "...perhaps the most subtle and elusive product of advertising is the attitude it engenders toward all activity of mind.

"In recent years Americans have speculated endlessly about the anti-intellectualism of our people, and about the apathy, confusion and alienation of youth. Yet it is a curious fact that in such discussions the influence of advertising, one of the most powerful value-creating instruments in world history, seldom is mentioned. Almost from infancy our children are exposed to the teachings of the ad man. He instructs them in the essential meaninglessness of all creations of mind: words, images, and ideas. The lesson is that they have no intrinsic importance, that they are merely instruments of manipulation. It is often said that, after all, advertising does no harm because no one really believes it. But of course that is precisely the point. In treating man as consumer we succeed in debasing what is most distinctively human."[56] When the imagination becomes a means for selling goods, when ideas become cliches about merchandise, when art becomes illustration of "items" and brand names, then the human mind is thoroughly degraded, and becomes superfluous.

In the corporate society, the public is converted into a mass. The "people," who were to control the press, have become its victims. The press is not merely unfree; it has ceased to be a means of communication, it is a means of mass manipulation. The degraded American "public" is not a democratic public. A mass of uninformed men bombarded with a fragmented world view, with only one organized theme cannot exert control over human affairs. A population of mis-educated men stormed with an infinite array of uninterpreted, irrelevant, sadistic detail designed to arouse desire and hatred, cannot possibly hold intelligent opinions on important public issues. Such a population does not rule, it does not constitute a "public"; it constitutes a mass—a controlled, systematically manipulated mass.

As advertising spreads, the ad-man mentality penetrates all facets of corporate life. The twentieth century American is not concerned with developing himself as a human being, but rather with "selling" himself. The time which other men spend enlarging their intellectual, artistic and imaginative faculties is spent by Americans in the acquisition of techniques of "self-selling." The content and quality of a human being cease to matter; all that counts is the label, the clothes, the fake smile.

The most glaring, as well as the most drastic, place where the ad-man mind has penetrated is the American government. Armed with weapons that could instantaneously incinerate all living humanity as well as all man's past achievements, the American government has become increasingly preoccupied with maintaining an "image" of competence and responsibility while pursuing an incompetent, irresponsible, and lunatic policy.

The official "image" depicts an America which is neither capitalist, nor corporate, nor hierarchic, and it is couched in terms that are familiar to the "average man." The result is illustrated by a New York *Times* article describing a digest "jointly sponsored by Yale University and the Advertising Council":

> "That the American economy is uniquely dynamic, that it has produced the highest standards of living, more widely spread, than the world has ever seen before, that it has come closest to a democratic, classless society and that this has come about through a fantastic increase in productivity made possible through greater mechanization—all this is well known to Americans, even though often but dimly understood abroad. 'People's capitalism' is increasingly used as a name for our economic system."[57]

(In fact, the name "People's Capitalism" is not "increasingly used" because the Advertising Council greatly overestimated its glamour. Using as a model the term "People's Communism," the Advertising Council neglected to find out how much of the world's population supports "People's Communism" not because of the glamorous sound of the words, but because of the quality of the dispensation, the degree of improvement in the human condition.) Since capitalists want neither to change their dispensation nor to legislate themselves out of existence, and since advertising experts are hired to juggle words and not to improve the reality underneath, they must continue to confine themselves to manipulating the Image. And the manipulation goes to fantastic lengths. During the Great Depression, the concept of "capitalist exploitation" was introduced into American thought by left-wing critics.

When the critics became respectable members of the New Deal administration, the term "exploitation" was dropped from the American vocabulary, and the System was known by the half-respectable title of "capitalism." When the Nazi War broke out and the System had to be defended, "capitalism" was replaced by the ultra-respectable title of "free enterprise." During the whole period, the highest corporate capitalists had been steadily consolidating greater power and control over the government. When, after the war, corporation-men replaced purged left-wingers, "free enterprise" became simply "freedom," and during the reign of John Foster Dulles, the capitalist countries as well as the feudal military dictatorships became "The Free World." This process is known as "face-lifting." Hitler's Propaganda Minister could hardly have done better. By 1960 there was no more capitalism. Only Freedom. Capitalists were so impressed by this manipulation of words they thought that by giving capitalism the name "freedom" they had thereby made it attractive to all the world's population. According to the New York *Times*,

> "Fifty leading United States business men presented ... a 'declaration of economic freedoms' to offset Communist propaganda at the United Nations...
>
> "The freedoms listed in the declaration were freedom of competitive private enterprise; choice of occupation; voluntary organization for private enterprise; contract; property ownership; freedom to produce, buy or sell; competition; trade; money, that is, a sound currency."[58]

At the time of writing this book, Cuba was invaded. The ad-man deceptions by which the American people were "informed" of this invasion bore a lurid similarity to the Nazi German accounts of their "liberation" of Europe. For years the American "free press" had supplied its readers with barely a mention of the atrocities, the brutality, the misery in Cuba under the dictator Fulgencio Batista and his administration of sugar planters, hired killers, and gamblers. Americans knew nothing about the oppression entailed in the fact that American corporations owned and operated Cuban sugar, land, electricity, telephones, and indirectly, armed forces. When revolution swept across Cuba and gained increasing support until most of Cuba's six million people were behind it, thus enabling it to rid Cuba of the planters' regime and the powerful army by which Batista had ruled, the American people were given an "image" of a coup d'etat in which a few hundred men had "overthrown" a few hundred other men. When the Cuban revolutionary government made education and culture available to men who had never seen a book and gave land and work and food to men who had never before been able to think or work because they suffered from chronic hunger diseases, the

American people were told by their "free press" that Cuba was "going Communist," and they were shown pictures of sad, wealthy landowners whose innumerable acres of land had been given to thousands of landless peasants. And when the Cuban government expropriated the American corporations whose huge profits had come from the raw materials and the cheap labor of a few million starving Cubans, the American people were told the familiar atrocity stories about priests and nuns which constitute the American "reading public's" knowledge of the non-capitalist part of the world. The American people were told virtually nothing of the reforms instituted by the Cuban revolution, of the housing, the education, the culture, the food which became available to Cubans—to some for the first time in their lives. They were told nothing of the enthusiasm of the Cuban people, of their revolution's ideals, of their plans. The American press, which daily consumes entire forests, directed itself to the constant repetition of charges that the Cuban Government was Communist, that it was "extracontinental," that it destroyed Inter-American Unity, that it undermined the Monroe Doctrine, and—when the "image" was "sold"—that it should be overthrown. When Cuba's Foreign Minister charged, at the United Nations, that the United States Government's Central Intelligence Agency was planning an invasion of Cuba, the press "explained" the charge to its readers as "outrageous," and as nothing more than a part of "Cuba's hate-America campaign." Yet in mid-April 1961, Cuba was invaded. Now the American newspaper readers were told that "Cubans" were liberating Cuba from "Communist Terror." At the same time, the American people were told that, though the United States Government had "sympathy" for the invaders, it was not giving them any aid; and they were also told that neither the United States nor any of its Latin American allies were allowing their territory to be used for the invasion: the "Cuban" invaders had presumably been holding their breaths under water off the Cuban shore while waiting for their chance to "liberate" Cuba. And then the American press, on the authority of the "Cuban Revolutionary Council," reported in front page banner headlines a sequence of events that was to lead to the "liberation" of Cuba by the "Cuban Freedom Fighters." The stories released to the press by the "Cuban Revolutionary Council" told that the Cuban people were about to rise against their government, they told that Cuban flyers had defected from the Cuban air force, they told of landings, and of victories. The day victory was to be proclaimed, the "liberators" were in the sea. The "Cuban Revolutionary Council" announced, and the press dutifully reported, that Fidel Castro had flown Russian Migs (fighter planes) and driven Russian tanks against the helpless "Freedom Fighters." The invasion failed. And suddenly the American press, with a few significant exceptions, became piously silent about the "liberation" of Cuba. One of the exceptions was the New York *Times*, which continued to run articles on Cuba until the American President reminded a conference of important newspapermen that the publication of information embarrassing to the United States Government was *not* one of the tasks of the Free Press. The *Times* revealed, though not in banner headlines, that "As has been an open secret in Florida and Central America for months, the C.I.A. planned, coordinated and directed the operations that ended in the defeat on a beachhead in southern Cuba..."[59] The "Cuban Revolutionary Council," it turned out, had not been in charge of the invasion. "On the day the anti-Castro forces landed in Cuba members of the Cuban Revolutionary Council were kept incommunicado by the Central Intelligence Agency in an old house near Miami ...

"The effect of not taking the Revolutionary Council leaders into confidence was to keep them from having any role in directing the landings..."[60] The reports supposedly issued by the "Cuban Revolutionary Council" about the landings, the fighting, the impending victory, the defections, the Russian Migs, had all come from the office of Lem Jones Associates, Inc., of Madison Avenue, New York—an advertising firm.[61] The invaders, it turned out, had not sprung from the sea, but from bases in Florida, in Louisiana, in Guatemala, and in United States-controlled Swann Islands in the Caribbean. The leading "Freedom Fighters" were those who regularly carry on the C.I.A.'s world-wide cloak-and-dagger operations. "A Filipino guerrilla specialist was in charge of some of the training. He was assisted by five or six instructors who are believed to be Slavs, perhaps Ukrainians, and who were assisted by interpreters."[62] The "defector" from the Cuban air force turned out to have flown an American plane with a Cuban insignia painted on it. "When ... one of the pilots who landed in Miami described himself as a defector from the Cuban Air Force, his picture, published in local newspapers, was promptly identified here [in Miami] as that of a Lieutenant from the Guatemalan camp. He has vanished."[63] And the "Russian Migs," which filled Americans with fear, frenzy and hatred, turned out to be "United-States-built T-33 jets flown by the Castro pilots."[64] By way of "explanation" of the furor raised by the front page scare-headlines about the Migs, the writer briefly commented: "It is thought that some of the insurgents, when surprised by these T-33 jets, believed they were Soviet-built Migs."[65] The "free press" of the United States did not tell its readers that the source of its "facts" on the Cuban invasion was a Public Relations firm on Madison Avenue, New York. But the "free press" did tell the American people, repeatedly and emphatically, that the Cuban government had "betrayed" the Cuban revolution.

"Alas! is it true, that ages are necessary to understand, whilst a moment will suffice to invent, an imposture?"[66]

The eighteenth century intellectual rebels were the Founding Fathers of American rhetoric, but the eighteenth century capitalists were the Founding Fathers of American practice. In American practice, the "democratic" participation is restricted to the marking of a ballot every two or four years. On the ballot are the names of men he does not know and has not chosen. He "votes" on the basis of no issues whatsoever, because no issues are presented. C. Wright Mills has summarized a typical ceremony. "In the 472 Congressional elections of 1954, for example, no national issues were clearly presented, nor even local issues related clearly to them. Slogans and personal attacks on character, personality defects, and counter-charges and suspicions were all that the electorate could see or hear, and, as usual, many paid no attention at all. Each candidate tried to dishonor his opponent, who in turn tried to dishonor him. The outraged candidates seemed to make themselves the issue, and on that issue virtually all of them lost. The electorate saw no issues at all, and they too lost, although they did not know it."[67] The candidate who succeeds is the one who can pay for the most lavish campaign and the cleverest advertising, who can best malign his opponent's personal traits, and who will best fulfill the role of courier for the vested interests of the rich. "Estimates of the cost of the 1952 presidential campaign ranged all the way up to $100 million. Frank Edwards, the former AFL radio commentator, said that the oil interests contributed half that sum, and all to the Eisenhower forces. There was no way to contest the statement, for no one in authority cared to flash a beam into the dark recesses of corporate financing of political parties."[68] The government "of the people" is quite openly a government of the corrupt and of the rich, yet it continues to call itself "democratic." America is a land where a very small group of men participate in the making of important decisions, where very few men's ideas carry weight and authority, where only the voice of the Celebrity is heard by All. "The people" have no greater participation in America's polity than in America's economy. "The top of modern American society is increasingly unified, and often seems willfully coordinated: at the top there has emerged an elite of power. The middle levels are a drifting set of stalemated, balancing forces: the middle does not link the bottom with the top. The bottom of this society is politically fragmented, and even as a passive fact, increasingly powerless: at the bottom there is emerging a mass society."[69] The democratic rhetoric hides a corporate state. The government "of the people" is a government of the rich. The people are told that by "casting ballots" for the rich they are somehow defending "Freedom." And the people acquiesce, and they thank the Founding Fathers, whose works they have not read, for having left them such a blessed political system.

5. CORPORATE DISPENSATION

The democratic ideal was an affirmation of human life. Democracy was to open for all men the possibility for creative development, imaginative exploration, experimental activity. Every man was to participate in the creation of the human community. Knowledge and technique need not have been put to the service of profits and slaughter. If taken up in a spirit that affirms human life, the sciences and technologies could be made to serve human ends. As Lewis Mumford has pointed out, "The ability to face one's whole self, and to direct every part of it toward a more unified development, is one of the promises held forth by the advance both of objective science and subjective understanding."[1] If put to the service of human development the science and technology which have come to the verge of annihilating mankind would enable men to "attempt enterprises that no civilization seeking mainly to exploit immediate economic advantages would entertain: launching projects and experiments whose outcome may await centuries...

The margin of free time, free energy, and free vitality that modern man may command is so great that, instead of devoting most of his days to mere biological survival, he now has capacities for self-development that were once confined to a minuscule ruling class."[2] In the democratic society, there would be science but no "experts," technology but no "technicians"; there would be no narrow, undeveloped, incomplete persons who are imbecils outside their own specialty: "the fragmentary man would be replaced by the completely developed individual, one for whom different social functions are but alternative forms of activity. Men would fish, hunt, or engage in literary criticism without becoming professional fishermen, hunters, or critics" (Karl Marx). The completely developed individual would not allow the instruments of human growth to fall once again into the hands of those who would use them for human oppression; such an individual would also have the intellectual power to undertake "ruthless criticism of everything that exists, ruthless in the sense that the criticism will not shrink either from its own conclusions or from conflict with the powers that be."[3] Giovanni Batista Vico long ago pointed out that man can understand and affect human history because it was made by man. On the same grounds, man can grasp all human knowledge because it is created by man. In a society which promotes wholeness and understanding, each individual would be able to do what any other can do. Thus each would be able to extend the frontiers of his own greatest interest, whether it is physics, poetry, or food preparation, and at the same time would understand, and participate in, the break-throughs of other frontiers. From early childhood on, men would participate in the important activities of the community, and thus would attach to them the naive curiosity and adventurous spirit which men reserve for the activities of childhood. There would be no "problem of leisure," which plagues societies that thwart imagination and creative energy, and reduce human activity to repetition and drudgery. Simone Weil has observed[4] that farmers who have participated fully in the life of the farm from childhood on consider their work, and not the escape from work, the meaningful facet of their lives. To force a man to carry on for thirty years an activity he has mastered in two would be considered a crime in a human dispensation: a crime as ugly as murder, for it kills the potentialities and thwarts the growth of the individual.

But the corporate dispensation is a negation of human life: it thwarts development, prevents wholeness, and nurtures fragmented "experts" and "professionals." Those who reject fragmentation are the outcasts of the corporate society. Yet the armies of incomplete men needed to support the corporate structure are at the same time its greatest danger: nurtured on ignorance, they are prey to a nihilist rejection of human life and a thirst for annihilation which, if allowed to erupt, will not exempt even the corporate masters.

The rich are the only beneficiaries of the corporate society. They are the Holders of all the projects, all the activity, all the rewards. The corporate society is their machine; it yields their profits. Contrary to their own claims, what the rich possess is not internal; it is not related to physique, or psyche, or intellect. The rich do not owe their wealth and prestige to themselves, but to their society and its institutions. In the excellent definition of C. Wright Mills, "the elite are simply those who have the most of what there is to have, which is generally held to include money, power, and prestige—as well as all the ways of life to which these lead. But the elite are not simply those who have the most, for they could not 'have the most' were it not for their positions in the great institutions. For such institutions are the necessary bases of power, of wealth, and of prestige, and at the same time, the chief means of exercising power, of acquiring and retaining wealth, and of cashing in the higher claims for prestige.

"By the powerful we mean, of course, those who are able to realize their will, even if others resist it. No one, accordingly, can be truly powerful unless he has access to the command of major institutions, for it is over these institutional means of power that the truly powerful are, in the first instance, powerful. Higher politicians and key officials of government command such institutional power, so do admirals and generals, and so do the major owners and executives of the larger corporations."[5] If the institutions rotted, or were abolished, the "elite" would not be elite; if they were eased to the bottom of their own market economy, the "elite" would probably be quite pathetic, since they would lack the training of other men to survive in such conditions. But such an eventuality is inconceivable to them, and since they stay by and large only among themselves, they are not fully aware that there is a bottom, they do not suspect that human beings live there, and they are not greatly concerned. Their world is a closed world; it is not a windowless world, but its windows look out only on lawns and beaches, not on slums. "They form a more or less compact social and psychological entity; they have become self-conscious members of a social class. People are either accepted into this class or they are not, and there is a qualitative split, rather than merely a numerical scale, separating them from those who are not elite. They are more or less aware of themselves as a social class and they behave toward one another differently from the way they do toward members of other classes. They accept one another, understand one another, marry one another, tend to work and to think if not together at least alike."[6]

The rich are born to wealth; thus they take wealth for granted, and do not feel concerned with wealth. They are born with their privileges, consequently they do not have to reach for privileges, and they can afford to look down on the "climbers" who do reach for privileges. Being themselves "well born," they feel no solidarity with those who are not "well born": they regard "the mass of mankind" with condescension and contempt. They do not identify with the goals or the problems of other men. Their own world, their "way of life," is made for them: it exists independently of their goals or their efforts. "Every member of the dominant class is a man by divine right," wrote Jean Paul Sartre. "Born into a society of leaders, he is convinced from childhood that he is born *to* command, and in a certain sense that is true, since his parents, who command, have engendered him to follow in their footsteps. There is a certain social function which awaits him in the future, into which he will slip as soon as he has come of age, and this function is something like the metaphysical reality of his person. And in his own eyes he is a person, that is, an *a priori* synthesis of fact and rights. Awaited by his peers, destined to take their place when the time comes, he exists because he has *the right* to exist...."[7]

The dominant minority of the rich consider themselves "the Nation." Born to command, born to privilege, they see their own welfare as "the welfare of the nation"; they see the defense of their privileges as "national defense." The welfare of others is a favor conferred by the rich. Other men do not have the right to exist: they are maintained, and kept happy, through the grace of their benevolent masters. And this grace must be repaid. The duty, the function of other men, is to maintain and protect the privileges of the rich. The ungrateful wretches who refuse must bear the consequences: they will not have jobs conferred on them, they will be unemployed, and to survive they will have to beg from their own lowly peers who are employed for the wages they turn down from the rich. Ungrateful or not, there must always be a certain minimum number of unemployed, between two and five million in the United States, for otherwise the employed would develop inflated conceptions of their own importance: they might become duped with ideas about the Welfare State, or worse. They might demand a greater share of wealth and privilege, and the rich know that "the mass of mankind" would only cut their own throats with greater leisure and wealth: they would not know what to do with it, and they'd commit suicide and increase the divorce rate. That's bad. "The mass of mankind" had best be kept in place. For the masses, the highest virtues are obedience and patriotism: these are the two components of nationalism. The educational system must see to it that obedience and patriotism are internalized, and that men are good workers. The good citizen is the patriot who identifies his own interests with the interests of the rich, who sees his duty as the defense of the privileges of the rich. And, as in slave societies, the slave must be taught to get vicarious joy from his master's Greatness and Power.

The corporate structure has irresponsibility built-in. Unlike other aristocracies, the dominant minority of corporate Holders do not have personal contact with those who serve them. This is the main psychological difference between the Holders of the corporate society and the earlier entrepreneurial capitalists. The entrepreneur was often the owner, the chief executive, as well as the employer. He was master over a relatively small number of men, and he was visible to them. The men knew he was the Boss: they were hired by him, supervised by him, reprimanded and fired by him. Or, in case there was a supervisor or a foreman, the men knew this was the second man, that he was the Boss acting by proxy. And the Boss had an equally clear view of his relation to "his men." Such an entrepreneur knew, for example, that when one of his "hands" fell into a meat vat, this was an unfortunate consequence of "the business." He may have greeted such an event with indifference, but the chain of responsibility was not hidden from him.

The corporate Shareholder, however, is completely removed from the activities of his corporation (or corporations, since most of the rich are Shareholders in many corporations, even "competing" ones). He has control over thousands of men, but is thoroughly unaware of his relation to them. This unawareness is built into the corporate structure itself. The Shareholder's money is invested for him by a high-priced specialist hired for that purpose. His corporation's activities are supervised by Executives who are paid to do that. He does not employ his own men, since vast "personnel offices" exist for that purpose. He does not advocate or advertise his products, since he pays ad men for that. He does not talk to people about his corporations, but sends hired public relations men to represent him. His only concern is to apportion money to serve one purpose or another, and he can hire an "expert" to do even that for him. If he chooses, he does not have to know what his corporations make. That, too, is his Privilege. He can literally allow his money to "work" for him, and can maintain complete ignorance about what his money "does." He may spend all his time travelling wherever he wants to go; he may collect art works, women, sport cars. He can "give" minute fractions of his wealth to Foundations, thus getting it tax-exempted and feeling like a humanitarian philanthropist devoted to "helping suffering humanity." He can, if he likes, run for political office, and thus extend the dominion under his control: he has the means to represent "the mass of mankind" in the legislature: the means to pay the party boss; to finance the advertising campaign; to hire the "writers" in the public relations firms whose "releases" inform newspaper readers of his candidacy, his honesty, and his devotion to "democracy."

The Holder lives in a world of privilege; he eats only the cream. He does not participate in the affairs of society. The corporation runs for his profit, but he does not design its product, does not produce it, does not distribute it, does not necessarily even consume it. The workers run for his profit, but he does not hire them, does not talk to them, does not share their concerns. Taught that all work is degrading, the Holder cannot imagine a state of affairs where work would be satisfying and ennobling. With absolute control over the projects of thousands of men, he is nevertheless deprived, by his ideology and his position, of the satisfaction that comes from the creation and carrying out of projects. His decisions are absolute, but they concern only money; he "sees" his corporations' activities only in the form of a financial report. The implementation is delegated to many men, none of whom fully comprehend the entire project. Tied to the financial end of all his activities, he does not, and cannot, get the understanding or the fulfillment of making, of creating—yet by fragmenting projects among hired servants, he deprives others of the joy of creation.

The financial masters of the realm are many times removed from the consequences of their decisions; they do not implement the decisions they make, or those made in their name. If one suggested to a Holder, for example, that most of his wealth came from a corporation that manufactured equipment for weapons of genocide, he could become righteously indignant: *he* doesn't have anything to do with genocide, he merely reads the "financial reports" prepared for him; he may not even read the "reports," since his subordinates are trustworthy, devoted men, highly trained to spend their lives increasing his wealth. He can continue his travels undisturbed. And his subordinates are not responsible either; they're merely hired to invest his money, and weapons happen to be the most profitable "item." Thus the Holders aren't responsible. And below the Holders, everyone is hired and no one is responsible. If an "accident" should take place, and if humanity should happen to be annihilated, no one will be responsible, no one will be to blame, no one will have caused anything. In fact, everyone will have been doing his best. The annihilation of mankind will not have been caused by a definite group of men, at a definite time, under definite circumstances, but rather, according to the Corporate Theologian Reinhold Niebuhr, the cataclysm will have been caused by Sin, and those responsible for it will be Collective Humanity: every human being who has ever lived anywhere will be equally responsible and equally guilty. Within the confines of the corporate structure, no solutions can be found—to anything.

Rich and removed, taking wealth and privilege for granted, the Holder feels no solidarity with other men. Any sense of obligation or responsibility is totally lacking. Men are not his brothers. He cannot feel equality towards "inferiors." He does not live in a community. Humanity is a fictional concept to him. He does not believe in sharing, or in cooperation. If he agrees to a project, he will do his part only if it pleases him. He feels no more reason to discharge obligations or promises towards "inferiors" than men feel towards dogs. But he takes it for granted that his reign constitutes the best of all possible worlds, that "Men of great property are deeply interested in the welfare of the states and they are the most competent judges of the form of government, best calculated to preserve their property, and such liberties as it is proper for the common and inferior class of people to enjoy. Men of wealth possess natural and acquired understanding, as they manifest by amassing riches, or by keeping and increasing those they derive from their ancestors, and they are best acquainted with the wants, the wishes, and desires of the people, and they are always ready to relieve them in their private and public stations."[8] The rich also take it for granted that "the mass of mankind," the hierarchy of hired servants, recognize and appreciate the superior wisdom, understanding, and benevolence of the dominant rich. However, according to George Bernard Shaw, the rich do not interpret correctly. "The taste for spending one's life in drudgery and never-ending pecuniary anxiety solely in order that certain idle and possibly vicious people may fleece you for their own amusement, is not so widespread as the papers would have us think."[9]

"They were offered the choice between becoming kings or the couriers of kings. The way children would, they all wanted to be couriers. Therefore there are only couriers who hurry about the world, shouting to each other—since there are no kings—messages that have become meaningless. They would like to put an end to this miserable life of theirs but they dare not because of their oaths of service."[10]

Franz Kafka's couriers carry many meanings into various realms and certainly they bring a glaring light into a corporate world where Holders are the hidden monarchs, Profits the aim of the realm, and Executives its most visible representatives. If the Holders get the privileges of the corporate society and the workers bear its physical brunt, the administrative couriers, besides being the society's most conspicuous members, bear its full psychological impact.

The new men in the capitalist economy—variously known as White Collar Workers, Minor Executives, Managers, New Middle Class—thoroughly upset and threw into confusion the expectations of traditional socialists. The drive for monopoly which propels all capitalists was expected, in time, to lodge great wealth and power in the hands of a few capitalists. This much, in fact, took place: "Slightly more than half [of American Industry] is owned outright by not more than 200 corporations."[11] However, it was expected that the property-less working class would grow larger and larger. In fact, the number of property-less men has increased. But it is not a working class. Seemingly out of nowhere, the White Collar men appeared on the scene, and before socialists could adjust their theories, these new men started to outnumber the workers. These men are property-less, they are often no better paid than workers, but they are not wage-workers, they do not produce anything, and they find solidarity not with each other, but with the corporations they serve. Even Karl Marx, the most far-seeing and imaginative of the founders of socialist theory, could diagnose only the coming of a monopoly capitalism where the greatest wealth would be concentrated in a few hands; his imagination was not cruel enough to visualize the plethora of lackeys who would be hired to preserve the higher privileges of their masters.

Every agrarian society has its officials and tax-collectors, every government its bureaucrats. In themselves they are not new. But a society where elaborate feudal hierarchies of bureaucrats exist to preserve and maximize the profits of private corporations—this is new. And the visibility of these people—the conspicuous roles which they play in every activity of the corporate society—this is new. In the past, kings displayed their military establishments but hid their bureaucrats. Farmers are never conspicuous; separated by patches of land, they are rarely seen in large numbers. Workers are crowded together, but hidden from public view by windowless factory walls. The factory owners are on their estates or recreational resorts set off from other men by fences marked KEEP OUT – PRIVATE PROPERTY – NO TRESPASSING. But in the cities, during the working day, the couriers are everywhere visible; they are the front of the corporate society; they are the department-store salesgirls, the door-to-door salesmen, the gas-station attendants, the bank clerks, office clerks, secretaries, higher secretaries, Managers, Supervisors, Directors, and entire schools of Assistants. In parts of New York City, there are banks on all four corners which have glass walls: inside, in full view of the thousands who pass daily, are the regimented rows of desks, each with its clerk. Skyscrapers with glass walls, gigantic rectangular filing cabinets in the "international style," are built constantly in the Empire City. Inside each of the thousands and thousands of slots, behind a large pane of glass, there is a manager, with his desk and his secretary. Thus an illusion is created that bank clerks exert some control over "their" banks, or salesgirls over "their" department stores, or gas-station attendants over "their" oil corporations. The king does not make public appearances, whereas the couriers are always on display. Thus the inhabitants of the corporate society are under the illusion that the couriers, the White Collar people, control the corporate economy.

 The administrative hierarchies are organized along military lines: they are pyramids where power is passed from the top down through an infinity of layers, which grow larger as they get lower. Each corporation has its own private hierarchy. However, unlike military armies, these hierarchies are composed of all officers and no soldiers. The actual top is invisible except to very special couriers, mostly lawyers. From the top down, each group has its rank, and each feels awe before the ranks above and contempt for those below. Next to the top are generally the Boards of Directors. These may be the Holders themselves, but generally they are glorified salaried-employees. These highest Directors may or may not hold stock in the corporation, they may or may not be independently rich, but some things they all do have in common: their one and only loyalty is toward the corporation, the only profits they work for are those of the corporation, the only wellbeing they know is the corporation's. Whether the corporation deals with steel or oil or food, the Directors concern themselves only with money—with maximizing profits that are not their own. High up on the pyramid, they are nevertheless couriers, not kings. They set the pace and hold up the image for all those below. Various types of subchiefs, Executive Directors, are the tops of the pyramids at a corporation's regional plants. The Executive Director is more visible than the Board. He generally has a local office. He is "benevolent" to those under him, but fearful of the Board. It is his task to implement locally the financial decisions of the Board. Hired and fired by the Board of Directors, the local Executive is the highest in the pyramid who has no view of the Holders.* From this point down, there are many couriers but no king. Immediately below the Executive Director, there is an intricate network of Assistant Directors, Associate Directors, Supervisors, Head Secretaries, Office Supervisors, and many, many other titles and sub-titles. The Office Supervisor is generally an efficient woman in middle-age, who is in charge of the secretaries, switch-board operators, typists, filing-cabinet experts, and filing cabinets. Generally prudish in her sexual habits, she finds her life's greatest joy in a one-sided Platonic intimacy with her immediate superior, the Executive Director. To her, the Board is a complex system of unapproachable deities. She speaks of "The Board," not as a group of human beings, but as an impersonal Thing that sits over and judges the affairs of her office. For her, the Holders no longer exist. The rich men at the top of her own corporation are as unreal to her as the rich men of any other corporation.

   The ranking system effectively prevents any unity, any feeling of solidarity. With awe for the top and contempt for the bottom, the White Collar people envy their own peers, and are in constant anxiety lest one of their co-workers "rise" above and one of those below rise to

---
*Unless he sits on the Board of Directors.

their own level. The master-servant relationship is hidden from their view. Each group's contact is limited to the rank immediately above, and that immediately below. The rest is shrouded in a deep fog. The top is above the clouds, the bottom below hell. The only solidarity, the only identification they feel, is toward the corporation they serve, but they do not know who controls the corporation, nor why.

Although they are as property-less as manual workers, the White Collar people do not make anything they neither produce nor create. They fill what are known as "Service Occupations." Their "service," as C. Wright Mills has summarized, consists of "handling" people and symbols. The symbols they handle are not those of the poet, but those of the filing-cabinet expert. Their relationship to the symbols is neither intellectual nor imaginative: it is a relationship of things to things, devoid of understanding, devoid of any human meaning. Trained animals or electronic machines could do their "work" much more efficiently, and the White Collar people know it: this knowledge is the basis of much of their frantic anxiety. Their relation to the objects of their world is a filing-cabinet relation. They sell articles they have not made. They file papers they do not understand. They answer letters they have not read. They file money they did not earn and will not get. They read forms in which they have no interest. They sit at the apex of uprootedness and alienation. Their frame of reference for understanding their relation to their work is the frame of reference of their particular filing cabinets. They live in a narrow one-dimensional world. The dimension is either alphabetical or numerical.

The Psychologists of the White Collar world fill their clients with an ideology of Interpersonal Relations precisely because the White Collar reality is completely alien to human relations. The Managerial and Secretarial people do not ever "relate" to human beings: they "handle" human beings. And their handling of people is modeled on their handling of things. People, in the administrative world, are merely another form of filing cards. If a man's name starts with Z, he cannot be "interviewed" until after the As, Es, Cs…. The salesman boasts that he has "contacts" with thousands of people—yet he neither understands nor communicates with any of them, because understanding and communication are undefined concepts in the world of the "contact" and the "pitch." The interviewer boasts that he "sees" hundreds of people every day, but he shares no dreams or goals or projects with them, because there are no projects in the White Collar world. A vast number of psychologists and analysts, equipped with a fictitious doctrine of Sigmund Freud and Ernest Jones which portrays the human mind as a bureaucracy, gain their wealth by tranquilizing the White Collar people. They tell their clients that "seeing" hundreds of people daily is an effective substitute for one true friendship, provided the clients swallow the "reality" of the Freudian doctrine. However, the tranquilizer is as spurious as the doctrine, and the lie does not effectively fill the emotional vacuum. In spite of all the psychological doublespeak, the White Collar people still suspect they are not fully human beings. Comradeship remains an alien notion in a world where men are objects to be classified or used. Communal sharing is a crime in a world where endless corporate appropriation is the only legitimate goal. Cooperative projects are impossible for men who have never initiated projects of their own, and who understand cooperation as a servile submission to mechanical routine. Under the ideology of Interpersonal Relations is a world of talk without communication, activity without human meaning, work without joy.

The White Collar hierarchies grow constantly; they are the front behind which every activity of the corporate society is carried on. The hierarchies are not restricted to Corporations. Government offices have always had their clerks. But today, labor unions are "administered" by clerks who are loyal only to their filing jobs, indifferent to the workers or their goals. Pre-university "education" has been effectively converted into a vast bureaucracy. All teachers must spend time at Teachers Colleges where they are taught how to administrate, not what to teach. The first result is that the imaginative spirits drop out to seek more adventurous pursuits, whereas the least intelligent and least independent receive their "teaching" licenses. The second result is that a vacuum exists in these people, the vacuum left by the knowledge they lack. While the "teachers" administrate, advertisers "educate" the students. The effect is a thorough indoctrination in the corporate ethic of profits and war. Even in the universities, teachers are being replaced at crucial spots by administrators. Thus even if a student has retained some intellectual curiosity and some imagination after a twelve-year Americanization through elementary and high school, he still hasn't much of a chance to become an educated man. Freed from the high school administrators, he will anxiously go to the University Admissions Office to seek enlightenment about the world of knowledge. There an Assistant Director will "counsel" the expectant student on the philosophy courses he should take, though to this Director philosophy is merely another classification in the catalogue; and the Director will advise the student about humanities, though this administrator's only "humanities" are the sex-crimes of the newspapers and the higher pornography of Hollywood movies. From then on the student will learn that in American universities, philosophy is a card to file, a grade to get, a requirement to fill, and no more. Reality is elsewhere—it resides in the corporate profits and the permanent war economy. From the administrator he has nothing to learn. The bureaucrat's advice comes from catalogues, his knowledge extends only to forms, his discourse is automatic repetition, and after the "job" he has nothing to say. Among high school students, many of the more intelligent quit school to become juvenile delinquents, and they try to find the adventure and meaning their society keeps from them by committing crimes against that society. Among university students, the few who retain a vestige of intellectual honesty and creative imagination become Beats, and they try to regain a worthwhile human community on the fringes of the corporate world, often succeeding in nothing more than becoming parasites of the corporate society and mirroring its values in reverse.

Because the White Collar people conspicuously occupy every niche and layer of the corporate society, because their work consists of "servicing, distributing, coordinating," their spokesmen have tried to build around them a halo of Indispensability, and to derive from this halo the claim that Managers would become the new ruling class. The assumption of this spurious theory is that the indispensable rule. C. Wright Mills has exploded the logic of this argument. In every society, workers, farmers, and slaves are the most indispensable members, since it is they who carry on the society's most basic activities. If indispensability were the mark of a ruling class, workers, peasants and slaves would have ruled every human society.

In actual fact, the indispensability of the White Collar people is a delusion limited to the White Collar people. The filing-cabinet has this delusion built-in. If a filing system is set up to classify trash according to certain characteristics, then of course each scrap has its "place," and the man who finds the "place" is indispensable. If the function of a system is to file all trash and to keep records and cross-references on it, then each of the millions of trash-collectors will derive his "meaning" and "station" from the particular type of trash it is his role to file. The illusion of indispensability can be maintained only as long as no one emerges from the system to question the human relevance of filing trash. As soon as someone asks, the halo of indispensability bursts, and the Administrators suddenly become parasites devoting life and energy to irrelevant and superfluous activity. The nihilistic literature of our time, best exemplified by Beckett and Ionesco, is addressed to this middle layer of the corporate society, to the men who neither initiate activity nor carry it out, but merely file and classify, service, distribute, and coordinate.

The people in the Service Occupations are runners—but they do the running for someone else. In the corporations, they have neither voice nor control. Service is the proper name for their occupations. They constitute the new feudal hierarchy. The couriers of corporate capitalism are servants: their task is to carry other men's projects, from those who initiate them to those who implement them; their function is to integrate the malfunctions of monopoly capitalism. Those who claim they'll rule the corporate society do not in fact even rule themselves. Their style of life is set by their status, the sole purpose of their lives is to rise, the meaning of life is to have a "place" in the hierarchy. The search for creative activity and imaginative adventure has been whittled down to a ceaseless preoccupation with rank, station, position. The International Business Machines have imposed their style of life on the men who run them.

Since life is identified with the slot one occupies, individuality and human dignity are taken to mean action that corresponds to the slot. When A Secretary becomes The Head Secretary, she must take on the style of life of the new station. She must talk and dress and walk like a Head Secretary. She must thoroughly familiarize herself with the habits, and even the main idiocyncracies, of other Head Secretaries. The advertisers and movie makers specialize in providing the models. Every American vehicle of public transportation advertises the Miss

Subways, Miss New York, Miss America, or Miss Alcoholic Beverage, and describes her main habits and activities for the edification of the millions who dutifully ape her style of life. As with "Interpersonal Relations," the White Collar people intoxicate themselves with an illusion of their Individuality precisely because they have no individuality. The Individuality of White Collar consists of thinking and acting like all others in the same Position. Thus "individuality" is identified with the most servile conformism. Within this conformism, the most disgusting characteristic of the "mass society," namely the search for invidious distinctions, becomes a mania. The runners accentuate their frantic conformism by lodging their "individuality" in the color of their cars, in the corporations that make their oars, in their ties, even in their names.

The mental and emotional vacuum of White Collar is where the "mass culture" finds a home. The world of comic strips, television heroes, and especially the world of the celebrities, are tailored for the personality-less couriers of corporate capitalism. Each Manager thinks himself the local incarnation of a celebrated movie hero; each secretary is the local Elizabeth Taylor or Deborah Kerr. When the actress Elizabeth Taylor was in a British hospital, New York office girls told each other they were "sick, just sick." And the American Press, Protector of the educated and informed public indispensable to any democracy, obligingly gave front page accounts describing every phase of the Celebrity's illness. When the movie actor Clark Gable died, Directors and Assistant-Directors all over the country "felt glum." Trapped by their filing-cabinet world, the White Collar people do their "living" by means of television and the movies. They live by proxy; Marlon Brando does the "living" for hundreds of thousands of minor executives and their assistants. Public Relations, Advertising and Communications men mould the ideas and ideals of the Masses in the Administrative Hierarchy.

A Bureaucracy is always a disguised servility to the status quo. A bureaucrat's greatest fear is a change of social institutions, although a change at the top is irrelevant to him. Predictability, Regularity, and Security are the absolute limits of the administrator's life, and any social change inevitably threatens all three. A man who has spent his life "working his way up" cannot conceive that the slot he has been aiming to reach might be abolished or replaced. He would then be nothing. The bureaucracy requires no talents and provides no training. A manager's only claim to relevance is his title. That the system of titles and ranks could be abolished is inconceivable to him: that would be the end of the world. The fact that the entire hierarchy exists to maintain the wealth and privilege of men who are not themselves within the hierarchy—this fact cannot penetrate the administrative mind without shattering it. Communication on these matters is impossible. Bureaucracy must be seen as part of the order of nature, as something that has always been and will always be. The White Collar man will be loyal to whoever protects the regularity, the routine, the ceaseless monotony, of his career. The subject matter of the forms is irrelevant, so long as the filing system remains the same. The purpose of the entire institution is irrelevant, so long as the ranks remain unchanged. The White Collar people would accept *any* regime so long as their "indispensability" was recognized. Among regimes, however, their preference is decidedly in favor of some form of military fascism. The White Collar people were Hitler's most enthusiastic supporters. In Nazi Germany they not only had their rank-system ensured by a military regimentation of all society; they also had a real-life comic strip hero whose lunacy they could ape, through whom the smallest clerk could "live" and feel powerful enough to destroy the world. In the United States, vestiges of an earlier entrepreneurial capitalism still send occasional anxiety through the White Collar world. But the consolidation of economic activity into the hands of a few corporations, the increasing militarization of American society, and the growth of the permanent war economy, are effectively giving the Managers the type of Security they desire.

"I do not want an economic system so grossly inefficient that, at its most efficient—in the U.S., with every child born to about five hundred times the natural resources a European child is heir to—it can achieve only twice the European standard of living, and then only at the cost of excluding three or four million citizens from work and spending over half the government's income on lethal ironmongery,"[12] wrote

Edward Hyams. In March 1961, according to official government statistics, five and a half million citizens were excluded from work,[13] and the expenditure on lethal ironmongery continued exceeding all previous bounds. The government's count of those excluded from work was challenged in many quarters. A *Monthly Review* editorial pointed out that "the government counts as unemployed only those who are (a) without any work at all and (b) actively looking for a job. Hence its figure leaves entirely out of account those who are involuntarily idle a part of the time and those who would like a job but are not looking for one (usually because they know from their own and others' experience that there is none to be had). It is not certain just how much should be added to the official figure to make good these omissions, but a careful study made by Philip Eden, economist for the West Coast longshore union, leaves no doubt that the needed adjustment is both absolutely and relatively large."[14] According to the adjusted figure, there were more than eight million unemployed citizens—which is 11% of the labor force. In other words, "with every child born to about five hundred times the natural resources a European child is heir to," more than one out of ten people were excluded from work. In December 1960, according to official figures, the percentage of white citizens excluded from work was slightly less than 6%; of non-white citizens, 12%. "Among non-whites the unemployment rate is thus *twice* as high as among whites," commented the *Monthly Review* editorial. "What a splendid advertisement for the affluent society in a predominantly colored world!"[15]

Since 1946, United States workers are told, the American economy has been following a "full employment" policy. However, it is not the workers who interpret the laws in America. The Employment Act of 1946 is implemented by businessmen—big, corporate businessmen. As interpreted by the men who run the government, the Employment Act doesn't really say anything: it speaks of maximum employment "in a manner calculated to foster and promote free competitive enterprise." Since "free competitive enterprise" is the polite name given to corporate practice, the law is unnecessary. The government of the United States has always acted "in a manner calculated to foster and promote free competitive enterprise." Obviously full employment would not "foster and promote" this ideal. In 1952, there were two million people without work in the United States. Paul Baran quoted a frank statement from *Business Week* which vividly demonstrates how the corporate businessmen dislike such "low" unemployment: "Unemployment remains too low for the work force to have flexibility. Anytime the jobless total is less than 2 million, even common labor is scarce. Many employers must tend to hoard skills. And certainly, the labor unions are in the driver's seat in wage negotiations. More workers can be had, to be sure. But only at considerable cost. And they probably wouldn't be of the skills most desired. There's no assurance against inflation like a pool of genuine unemployment. That's a blunt, hard-headed statement, but a fact."[16] In 1961, the businessmen got their with a "pool of genuine unemployment" containing eight million people "calculated to foster and promote free competitive enterprise." Clearly, the Employment Act does not mean what the poor read into it; the Law is not designed to upset the status quo, but to maintain it; when "unemployment remains too low for the work force to have flexibility," it is not consistent with "free competitive enterprise." As the satirist of the Constitution wrote in 1788, "debtors might safely trust to the humanity and clemency of their creditors who will not keep them in gaol all their lives, unless they deserve it.... Men of great property are deeply interested in the welfare of the state; and they are the most competent judges of the form of government, best calculated to preserve their property, and such liberties as it is proper for the common and inferior class of people to enjoy."[17]

For the American worker, the "free competitive enterprise" of the corporations means constant anxiety, intellectual and psychic fragmentation, and incomplete development. The constant threat of unemployment is accompanied by constant pecuniary anxiety. A man beset with rents, bills, food expenditures, automobile maintenance, and contingencies with no end, does not have the conditions required for creative contemplation or intellectual development. Unless he is very unusual, his circumstances will not permit him to seek to extend the frontiers of human knowledge, or to devise projects for community participation. If he has time-off, he will seek to forget the rents, bills and contingencies, and the best way to forget is to immerse himself in mindless activity. The Coney Islands of the corporate world are the epitome of mindlessness available to anxiety-ridden men trying frantically to forget they have no control over their lives. If the worker's hours are shortened, he will seek to lessen the anxiety of rents, bills, contingencies, by getting an additional job and spending his life in endless accumulation for "in case." Money is made the condition for survival, and then workers concerned with survival are roundly condemned for their lack of other interests by the rich who have no need to be concerned. To survive, a worker must have a "job" and each "job" requires a "skill." In order to have a "skill," a worker must have spent a portion of his life pushing, pulling, pressing, stamping, filing, shaking…. Those who have no "skill" are not exterminated in the corporate society: they are allowed to live and sleep on the sidewalks and doorways of the Bowerys and the Skid Rows of the cities. It is the "skill" that defines the humanity of a worker; without it, he's an animal, as useless to himself as to the corporate masters. It is the "skill" that makes a worker *someone* at the employment offices: there a man is not asked about his ideals, his goals, his projects; he is asked "what's your skill?" In the corporate society, Socrates would be doomed to speak to the drunken wretches of the Bowery. Socrates did not have what the employment offices consider a "useful skill." The developed human being cannot survive in the world of skilled employees. Only those who successfully transform themselves into "hands" can survive. The most employable worker is the one who has devoted his life to one "skill," and who has effectively suppressed his intellect and imagination to the point of being able to put up with the drudgery and boredom of the one-skill life.

The Advertising Council, however, by means of the "free press," informs the world that America is a "People's Capitalism," and that the United States "has come closest to a democratic, classless society..."[18] and so on. In short, Everyone has a Share in People's Capitalism, America is a Shareholder's Democracy, and, if it weren't for the unions and their constant grasping for bigger Handouts, America would be Paradise. However, according to the 1953 Economic Report of the President to Congress, "average hourly earnings in manufacturing, adjusted for consumers' price changes, have not risen faster than the economy's real productivity gains, but instead apparently have lagged significantly."[19]

In other words, in spite of their endless grasping, the unions have not even succeeded in maintaining their members' share of the wealth; they've let it get smaller. But the profits of the Holders don't get smaller: they've been going uphill since 1787. And not all the 180 million Americans are Shareholders, nor do the relatively large number of Shareholders own a significant number of shares. Paul Baran quoted a Brookings Institute study on Share Ownership which contained the following statistics: "...2.3 percent of all stockholders in manufacturing corporations account for 57 percent of the total number of those corporations' shares. In the field of public utilities 1 percent of shareholders own 46 percent of all shares. In finance and investment 3 percent of shareholders control 53 percent of the number of shares, and in transportation 1.5 percent of shareholders hold 56 percent of stock."[20] Thus the Advertising Council was fibbing; its account of the "democratic, classless society" was neither history, nor science, nor truth. But advertisers will be the first to admit that corporations would not hire them if they dealt with history, or science, or truth. Any advertiser "who would be so foolish as to write his honest opinions would be out on the streets looking for another job."[21] If such demands were made of advertisers, unemployment would rise yet higher.

The Advertising Council's "democratic, classless society" is an undemocratic class society. If America is a Shareholder's Democracy, then it has a far smaller proportion of Citizens than ancient Athens, which was a slave society. Less than 4% of the United States population own shares,[22] and of this four percent, less than three percent own a tremendously large proportion of the shares. At this rate the modern Athens that calls itself a Shareholder's Democracy can only boast that one out of every 750 members of its population is a Citizen. The "democratic, classless society" and the Shareholder's Democracy" cannot stand to be scrutinized. Scrutiny takes patience, effort and time. It is far easier for an advertiser to make claims than for a scholar to disprove them. The advertiser has merely to say so, and it is so. The scholar must spend years of study, thought and analysis to say it is not so—and then he's not as well rewarded, if rewarded at all.

The North American Paradise is heavenly only for the chosen few who, through the grace of Mammon, were hoisted up into Eden at some historical point. This garden, too, is confined to those whom Gerrard Winstanley called the "Adams of the earth." For the rest—those whom Hamilton called "the mass of mankind"—Heaven still lies in the grave. In a recent study, Leo Huberman compared some significant statistics about the unheavenly circumstances most people are born to in "People's Capitalism." There are a few Adams in America who are billionaires: that is, there are a few men whose personal incomes are greater than the total value of all property in the United States at the time of the American Revolution. These are the heirs of "five hundred times the natural resources a European child is heir to," And yet, one third of all American families receive incomes of less than $4000, and one fourth, less than $3,000.[23] According to *Fortune* magazine, "families with after-tax incomes under $4000 are obliged to spend just about everything on the necessities of food, clothing, shelter, transportation, and medical care."[24] Consequently, while wealthy Adams dress and keep their garden of Eden, the other "creatures" crawl from slum to slum. Huberman quoted the following from the editor of *The Housing Yearbook*: "New slum areas are found in every large city. Families displaced by slum clearance have to move elsewhere, and Congress sees to it that there isn't enough low-rent public housing for them. So they go into the big old houses of the 19th century, with a dozen families occupying space designed for a single household. Or they find shoddily built little houses on a 25-foot lot."[25] And a West Virginia Congressman, representative of a "distressed area" outside of Eden, said in 1959: "In areas of chronic unemployment I have talked with families who have not had fresh milk, eggs, meat, or citrus juices for periods ranging up to 2 years. These

Americans actually exist on a diet less than half as nutritive as that provided for the occupants of displaced persons camps in Europe after World War II."[26] The original Lord had given the Adams dominion over all other creatures; He had, however, made the following proviso: "Of every tree of the garden thou mayest freely eat; but of the tree of the knowledge of good and evil, thou shalt not eat of it; for in the day that thou eatest thereof thou shalt surely die." And between twenty-four and twenty-nine centuries later, the Digger, Winstanley, amplified the Lord's saying in the following terms: "O you Adams of the earth, you have rich clothing, full bellies.... But know ... that the day of judgment is begun.... The poor people whom thou oppresses shall be the saviors of the land."

The new Adams have not been unmindful of old Jehovah's warning; with the help of Mammon they have converted Eden into a Crystal Palace with floors of asphalt and concrete, walls of steel and glass. The tree of the knowledge of good and evil cannot grow on glass, steel and concrete. Consequently, the Adams will not eat from the tree, and they will not die from their knowledge of good and evil. They will perhaps stifle from the lack of earth and air and men, but they will not die from knowledge. On their Park Avenue, the Corporate Adams have confined the earth to a "park" which separates two asphalt roadways—the "park," in Percival Goodman's measurements, "consists of little islands 16' wide." On the far sides of the asphalt stand the monuments which advertise the corporate products: whiskey, soap, money.... And inside, "people in the thousands sit in mechanically controlled atmospheres handling endless pieces of paper. In the hushed quiet of acoustically treated spaces, they talk to a variety of instruments from silken blondes to black telephones. In these great aquaria, sportsmen fish in stenographic pools. Most everything is brittle, transparent, brightly lighted, invisibly operated, synthetic. But the carpets are deep, soft to the spiked heels and extended endlessly from wall to wall. Outside the trains rumble underground and on the street no one wants to linger. The shards of glass are paper thin."[27] The architectural advertising in the Empire City grows with unprecedented speed: the cost of the corporate showhouses on Park Avenue represents potential housing for millions of homeless Indians. Looking at the world from air-conditioned rooms through steel-lined panes of glass, however, the chosen ones are not likely to discover their relation to the burning heat outside. To them, the New Freedom is real. Not only have they been assured financial "security," far more lucrative than was enjoyed by the Krupps and Farbens of the earlier Nazi version of a corporate capitalism. The New World's Adams have also streamlined their manipulative techniques to heights never reached before. Robert Jungk, a German journalist familiar at first-hand with the Nazi version of the nation of obedient servants, was astounded by the extent and direction of North American progress in manipulation. In a book entitled *Tomorrow Is Already Here*, Jungk described, not the police brutality, the political persecutions, or the other extreme situations which are localized in area and restricted to few people, but the subtle, widespread phenomena, the little things with which every worker is familiar: "…the far more innocent and ethically unobjectionable techniques of counselling, the public opinion polls and the promotion of happy industrial relations, have indirect effects all too reminiscent of similar phenomena in the totalitarian states. Knowing that before and during their employment they are being watched by people in whose hands lies their economic fate, many who wish to keep their jobs speak in a way that does not reflect their true feelings.

"Millions of Americans, as soon as they cross the threshold of their place of work step, partly consciously, partly unconsciously, into roles which correspond to what the soul engineers expect of them. They are happy, and 'keep smiling' even when they do not feel so inclined. They act as though they were 'well balanced' and 'perfectly normal' even when they have a tremendous urge to kick over the traces. They strain every fibre to suppress their natural aggressiveness and to be 'good companions' with whom everyone easily gets along, even when they would like to break into loud curses at the next desk. And above all they behave as though they were loyal to the firm through thick and thin, even if they find more to criticize in it than to praise.

"This standard mask of the 'jolly good fellow', of the 'easy going guy', of the 'sweet girl', grows on to some of them as a second face…."[28]

The upkeep of the Crystal Palace, its masters, and its "soul engineers," is an expensive proposition, and the toll is not confined to the "natives" of Asia, Africa and Latin America. The cities of the corporate paradise also contain unprivileged "natives." According to the Chairman of the City and Regional Planning Dept. at Harvard University, "Despite all efforts being made by public and private enterprise, cities are deteriorating at a faster rate than they are being renewed through new construction, repair or maintenance. Not one city is known to have a program so complete as to be able to renew at even the same rate that its deterioration takes place."[29] Millions of incomplete, manipulated, faceless men, each with his "skill," travel obediently through underground tunnels from the slums in which they live to the factories or air-conditioned rooms in which they work. Perhaps they are dead. Maybe they are only asleep, and maybe when they wake and realize they've been robbed of their humanity, they will not wait for their birthright until the day when their masters eat from the tree of the knowledge of good and evil.

The Crystal Palace, with the slums that house its window-cleaners, its unskilled workers, its outcasts, is not self-sustaining. A world-wide proletariat supports the luxurious skyscrapers along Park Avenue. This symbiotic relationship between domestic wealth and external misery was keenly understood by an early advocate of the Constitution, who in 1787 urged his countrymen to adopt the document so that "The spoils of the West-Indies and South America may enrich the next generation of Cincinnati."[30] According to "a Discussion Prepared for Leaders of American Industry" by three United States scientists, "At one end of the economic scale we find the people of the United States, representing but 6 percent of the world's population, able, largely as the result of the high level of industrialization and the abundant resources with which the land was originally endowed, to consume about 50 percent of the goods produced in the world."[31] And a British scientist, J.D. Bernal, has estimated that the capitalists who consume half the world's spoils, could easily undertake to feed, house and educate the millions whose sacrificed lives are displayed on Park Avenue. "The great monopolies that directly or indirectly control the whole of capitalist industry have ample means from their internal reserves not only to remodel but vastly to extend their production so as to be able to provide enough for the whole rest of the world. They could easily finance the industrialization of all the underdeveloped countries..."[32] If they chose to do so. Bernal is well aware, however, that the beneficiaries of half the world's wealth are interested in profits, not in world wellbeing. "Inexorably, all their activity—the volume of production, the rate of capital investment, the flow of development and research—is at the mercy of the state of the market and the estimates of profit margins. It would seem on the face of it that there was something radically wrong here. The new scientific, productive machine has already outgrown the financial system that first brought it into existence. If we have bigger capacity than we had dreamed of before, we must have bigger aims. The objects of profits, even big corporation profits, are trivial compared to the real benefits measured in human wellbeing, that could be poured out if the new methods were allowed to be freely used and developed at evergrowing rate. If this cannot be done because of the laws of economics, then it is about time those laws were looked into. People are asking if they are really laws of Nature or conventions to protect particular interests, and whether in either case they have any relevance to a world of free power and unlimited automation."[33]

The "laws of economics" which sustain the empire of corporate wealth and world wretchedness are a vast mystery. They are not natural laws, since they are enforced by armies of men. They are not human laws, since they do not promote justice. The capitalist "laws of economics" are not laws at all; they are fictions by means of which capitalists justify taking for themselves what belongs to all men. For the corporations, the world is a vast arena for profits. In corporate anthropology there are no cultures, civilizations, histories or traditions; there are only sources of raw materials, sources of cheap labor, and markets. Most of living humanity, except those who have extricated themselves from this net of "laws," fit one of these categories; some fit all three. Corporate practice consists of taking the raw materials of other continents cheaply, processing them, and selling the finished products very expensively. This "law of economics" is very lucrative for the corporate Holders. According to statistics given in a *Monthly Review* editorial, "As of 1959 total United States private investment abroad was $448 billion.... Total sales by American-owned enterprises abroad in 1957 came to $32 billion.... Sales of American-owned manufacturing firms abroad in 1957 were 50 percent higher than experts of comparable goods from the United States. In other words, for American business as a whole foreign operations are much more important than export trade."[34] According to *Business Week*, "of the 100 largest industrial corporations (ranked by 1957 domestic sales) 99 are involved today in one or another kind of overseas operation.... All told, at least 3,000 U.S. companies have money invested directly in foreign production and distribution. Working alongside these operating companies are dozens of U.S. engineering and contracting outfits, management and marketing consultants, and the foreign branches of U.S. banks."[35] All these "investments" get very profitable "returns" because the overseas workers, being "natives," are considered sub-human, and consequently are paid less than American workers; sometimes they are barely paid at all. The raw materials so cheaply acquired and so cheaply processed are then sold at the highest price they fetch in the United States. The difference between what the "item" costs to produce, and what it sells for, does not reach the men in the Philippines, Peru or Venezuela; the difference goes as profit to the corporate Holders; some of it is used to broadcast "free enterprise" and "free world" propaganda over the corporate media of communication. In order to sell their products expensively, the corporations must have markets. At this juncture their "laws of economics" muddle their interests somewhat. One of the main advantages of the "foreign investments" is that they work for almost nothing. The outcome, however, is that the "natives" remain poor, and poor men do not constitute a market: they cannot afford to buy the corporate goods. Consequently, the U.S. corporations that produce goods abroad sell a substantial amount of these goods to consumers in the U.S. This may sound a little silly, but it is profitable to the corporations, and consequently is a "law of economics." For example, the United States has one of the world's largest oil deposits, but much of the oil in American cars comes from Saudi Arabia, Kuwait, Venezuela.... U.S. inhabitants, however, constitute only 6% of the world's population, and can only consume 50% of the world's goods. The rest must be sold elsewhere. Since the starving wretches in the "underprivileged nations" cannot buy very much, the capitalists are in a rut. If they produce more than they can sell, then the market will be glutted, and prices will fall, and profits will fall—God forbid! that's precisely what the "laws of economics" are designed to prevent!

Profits never fall. The brunt filters down to the internal proletariat, who are better paid than the overseas "natives" and so must be "laid-off," and domestic unemployment climbs to 8 million. The capitalists will not give their goods, or sell them cheaply, to men who need them. That's not profitable; it's not a "law of economics." Consequently, to maintain the price that fetches big profits, the domestic proletariat is laid off work, the external proletariat is left in a state of misery, and the vast technological heritage which could forever abolish both the unemployment and the misery, is left idle. The minimum number of calories required for healthy life is set at about 2700 per day; below that number, deficiency diseases take hold of the human body, dull the intellect, and shrivel the imagination. Within the capitalist imperium, the so-called "Free World," there are few outside of Western Europe and the United States who consume 2700 calories, but many who consume less than 1500. The freedom to eat, live, think and learn, are not provided for in the corporate "laws of economics;" they are not the freedoms found in the "Free World."

"I do not want an economic system which, while paying farmers not to grow food in fertile land, desperately urges others to plant food crops in unfertile land, and, with huge food surpluses which it fails to distribute, leaves half the world's people on the edge of starvation," wrote Edward Hyams.[36] The marvelous "laws of economics" are such that, while most of the world's population are unfed, unhoused, untaught, wheat and corn and fruit are fed to animals in the United States, and sometimes even destroyed—to keep the prices high. The *Wall Street Journal* described the workings of this "law" with regard to peaches: "California canners and growers agreed to destroy about 18 percent of the state's estimated 705,000-ton cling peach crop to prevent a market glut.... The previous high cling peach pack in California, one of the largest peach producing states, was 552,000 tons last year. Each year the state sets a limit on the amount of cling peaches which may be canned after receiving recommendations of canners and growers. The quota is designed to keep supply from exceeding demand and, in effect prevents market prices from falling."[37] With respect to automobiles, the *Wall Street Journal* had the following advice: "What is really needed, obviously, is some 'crash' legislation by Congress which would have the Government buy two million cars and dump them in the middle of the Atlantic."[38] Obviously, the capitalists would readily line the bottom of the sea with automobiles, if that fetched the high price. They do not care who needs their products, nor what use their products have, so long as the profits keep climbing.

The obedient "masses" of "People's Capitalism" are told, by the corporate media of communication, that the misery, the plunder, the waste, are all "in the national interest," that the destruction of food and vehicles is a protection of Our Way of Life. And the Americans acquiesce and believe what their corporate masters tell them, because Americans have for many generations been trained to believe all that their corporate masters tell them. When Woodrow Wilson, early in this century, urged his countrymen to participate in "The New Freedom," he roused many Americans, especially corporate ones, to enthusiasm. The historian William A. Williams has shown, however, that Wilson did not refer to anything new, nor to freedom—unless freedom is taken in its peculiar American definition, where it means the "freedom" to plunder, the "freedom" to expand the corporate empire. Wilson's New Freedom referred to "the market to which diplomacy, and if need be power, must make an open way."[39] This open way was to be realized by very ancient means, namely force: "it is evident that empire is an affair of strong government."[40] Secretary of State Bryan explained the meaning of Wilsonian "freedom" even more clearly: it meant to "open the doors of all the weaker countries to an invasion of American capital and enterprise."[41] President Franklin Delano Roosevelt was not unclear about America's foreign policy either; he set out "to secure a lowering of foreign walls (so) that a larger measure of our surplus may be admitted abroad."[42] As Williams points out, "freedom," in the modern American vocabulary, has been made synonymous with trade, and "inherent in the approach was a definition of trade that went far beyond the idea of an exchange of commodities and services. The denotation of the definition emphasized trade as the expansion of markets for America's corporate *system*; while the connotations stressed the control and development of raw-material supplies."[43] This program can only be carried out in a world where "doors" are "open" to American investments; where laborers are "free" to work for small wages; where markets are "open" for high priced corporate products. This section of the world has been named the "Free World" for the past fifteen years, and its "freedom" has been safeguarded by an ever-increasing tempo of violence, terror and annihilation. The "Free World" is the outer limit beyond which the corporate system cannot expand, and the maintenance of this "freedom" has become the sole international concern of latter-day capitalism.

Yet in spite of all the ironmongery designed to protect with violence, the "Free World" constantly diminishes in size. This happens in spite of the fact that capitalists are under the impression that they give "aid" and the "blessings of civilization" to the world's unprivileged. That the aid, as well as the blessings, serve only to enrich the corporations, while yet further impoverishing the "natives," does not seem to penetrate the corporate consciousness. The hungry men in the colonies cannot help but notice that many of the defectors from the "Free World" are on their way towards the creation of human economies, and they cannot help but notice that their own misery is related to the corporate "operations" in their lands. The "natives" grow restless, they start to clamor for food, life and decency, they start to resent being martyred to the American Way of Life. The clamor of the "natives" alarms the corporations. To abolish the unrest, the corporations seek frantically to increase their "development" and "aid" programs. They push through Congress vast Housing Programs for Peru or Puerto Rico. Big United States investors are sent to the "underdeveloped nation" to buy the land, to raze the slums on it. Big United States contractors, architects and engineers are sent to build the houses, the roads, the shopping centers. Big public relations firms are hired to advertise United States generosity towards the world's "natives." And yet, every investigation of such "development programs" reveals that the houses are so expensive only United States executives and wealthy local capitalists can rent them; that the wretches whose slums were razed to build the houses are left homeless; that the only beneficiaries of the "aid" were the American investors, the American contractors, architects, engineers—plus perhaps a few wealthy local landlords. Public money is transferred to the pockets of the rich, but the American people are told they must sacrifice a portion of their taxes to "benefit mankind." The American people, mis-educated, misinformed and obedient, acquiesce in the higher wisdom of their masters. The "natives," however, though they are no better educated or informed, cannot so easily acquiesce: the hunger is too real, the plunder too visible. Men whose misery increases daily, year after year, generation after generation, cannot effectively be told they are being "aided," "benefitted," or "developed." The misery grows and the unrest grows, and a point is reached when misery becomes unbearable and the restlessness becomes revolution.

And then comes the grand explanation. Since the capitalists are convinced they have been doing all they could for the world's "natives," then obviously *they* cannot be responsible for all the tension, the unrest, the revolutions. Clearly if the capitalists are not responsible for the unrest in the colonies, then someone else must be responsible. Since all anti-capitalists are called communists, and since communists openly advocate the overthrow of capitalism, then clearly they are the single cause of all the world's unrest. The communists "exploit" the misery brought by the corporations, and thus "instigate" demonstrations, riots, and revolutions. This type of reasoning used to be called totalitarian logic by Americans of a former day. Today it is called Freedom and everyone believes in it. The "explanation" does not explain anything—rather it explains everything away—but it is enforced by the world's greatest military Power, and thus cannot be doubted without risk to life, liberty, and happiness. As soon as the grand explanation is applied, there's no more need for "aid" and "development" programs. If the "Communists are taking over" it is pointless to build more houses for corporate executives. From that point on, the only "aid" sent is military "aid." The "communists" must be suppressed—even if the "communists" comprise an entire nation of miserable wretches who ask no more than bread and homes. Senator Hubert Humphrey seemed highly stunned when he recently found out the purpose of American military aid. The innocent Senator exclaimed, "Do you know what the head of the Iranian Army told one of our people? He said the Army was in good shape, thanks to U.S. aid—it was now capable of coping with the civilian population. That Army isn't planning to fight the Russians. It's planning to fight the Iranian people."[44]

The "solution," however, doesn't work. The unrest caused by the misery cannot be abolished by violence. The revolutions are postponed, the bloodshed is increased, the terror is intensified, but the unrest is not abolished. The local armies are not stable; they cannot effectively be taught that the profits of American corporations are synonymous with the "freedom" of their starving countrymen. The local soldiers, after all, are themselves members of the population they are hired to repress, and they cannot effectively be brainwashed to believe they can "save" their countrymen by exterminating them. Consequently, the unrest grows, and the revolutions take place in spite of all the massive military "aid." The military "aid" is stepped up astronomically, men are slaughtered in ever-increasing numbers, and yet the unrest becomes ever more profound, ever more widespread. The military metaphysicians of the Pentagon and the C.I.A. become frantic; they cease to cope rationally with events. Within their narrow ideological walls, they cannot understand how unrest can continue even after all the "agitators" have been put to death. Since they take the profit-world for granted, they do not look *there* for the cause of unrest; consequently, they cannot find the cause of all their failures. Yet the military metaphysicians of the corporate society, the self-proclaimed "realists," continue to believe there is *one cause* behind all their failures. If ye seek ye shall find—and they do: every demonstration anywhere in the world originates in Moscow; every setback to the corporate imperium originates in Moscow; every revolution originates in Moscow. *Sancta Simplicita*. The "Free World" grows ever smaller, and the communists are blamed—or rather, praised—for every event. If the miserable millions of the world believed American propaganda, they would picture the communists as heroes, liberators and saviors. Washington's propaganda, coming from the mouths of those who profess to hate the communists, is far more effective than any propaganda the communists could devise. The American propaganda media attribute to "the men in the Kremlin" an all-but omnipotent intelligence, and an iron determination to "nibble away" at the corporate empire. With such an advertising campaign, there would be communist revolutions even if Moscow didn't exist.

Capitalists grow frantic. They see men everywhere abolishing private property, expropriating corporations, building economies which distribute wealth, goods and opportunities more equally. They see, in short, that the "Free World" grows smaller and smaller, while the circle of men who refuse to call the freedom of the few freedom, grows larger and larger. The rejections of capitalism take many different forms and have little in common, except their determined rejection of capitalism.

Yet in the corporate philosophy every rejection of capitalism, whatever its differences and whatever its similarities to all the others, represents always the same thing: the International Communist Conspiracy. So defined, all the revolutions are unintelligible to the corporate experts. The latter-day "realists" first define revolutions as the outcome of the great conspiracy—of the fiendish machinations of Moscow. They then seek to interpret the revolutions in terms with which they are familiar, that is, they expect the communist "conspirators" to work the same way their own cloak-and-dagger outfits work. Thus they expect regimes ruled by a Conspiracy to be highly unstable and to collapse. They expect, in other words, that the social revolutions will be as unstable as the regimes ruled by the United States Armed Forces and the C.I.A., such as South Korea, Formosa, South Vietnam, regimes where the State Department does not insist on "free elections." Yet the instability is all on one side. The societies that have emerged from social revolutions are among the stablest in the world,* whereas the Koreas, Iraqs, Irans, Vietnams, Formosas, Guatemalas, Congos, Laos, comprise a full history of unrest. The corporate explanations leave the revolutions unexplained. Every charge the capitalists make bounces back at them. The professional counter-revolutionaries predict that non-capitalist societies could never achieve the material prosperity of the capitalist paradise; when some of them do so, in fractions of the time it took the United States to do so, they drop the charge. They next claim that communist, socialist, "neutralist," and other non-capitalist societies can never achieve the level of employment achieved in paradise. Yet the chronic unemployment turns out to be confined to the corporate empire; most of the socialist societies have a shortage of labor, and the other non-capitalist societies seem to be coping with unemployment with far greater seriousness than the United States.

---

*Hungary and Eastern Germany did not emerge from popular social revolutions, but from what Marxists call "palace revolutions." In both cases, unpopular regimes were imposed on them by the Soviet Union after the defeat of Nazism in 1945. In both regions, Nazism was the most popular and the most desired social system. That they are both unstable, there is no doubt, but they cannot be used as examples of societies that emerged from social revolutions, and a thorough study of their instabilities and problems is out of place in this book, which tries to confine itself to the instabilities and problems, foreign and domestic, of corporate capitalism.

None of the revolutions achieve Utopia, and ugly remains of archaic institutions undoubtedly hamper all of them; the revolutions do not transform mere men into saints and angels. But among the defectors from the "Free World," prices get cheaper and cheaper, education becomes widespread, food becomes universally available, and houses become gradually accessible to all: the overall improvement in the condition of life is unquestionable. Thus the capitalists are deprived of all their charges, and thus as a last resort they level their foulest claim: the populations of the non-capitalist societies do not enjoy the "freedoms" which are available to capitalists in the corporate society. King Louis could well have groaned that the French revolutionaries were depriving themselves of his extravagant tastes. The loss of "freedom" for the few to enrich themselves at the expense of the many is not a tragic loss. The language in which this charge is couched, however, threatens to submerge in a dark age one of the fine human ideals. For the capitalists identify their "freedom" and their dispensation with the freedom of the democratic, equalitarian, classless society described by Babeuf, Jefferson, Taylor, Marx. Too many of the anti-capitalist revolutionaries take the capitalists at their word, and they reject the capitalist version of "freedom" by rejecting the democratic ideal as well. Yet if the revolutionary societies achieve equality, if they make abundance available to all, and if on such a ground they open the avenues of creative participation to all their members, then they will have personal freedoms and civil liberties such as never existed under capitalism. Such a society is still today Utopia, but the seeds of Utopia are being sown, and should any of them sprout, the calls of derision from those who claim a private monopoly over Utopia will fall on deaf ears.

The corporate society is in fact seriously threatened by Russia, China, Yugoslavia, India, Ghana, Indonesia, Poland, Cuba—but not because of the reasons given by the capitalists. It is not Russian or Chinese or Cuban military strength, or rockets, or "conspiracy," that threaten the capitalists. The threat comes from the fact that all of the world's non-capitalist societies offer mankind models, however half-baked, of alternatives to capitalist plunder, nihilism, and dehumanization. The capitalists do not fear what is bad in the revolutionary experiments: the coercion, the censored press, the secret police with which to battle real and imagined terrorism. All these things have by now become permanent institutions of the corporate world. What the capitalists fear is precisely the good, the promise and the hope, of the social experiments: the equality, the participation, the joy of creation. Why? Why do the capitalists ape the worst and fear the best institutions growing out of the revolutions? Because if the experiments should succeed, then the hungry, the unhoused, the uneducated, will defect in mass from the "Free World." Because, if the experiments should succeed and be followed by more, then the slums of the Corporate Heaven will be the ugliest in the world, the inhabitants of "People's Capitalism" will be the least educated, least informed, least creative inhabitants on the planet. If too many "natives" defect from the "Free World," then the corporate profits will fall, and the architectural advertisements on Park Avenue will deteriorate into ugly, monstrous boxes of rusted steel and filthy glass, and the gaudy billboards with the legend "Money Works For You" will be tasteless reminders of the inhuman criminality of the Holders' and Bankers' Paradise.

To ward off the vision of a deteriorated Eden, the capitalists can only strike out with hatred, violence and destruction. To preserve a system of plunder which all humanity is rejecting, the capitalists have frozen themselves into a military society which increasingly rules out all aims and projects inconsistent with annihilation. Unable, at the end, to solve their problems rationally, the capitalists have at last abandoned rationality and sought "solutions" of all their problems in a permanent war economy. Domestic and external profits, the safeguarding of investments, the repression of unrest, the prevention of revolutions, are all synthesized by the permanent war economy, although psychotically. To prolong the life of corporate wealth and privilege, the corporate rulers have transformed their society into an armed camp where men are employed, directly or indirectly, in the manufacture of instruments of death. The rulers of the corporate empire are determined to continue taking "freedoms" that mankind is no longer willing to relinquish; they are armed with the power to annihilate all life; they are supported by a vast population thoroughly indoctrinated to impose the will of its corporate masters over the rest of humanity.

"World Trade means World Peace" to the corporate rulers, but only on the terms of the "tradesmen," and at the point of a gun. The absolute monarchs of former days waged innumerable bloody wars and dispensed a great deal of misery. But the absolute monarchs would not have dared to decree involuntary conscription for fear their populations would rise in rebellion, and they would not have thought to willfully destroy civilian populations for fear their kingdoms would topple. In the era of Capitalist Freedom, however, the soldiery ceased to be confined to volunteers, and armies ceased to be the only victims. The businessman's peace is rising profits, and he can neither attain nor protect his peace except with the sword. Since every material object that can be captured is an object of profit, the outer limit of capitalist "peace" cannot be reached until the businessman has absolute "freedom" over all the world's material objects. At the beginnings of America's commercial career, the great capitalist political theorist Alexander Hamilton outlined with unsurpassed clarity the relationship of commerce to war. "Has commerce hitherto done anything more than change the objects of war? Is not the love of wealth as domineering and enterprising a passion as that of power or glory? Have there not been as many wars founded upon commercial motives, since that has become the prevailing system of nations, as were before occasioned by the cupidity of territory or dominion? Has not the spirit of commerce, in many instances, administered new incentives to the appetite…?"[45]

Until the advent of Fascism in the twentieth century, capitalists had regarded war as an auxiliary means to achieve their ends, and they turned to war as a last resort. The rise of Nazi Germany, however, brutally put to death all Humanist traditions that had restrained the greed of businessmen, and made war the central institution of capitalist society. The rise of the permanent war economy in Italy, Germany and the United States, established war as the most "efficient" means by which capitalists could attain their goals, as well as the only means by which the corporate system could be kept from collapsing.

Internally, the permanent war economy has become the main source of corporate profit as well as the only alternative to catastrophic depression. The manufacture of weapons is today the most lucrative business, by far, of the corporate society. The entire nation of 180 million people—farmers, workers, white collar clerks, shopkeepers—are taxed by the government. The taxes are tremendous: millions of men pay them, and each pays an average minimum of one fourth his wage; many pay a great deal more. The government spends this money—amounts which cannot be counted or even clearly conceived—to buy weapons of extermination. According to *Business Week*, "No matter how it's described, the business of piling up weapons is bigger than any other industry. It runs to $14.5 billion a year, if you count only major military hardware contracts. It climbs to $25 billion a year when you add research and development, operation and maintenance of such vast systems as the DEW line, and construction of airfields and missile launching bases. It hits around $41 billion a year when you include everything else on which the Defense Dept. spends money. By way of a yardstick: the international oil business, the largest single industry, pumps up around $10 billion worth of petroleum a year."[46] No matter how it's described, the business of extermination is for the corporations the biggest pot of gold ever created by men. For the biggest corporations get the biggest war contracts, and they are paid with money contributed by the entire population. When a government of the rich funneled the taxes of the population into their own private vaults for the first time in American history, a Congressman had exclaimed with indignation: "We shall return to the mass of the people, and participate in the burdens we impose. When the cool hour of investigation arrives, happy indeed will it be for us if, amidst the murmurs of an oppressed people, we have not to say, in self-condemnation, I too have been guilty of bringing this load of fetters on the people. America, sir, will not always think as is the fashion of the present day; and when the iron hand of tyranny is felt, denunciations will fall on those who, by imposing this enormous and iniquitous debt, will beggar the people and bind them in chains."[47] The denunciations have not yet fallen, and even the indignation is no longer expressed. The "iron hand of tyranny" is far too profitable, even for its smallest beneficiary, to be denounced. The permanent war economy is a fountain of never-ending wealth, and those who drink from it drown forever all protest, all indignation. The market for weapons is literally bottomless, and the weapon of extermination is the most profitable commodity yet devised by profit-seekers. Automobile manufacturers build "obsolescence" into their vehicles: they hire large research staffs to see to it that the damage is beyond repair; and yet clever Americans outwit the corporations and maintain automobiles for as long as five years. The weapon-makers, however, cannot be so outwitted: their products can neither be maintained nor repaired, but must constantly be discarded. In an age of frenzied technological change, a weapon is obsolete long before its manufacture is completed. The *Wall Street Journal* had urged that "the government buy two million cars and dump them in the middle of the Atlantic."[48] This is precisely what is accomplished by the permanent war economy. Faster planes, bigger ships, deadlier bombs, rockets, submarines, gasses, are constantly developed by the Scientists of the corporate society, the older versions of the weapons are discarded, the corporations are paid to manufacture the "latest" weapons, and these in turn are discarded before they are finished. The bottom of the sea becomes increasingly lined with the "commodities" around which the corporate economy revolves.

The permanent war economy has become the central institution of the corporate society and the only means for capitalist survival. Without recourse to the war economy, capitalism would collapse from a catastrophic depression of far greater dimensions than the Great Depression of 1929. The productive facilities are today so great they can produce infinitely more goods than anyone can buy. There's a crying need for goods in all parts of the world, but the world's poor cannot afford to buy them. The corporate society is faced with three alternatives. Its productive facilities could be used to make goods for free distribution to all in the world who need them, or to make goods which the government would buy and dump into the sea, or to make weapons. Without resort to one of these three alternatives, there would be depression and collapse: the goods would accumulate and none in the world would buy them—there would be a glut; to prevent a fall in the profits of the Holders, the corporations would lay off workers; the unemployed would not be able to buy the goods of other corporations, and these corporations in turn would lay off workers. The process is familiar to all American workers and farmers over thirty years old, but Americans seem to have phenomenally short memories—or else they've been taught to believe the depression was not brought on by capitalism, but by visitors from Mars. Of the alternatives to depression, the corporate "elite" prefer the third: to turn

America's productive facilities to the manufacture of weapons. The production and free distribution of goods for those who need them is completely alien to the corporate way of life. In the world's wealthiest land, not even medical treatment is available to men who cannot afford to pay the high prices demanded by the Association for Medical Appropriation. It can hardly be expected that capitalists would willingly distribute their goods among those who need them. The entire institutional complex of the corporate society is nothing but a vast machine which lodges the world's wealth, privilege and property into the hands of the rich. If privilege is distributed among the unprivileged, it ceases to be privilege. If the capitalist society distributed its goods among the world's poor, it would cease to be a capitalist society. Rational distribution to fulfill human needs and abolish misery might bring the world not only socialism, but democracy as well. Such an alternative is clearly inconsistent with the central tenets of the acquisitive society. The second way to dispose of capitalist surplus goods would be for the corporation-men in the government to use public tax money to buy corporate products, and to dump the products into the ocean, or let them rot. This is in fact done: farmers are paid not to grow anything on fertile soil; fruits are destroyed; food is bought, stored, and allowed to rot. This alternative, however, does not appeal to the capitalists either. It is too clearly waste, and it cannot be justified. The third alternative—to use the world's greatest productive facilities for the production of weapons—is the only alternative acceptable to the corporate "elite." The market for weapons is a bottomless pit, and thus there will never be a "glut" on weapons. Depression is kept away, unemployment does not reach revolutionary proportions, and profits are extremely high. What is more, the manufacture of weapons can always be justified in terms of National Greatness and National Defense. Thus the corporations can appropriate public taxes from the sale of goods to the government without any danger of socialism or democracy, since the weapons sold to the government serve the double purpose of increasing the profits of the rich while at the same time protecting those profits. John Taylor had observed, a century and a half ago, that the capitalists "will finally avow and maintain their corruption, by establishing an irresistible standing army, not to defend the nation, but to defend a system for plundering the nation."[49]

The war economy is thus primarily a "solution" to the economic problems of the corporate society. What the capitalists cannot admit is that the war economy has become a permanent feature of latter-day capitalist society; the manufacture of instruments of death would increase *whether or not* there were external enemies to "justify" the making of weapons. The fact that the war economy is a purely domestic affair of the corporate society was recently brought out in a series of questions addressed by a Harvard University instructor in a letter to the New York *Times*, questions which could not be answered within the corporate framework: "What Senator or Representative from New England would announce himself in favor of the immediate cancellation of all military electronics contracts? How would the powerful aircraft industry greet a proposal to discontinue the production of all war-planes and missiles? How many Congressmen could watch with equanimity as two million soldiers, sailors and airmen were released to flood the job market?

"How would the Pentagon react to the prospect of closing down West Point, Anapolis and the newly created Air Force Academy, pensioning off the officer corps, and sending home the Chiefs of Staff? Just how great would be the rejoicing as community after community, industry after industry, saw itself deprived of the contracts, installations, subsidies, which have meant economic life or death for the past twenty years?"[50] The "how" in each of the questions cannot be answered, because the society based on private profit can no longer survive without its war economy. Its only alternative would be to distribute its goods among those who need them, regardless of profits; if that were done, the United States would become an important member of a commonwealth of all mankind; if that were done, however, the United States would cease to be a capitalist society, and its Shareholders would have to seek productive employment because money would no longer "work" for them.

While Shareholders and their lawyers constitute the government, the possibility of world-wide distribution of goods is far-fetched. The war economy will be maintained, and to justify the war economy, enemies will be created. It is conceivable that, with the vast propaganda network at their disposal, the corporate rulers could convince the American population of the necessity of weapons even if the corporate society had no enemies. That, however, is not necessary. The enemies, the tension, and the pretext for war can be endlessly re-created and maintained. All around the globe, capitalists are engaged in taking the raw materials and cheap labor of a region, and leaving human misery in their train. The victims of corporate enterprise invariably seek a way out of their misery by means of rebellion and revolution, and after locating the central cause of their misery, the "natives" seek to expropriate the corporations. Whenever their victims rebel, the corporations invoke the International Communist Conspiracy, appeal to National Toughness, National Greatness, and National Defense, and again enlarge the military budget. Since the potential "field" for corporate enterprise is the entire world, and since the victims of the "enterprise" will rebel so long as they remain human, the tension, the "plots," "threats," and "conspiracies" by which the war economy is justified will be permanently available. And as the world's "natives" become increasingly aware that the expropriation of corporations is within the realm of possibility, the "threats" and "conspiracies" against the corporate way of life become ever more frequent, International Communism is invoked with growing frenzy, war contracts and war profits climb inconceivably. By 1961, it already appeared that in a very near future the American people would be asked by their corporate rulers to "sacrifice" all projects which are not related to the manufacture of weapons and the planning of extermination.

The permanent war economy, though designed to maintain and perpetuate the corporate society, begets an unintended creature which in time turns against the hand that feeds it, and converts the society into a garrison state. The unintended creature is militarism, and the power which is given to the military, for the defense of corporate profit, threatens to overwhelm the very capitalists who have entrusted their fortune to military power. Although most of the military chiefs have been corporate capitalists, and although the entire military establishment is imbued with the ideology of profit, the morality of personal gain is nevertheless alien to the military hierarchy. Guided by a military definition of reality, by what C. Wright Mills has called the "military metaphysic," the rulers of the corporate society have severely curtailed the chances of human survival. In the military metaphysic, the world is divided into two camps: allies and enemies. At first, everyone opposed to corporate plunder was an enemy. Later, all men who protested against the hunger and misery of their own lands were added to the list of enemies. Today, even those who are opposed to American militarism are listed as enemies. Thus by 1960 the United States was committed to a "cold war" against the majority of mankind. Within the rules of the military metaphysic, foreign policy consists of a "game of poker" in which bombs are the cards and annihilation the outcome. Non-military methods of solving problems are increasingly ruled out, and violence becomes the only response of which the United States is still capable. The technicians of annihilation are hired to "win wars," and those among them who do not believe that nuclear wars can be "won" must perforce resign from their jobs. Thus the military hierarchy is manned by institutional lunatics who are prepared to launch a war which would mean the extermination of all life, while the "experts" in charge of American foreign policy confront every event on the globe with concepts of Deterrence, Retaliation, and Toughness. The "poker game" which the military technicians play is a terrible nihilism in which human considerations are irrelevant. Along with ancient Sparta, fascist Italy and Nazi Germany, the United States has become a military society whose sole "national purpose" is the death of human beings. With its war economy, its militarist attitude, and its orientation to violence, the United States does not substantially differ from Nazi Germany, except that the Nazi military machine did not have the power to destroy all life on earth. And the American population has been trained to unquestioning obedience. When sirens ring, the American people submissively crawl underground to "practice" for the day when the holocaust is set off. They will suffocate in their underground "shelters," since the heat caused by an atomic explosion will suck up all the oxygen. The Americans still pay lip-service to the Christian hero Jesus of Nazareth who, if he lived today, would lead them to the chambers of the corporate rulers, turn over their "poker" tables, and hurl their weapons into the sea. But the American people do not travel in mass to their Pentagon to hound out the crackpot "realists" who play "poker" with their lives. The American people crawl obediently into underground "shelters." And those few—very few—who refuse to "practice" for the annihilation of mankind, and refuse to crawl into the underground "shelters," receive jail sentences in criminal courts from judges who are only enforcing the "laws" passed by their superiors. The Adolf Eichmann's of America will doubtless plead they were only obeying the orders of their superiors, but there will be no audiences to hear their pleas. Judges and soldiers, scientists, engineers and weapon-makers, will all have been doing their jobs, obediently defending the corporate way of life, when all life is incinerated with thousand degrees of radioactive heat.

While the physical annihilation of all life has become the aim of corporate "foreign policy," the psychological annihilation of human beings has become the aim of "domestic policy." All human activity is trivialized, ideals are degraded, men are dehumanized, reason is put at the service of irrationality, and total annihilation is a game, in the society that calls itself The West and speaks of itself as a "civilization."

The all-embracing nihilism of the garrison state is perhaps an unintended outcome of corporate "freedom," but the negation of human needs and interests has always accompanied an aristocracy of wealth and privilege. Obviously "the few" can maintain their privileges only by taking them from "the mass of mankind." Perhaps the peculiarity, as well as the power, of the American aristocracy, can be traced to the effectiveness with which the American people were trained to identify their interests with the interests of the rich. Previous aristocracies had openly avowed their plunder of the rest of humanity, and had claimed to have a *right* to plunder, generally "divine." The capitalist aristocracy, however, did not avow its plunder; it claimed, in fact, to act in the interest of all other men. Thus, instead of banishing the ideals of other men, as previous aristocracies had done, the capitalists identified with those ideals, and claimed to fulfill them.

In the eighteenth century, the democratic ideals were not discarded, as the straightforward Hamilton and his aristocratic followers would have wanted. On the contrary, capitalists claimed the democratic ideals had been fulfilled by the capitalist coup d'etat of 1787. The aristocracy of wealth claimed to fulfill ideals and needs while at the same time manipulating those very ideals and needs.

For more than one and a half centuries, American capitalists have justified the regime of profit-making by citing Elections, Representatives, and Political Parties. The subject has gathered so much fog during the history of American capitalism that it would be worthwhile to review the eighteenth century view of these institutions, and to try to ascertain whether capitalism fulfilled or betrayed them. In a democratic context, each was to participate in the creation of the human community. The imaginative insights of any man were to be judged in terms of their own value, not in terms of the man's power or wealth. Since, however, there were too many citizens in the United States for all to meet in one place and enact their will directly, men delegated their powers temporarily to their peers, and the delegates were to be responsible representatives who would enact in small numbers what all would have done directly. Clearly these ideas were not located in an aristocratic context. No one was under the illusion that elections, representatives, or any other democratic institution could function democratically if an aristocracy of wealth existed. It was obvious that institutions designed to preserve equality and participation could have no meaning where there existed no equality or participation to preserve. Human history overflows with instances when the content of ideas changed; but in America the content of democratic ideas was actually reversed. The fact that men of wealth could not possibly be "representatives" that they would govern exclusively in the interest of wealth, was not first discovered by Karl Marx. The conservative second President of the Republic, John Adams, expressed himself unambiguously in this regard, "It is not true, in fact, that any people ever existed who loved the public better than themselves, their private friends, neighbours, &c. and therefore this kind of virtue, this sort of love, is as precarious a foundation for liberty as honour or fear."[51] Adams' agrarian opponent John Taylor expressed this insight even more forcefully, "It is a matter of surprise that mankind should owe their greatest calamities to the two most respectable human characters, priests and patriots, from a political gluttony, like that of swallowing too much food, however good. If responsibility to God cannot cure priests of the vices which infect legislative parties of interest, what security lies in a responsibility to man? If the love of souls cannot awaken integrity, laid to sleep by this species of legislative patronage, will it be awakened by a love of wealth and power?"[52] "It is the same thing to a nation whether it is subjected to the will of a minority, by superstition, conquest, or patronage and paper. Whether this end is generated by errour, by force, or by fraud, the interest of the nation is invariably sacrificed to the interest of the minority."[53] Political parties and electoral machinery which flourished in an acquisitive context would invariably be founded on accumulation. Such parties and elections would become instruments of plunder. Ancient Rome had two parties, and it had elections, but ancient Rome has never been hailed as a model democracy. According to the Federalist Adams, "Speculation and usury kept the state in perpetual broils. The patricians usurped the lands and the plebians demanded agrarian laws. The patricians lent money at exorbitant interest and the plebians were sometimes unable and always unwilling to pay it. These were the causes of dividing the people into two parties, as distinct and jealous, and almost as hostile to each other, as two nations."[54] And John Taylor analyzed America's "two-party system" long before the system had acquired a history, and his observations were little short of prophetic, though perhaps any intelligent observer might have reached similar conclusions. Political parties, and the electoral machines by which they come to power, will not serve democratic purposes in an acquisitive society, but precisely the opposite: "...being in truth produced by the mass of property transferred by funding, banking and patronage, creating (to borrow Mr. Hume's phrase) an aristocracy of interest, they yet exist, because these laws divided the nation into a minority enriched, and a majority furnishing the riches; and two parties, seekers and defenders of wealth, are an unavoidable consequence. All parties, however loyal to principles at first, degenerate into aristocracies of interest at last; and unless a nation is capable of discerning the point where integrity ends and fraud begins, popular parties are among the surest modes of introducing an aristocracy."[55] Taylor's conclusion is that political parties are an offshoot, not of America's democratic ideal, but of its capitalist reality. "In whatever numerical class a government is arranged, a power of advancing the wealth of one part of the nation, by civil laws, will be used by its successive administrators to obtain a corrupt influence, wholly inconsistent with any good moral principles interwoven in a constitution, and certainly destructive of them.

"Every party of interest, whether a noble, a religious, or a military order; or created by a corrupting degree of legislative or executive patronage; or by usurping a power of regulating property by means of paper credit, charters or fraudulent wars; is the instrument and ally of the power by which its interest can be fed or starved. It must acquire an influence over legislation, both to do its own work, and the work of the power it serves....

"This game between political and pecuniary parties, is precisely the cause by which free, moderate, and honest farms of government are destroyed..."[56] And worst of all, perhaps, is the fact that even those who may start their political career with a sincere desire to serve the public good, are corrupted after joining the institution and partaking of the plunder which the parties offer. "These parties plead patriotism to ignorance and credulity, and offer wealth and power to avarice and ambition. The most fraudulent is loudest in professions of zeal for the publick good ... because the vicious principle of creating wealth by law, having debauched the minds of the audience, no dishonesty appears to be attached to any excesses of legislative robbery. Audacity or delusion at length inculcates an opinion, that he who refuses to surrender his conscience and his understanding to some party, is a knave or a fool; a knave, in pretending to honesty under a legislative distribution of wealth; and a fool, for preferring hopeless efforts to serve the publick, to his own aggrandizement at the publick expense. Thus the maxims taught by the legal intercourse between political and pecuniary parties reverse the dictates of common sense and common honesty. Knaves or fools only, surrender their duties and rights to party despotism. Knaves, to get a share in its acquisitions; fools, because they are deceived. Can an honest man of sound understanding think himself bound by wisdom or duty, to give or sell himself to one of two parties, prompted by interest and ambition to impair the publick good? Are men bound by wisdom or honour to take side with one of two competitors, if both are robbers or usurpers? On the contrary, as neither could succeed except by dividing the national force between them, a nation of fools only could be drawn into a division, in which the success of either party, is a calamity to a majority of both.... Parties, like usurpers, acquire nothing from each other. The rich spoils of a gallant but deluded nation, were the fruits gathered by the whig and tory parties from the opinion—that it is knavery to adhere to the publick interest, and folly to exercise one's own judgment. Thus election, designed to advance this interest, is converted into an instrument for parties; and that which is successful, hastens to reap the transitory harvest by legislative abuses, during the delirium of victory, until the crimes make room for a rival, equally unrestrained, which follows its precedents, repeats its frauds, and experiences its fate. By considering zeal for party as more wise or honourable, than a zeal for good or bad laws, a nation is thus perpetually suspended in a state of political warfare, pregnant only with aggravations and calamity."[57]

The parties quickly ceased to reflect anyone's ideals and became political factories for the production and sale of votes and candidates. And the dilemma of choosing "representatives" was "solved" by the appearance of the Party Boss. The Boss, whom Max Weber has appropriately called a political capitalist, is a man whose only interest in political issues is their popularity; for whom a principle is a commodity valued in terms of the votes it will fetch. Though himself neither elected nor selected nor approved by the public, he makes the choice of the candidates for whom the public will "vote." The Boss chooses a candidate not for his principles but for his "appeal." Generally tied, directly or indirectly, to the staggering American "underground" of gambling, racketeering and graft, the Boss will occasionally put up for election even a candidate who opposes Bossism and Graft, provided such a candidate can be made to "appeal" to the voters, and on condition that the candidate give up his pre-election rhetoric after the election. Idealism and dedication are never found in American politicians; such "sentimentality" cannot coexist with the Boss. Sociologists who are trained to believe this is Democracy claim to be appalled by the indifference and apathy the American citizen displays toward his Great Democratic Heritage. Apologists claim that through this process, "contending factions" somehow attain a "balance of interests." There are many theories of Balance, ranging from the elementary-school textbook doctrine which equates the American with the ancient Roman system of Checks and Balances brought about by "independent" executive, judicial and legislative departments, to the more esoteric sociological theories which claim that a "plurality of interests" "countervail" against each other and thus create a political balance similar to the economic "balance" achieved by Adam Smith's

Invisible Hand. What the elementary school theory does not teach the young is that if the same interests are in control of all the "independent departments" then there could be fifteen instead of three departments and the "checks and balances" would still favor the same group of men. And what the Sociologists forget to mention, as Adam Smith also forgot to mention, is that within the "plurality of contending factions," the factions that contend most effectively are those that can financially afford to do so, and that the wealthiest have the best leverage for a favorable "balance." The fact that the rich contend with each other for the greatest favors does not further the interests of the poor, either in America or in Rome. Under feudalism, too, factions of noblemen contended for the king's favor, but this did not make feudalism democratic. As Taylor pointed out, this process is no more controlled by, nor more beneficial to the American population, than the laceration of an individual's bowels is controlled by, or beneficial to the individual. "If you had seen the vulture preying upon the entrails of the agonized Prometheus, would you have believed, though Pluto himself had sworn it, that the vulture was under the control of Prometheus? If you could not have believed this, neither can you believe, that the concubinage between a government, and the system of paper and patronage, is an organ of national opinion, or of the wealth, virtue and talents of the nation, and not a conspiracy between avarice and ambition; because, it is as impossible that a nation should derive pleasure from a government founded in the principle of voraciousness, as the man from the laceration of his bowels."[58]

Yet the laceration of the bowels has become systematic in the United States; it has become a science. Large "fields" of research and calculation investigate the means to manipulate the irrationality, gullibility and insecurity of American "voters" to get them to "eject" candidates on no issues whatever. Vast political machines exploit fear, envy, hatred, and desire for self-aggrandisement. This refinement and stimulation of the worst human traits is what remains of the "balance of conflicting interests." The American Citizen is condemned to carry on activities he has not chosen and does not understand, while being "represented" by the very men who plunder and manipulate him. Such a Citizen does not participate. He is used. Yet, unlike his revolutionary predecessors, the American Citizen does not rebel. He stands silently on long lines in the employment offices and waits patiently to be granted permission to work for one or another capitalist. Once hired, he does not question his boss's right to employ (use) him; rather he is grateful to have found a capitalist who can use him. After all, the system is so vast, so all-pervading; the ideology is so effectively internalized. What is so obvious to an external observer is so befogged with a myriad of obscurities to those inside. If a factory owner asked "his" workers to "vote" on which of his two sons should be the next owner, the workers would laugh. If the capitalist then asked the workers to contribute from their wages to support this ceremony, the workers would refuse. If, after such an "election," the capitalist claimed the workers had chosen the "representative" who should be boss over them, and consequently that the factory conditions are their own fault, that the capitalist is doing his best for them, the workers would seethe with indignation. And if, finally, the workers were told that the only way they could change their conditions would be "voting" for the capitalist's other son at the election, the workers would rebel; they would demand that, if the factory conditions depend on them, then they should themselves run the factory. Of course, no capitalist would dare to claim that "his" workers run "his" corporation. Capitalists reserve this fantastic claim for the national government, and on that level the issues become so large, so obscure. The American people not only take their "ballot-boxes" seriously; they go obediently to them every two or four years to cast their votes; they give from their wages to support the parties; and in the end they are proud of the capitalists they've "elected" to run over them. And anyone who should call the bluff, who should dare to take the democratic professions seriously, can be called before the Subversive Activities Control Board to answer for the crime of having "dangerous thoughts"; anyone who should dare to urge men to discard the fraudulent "freedom" they've been brainwashed to accept, can be made to answer with his life in Democratic America. In the corporate society, each man is not the master of the conditions of his life; men do not share equal wealth, power and influence. As in the slave and serf societies of former times, masters set the conditions, and slaves fit themselves to the conditions; masters direct and control, while slaves do the work. Slaves are not participants in the creation of their community; they do not exert control over the important affairs of their society; even their right to life is a favor bestowed on them by their masters. The American atomic arsenal is described as a guarantee of Human Freedom and Dignity, as a protection of Democracy. Yet is this the democracy which can justify the burning of humanity with megaton bombs? Is this the freedom whose protection could warrant the taking of a single human life?

The taking of life is not a crime in the corporate society, provided it is taken on a large enough scale. Life has been de-valued; the degradation of human ideals has been accompanied by the dehumanization of men and the trivialization of men's activities. In the corporate society, all activity has been reduced to market activity: the relations of buying, selling and profiting have imposed themselves into all facets of human life. Political activity as a means of changing the basic conditions of life does not exist in the land that lists Thomas Jefferson among its Founding Fathers. The conditions of corporate life—buying, selling, and profit-making—are accepted as God-given, eternal, and unchanging, and they are never questioned; they are accepted as if buying, selling and profit-seeking were the eternal patterns of all nature, and of the stars as well. With the conditions thus accepted and internalized, that is, within such an ideological context, politics becomes merely another means of acquiring wealth and power. As a result, American politics takes form in vast hierarchies of power with no overt political philosophy and no political purpose. The purpose of the political hierarchy is as unquestioned as the purpose of the corporate hierarchies of couriers and filing experts. Everyone is "in it" to get "his," and no one cares what the whole damn thing is for. As in the corporate hierarchy, everyone in the political hierarchy serves someone else, and no one is responsible. Probably the Boss is the most powerful figure in the political hierarchy, but the Boss is not elected, he is not seen; according to official mythology, the Boss does not exist. (Occasionally the mythology is embarrassed, especially when certain bosses go out of their way to make public appearances and get their pictures in newspapers.) The Boss may have the power, but his interests are all non-political; his function is to suck as much wealth as possible out of his machine. The more visible politicians have little to do with politics: they are business men and corporate lawyers, concerned with the profits of their corporations; political issues do not concern them except as possible threats to corporate profits, and in any case, caught as they are between boss, expert and bureaucrat, they can hardly feel urgency about problems that seem so remote. Below the politicians are the various types of administrators, judges, policemen, all of whom are concerned with the management and maintenance of existing power relations. From top to bottom, the political hierarchy is a system for preserving the social and economic relations of corporate capitalism. Those concerned with changing the conditions of life are excluded from American "politics."

In the society devoted to buying, selling and profit-making, education and knowledge are reduced to financial "assets." A student is someone who "invests" in education. An educated man is esteemed for the size of his income, the price of his car, the "name" of the school or corporation he works for, and the number of men he's in charge of. Chemistry, physics, mathematics, engineering, are converted to instruments for the manufacture of commodities and weapons. The scientist, whom Western tradition had crowned Pursuer of Truth, today sells his knowledge to the corporation or military branch that hires him, and teachers of science train their students in the arts of making commodities and bombs. The scientist's knowledge does not serve to ennoble, but to degrade man. And the scientist has been effectively taught that the *use* to which his knowledge is put is not his "field." The useless gadgets, the megaton bombs, the poison gas, are graciously given over to the manikins in the corporate and political hierarchies. The scientist, too, is merely hired, and not responsible.

The great achievements of human imagination and reason are put at the service of irrationality. The pattern of capitalist production has become the model for all activity. The irrationality of production-for-profit has become all-pervading. Capitalist production is unplanned and uncoordinated; it has no view to human needs. More is produced than people can buy, and so to keep the market open, "obsolescence" is built into the goods so they will wear out quickly and have to be replaced. Capitalists outrun each other in producing what no one needs. The goal of all the activity is inhuman and absurd: the whole society is made to run a frantic race whose outcome is the profit of the rich. Yet every single phase of the process—the production, research, marketing, advertising—contains all the rationality and knowledge developed by millenia of human beings. The American educator Robert Hutchins described the process lucidly in an address he delivered in 1959. "Our real problems ... concealed from us by our current remarkable prosperity, which results in part from the production of arms that we do not expect to use, and in part from our new way of getting rich, which is to buy things from one another that we do not want at prices we cannot pay on terms we cannot meet because of advertising we do not believe."[59]

The contrast between rational means and irrational ends has been termed by Paul Baran a clash between "micro-sense" and "macro-madness." Baran has pointed out that both parts of the relation advance simultaneously, thus leading human consciousness into absurdity at one end and meaninglessness at the other. "Whereas the irrationality of the whole must be constantly maintained if exploitation, waste, and privilege, if—in one word—capitalism is to survive, the rationality of society's individual parts is enforced by the drive for profits and the competitive necessities of capitalist enterprise. Thus this partial rationality continually edges forward—albeit jerkily and unevenly—but the advance takes place at the cost of its being warped, perverted, and corrupted by the irrationality of the surrounding social order."[60] This process is obviously hard on the human personality. A person trained to exercise his reason on details, as he perforce must be to carry out his task effectively, will naturally be disturbed when he confronts the irrationality of the entire process. The prevention and control of such disturbance is the crucial role Psychoanalysis plays in the corporate society. The psycho-analyst takes the irrationality of the profit-society for granted; his function is to "fix" those who do not take this irrationality for granted. The psychoanalyst seeks to "adjust" the personality to the "macro-madness" by means of "micro-sense." How this is done, and the effect of the "treatment," has been described by N.S. Lehrman, himself a psychoanalyst. "The analyst, 'high in a tower up a chamber to the east,' doubts the existence of harassment in the present, suspects the patient's reaction is 'paranoid' and assumes that the roots of the fears of the present lie somewhere in the past. The patient accepts this concept and withdraws interest from the present in order to examine the past. Amorphously and sincerely, analyst and patient then go to work examining the latter's childhood.

"The paralytic effectiveness of the treatment is maximized by the fact that both the patient and the analyst sincerely believe the treatment to be efficacious and scientific.

"And while the patient searches his past, the world goes on and opportunities are missed. I have often wondered what the role of the flourishing Berlin Psychoanalytic Institute was in 1932 and 1933, with particular reference to the paralysis of intellectuals of the Social Democratic Party."[61]

Psychoanalysts confess the ineffectiveness of their "cure" on real mental patients. It is not mental illness they are equipped to "heal." Their only targets are those persons who are fed up with capitalist "reality." Since the Psychoanalysts are victims of capitalist ideology, as well as being hired and maintained by the corporate society's masters, they cannot afford to question the human relevance of corporate capitalism. Consequently, they must attribute the irrationality of capitalism to the individual patient's "subconscious." *That* is their ideology. The psychoanalyst first of all reduces his "patient" to utter helplessness by "opening him up"—by allowing the "patient" to pour out the contents of his consciousness, systematically mixing triviality together with choices and goals. After months of such "treatment," during which an individual's reason and self-control are thoroughly undermined, even the strongest can be driven into an imbecile fear of the inexistent "subconscious." Once the individual's faith in his own rationality is undermined, once he is made to believe that his ideals, thoughts and wishes all emanate from the uncontrollable pit the psychoanalyst calls the "subconscious," the individual is paralyzed. Having reduced the "patient" to helplessness, the psychoanalyst then leads him back to "reality"—which means, to an unquestioning acceptance of *all* the irrationalities of the capitalist society. The individual so "treated" emerges with the belief that irrationality is the order of nature and society, and that those who demand rationality must be examined. The "patient" learns from his "treatment" to look with contempt on all criticism of the corporate society, because he now "knows" that the endless accumulation of gadgets, the bureaucratic crawl, the permanent war economy, the world misery, constitute "reality." The effectively psychoanalyzed "patient" learns that one who criticizes "reality" does not "really" criticize the inhuman brutality of corporate capitalism, but merely expresses a "father complex" of one sort or another. And the "cured" individual learns from his psychoanalyst that the roots of the illness described by a critic are not to be sought in the society the critic describes, but are rather to be sought in remote, or even contrived, "incidents" in the critic's childhood. Having channeled an individual's concern with his community to a self-indulgent preoccupation with childhood memories and mythological "explanations," the psychoanalyst proceeds to train his "patient" to spread the "cure" among other disaffected members of the corporate society. The only bright feature of psychoanalysis is that the Freudian theory on which it stands is neither original nor imaginative, and thus cannot, on its own merits, be spread very readily.

Community is banished, ideals are degraded, men are dehumanized—and cultural activity is trivialized. Culture is man's permanent intellectual and imaginative contribution to human ennoblement. The corporate society can boast only great critics of its "way of life"; great spokesmen it has none. The literature, music and art of the corporate society are grounded on nihilism. Nihilism is not culture; it is a negation of culture. North America's greatest architect, Frank Lloyd Wright, built on the outskirts of the corporate society, openly defiant toward corporate demands. The Crystal Palace does, however, have a pseudo-culture, the so-called Mass Culture, which is no culture at all, but a business. The mass culture is another means of acquiring wealth. Modeled on the capitalist industrial plant, mass culture consists of the manufacture of entertainment-commodities which are for sale to consumers. The goals are sale and profit; the effects are degraded intellects and infantile imaginations. That a vast and largely literate population could be trained to "consume" the "commodities" of the mass culture is nearly incredible. The conditioning of almost 200 million people into swallowing sham literature, sham music, sham art, as a substitute for genuine cultural creation, has no historical precedents. It was once thought that what Pavlov did with dogs could not be done with human beings, but capitalist achievements are not bound by human limits. If food is placed before a dog, the dog salivates. In one of his experiments, Pavlov placed food before a dog and simultaneously rang a bell: the dog salivated. He rang the bell at every meal-time, but did not always bring the food, yet the dog continued to salivate. Soon Pavlov rang only the bell, and did not bring the food, yet the dog still salivated. The dog had been "conditioned" to associate the bell with food; it had been taught to "digest" the bell instead of food. Once under the impression that the bell constitutes food, the dog would continue to "consume" the bell until it contentedly starved to death. In the corporate society, the American people are substituted for Pavlov's dogs, and sham culture is the bell. Genuine culture-whether it is expressed in drama, music, painting, sculpture, architecture—provides intellectual and emotional satisfaction by communicating content from artist to audience. In genuine culture, the words, sounds, movements, or forms, are irrelevant if divorced from the content. Yet in the corporate culture, the sounds and forms have been effectively dissociated from the content. Millions of Americans watch movies and television, listen to music, which has no content. They have been taught to consume words, sounds, movements and forms, in which nothing is communicated. They have been taught to salivate from the bell, to digest words without meaning and forms without content. Capitalists quickly applied this principle in their factories; guided by "industrial psychologists," they painted factory walls and had music played during work-hours, so that workers would get the impression they were not working but relaxing, and could thus be made to work harder. Most of the big corporations have adopted paternalistic "benefit" programs which shower workers with insurances of different kinds, wage increases, paid vacations, relaxation rooms—all the trappings of life except life, all the "benefits" except meaningful participation. The workers salivate as if they were fed, but their intellects decay, their imaginations deteriorate, because the food they are given is not human nourishment. Paul Goodman, in *Growing Up Absurd*, quotes surveys in which workers place Interest high on their list of needs. Interest cannot be provided without genuine sharing and participation. The workers are fed many "benefits," and more are constantly added; yet, as Goodman points out, the job "is not interesting; it is not his, he is not 'in' on it; the product is not really useful."[62] With the help of psychologists, palliative "benefits" are increased to quell all dissatisfaction; what is not given, and cannot be given by the corporate Holders, is human justification and relevance, what Goodman calls "the sense of being needed for one's unique contribution." The intellects and imaginations of Americans salivate from the bell, and food need no longer be brought. The result is "a mind bemired in fact, an imagination beslimed with particulars."[63] Yet a land of scientifically created imbeciles cannot long survive; the cultural needs of men cannot long be suppressed without far-reaching repercussions. The salesmen of mass culture claim that the people "want" the type of food they are fed. No doubt Pavlov's dog, after he learned to associate the bell with food, also "wanted" to "eat" the bell. By acquiring such a "want," however, a dog starves to death.

An organized society, with all the complication and sacrifice it imposes on its members, can only be justified if it provides for the fullest possible creative and intellectual development of each individual. The corporate society, where reason serves no rational purpose, where "micro-sense" is devoted to "macro-madness," cannot claim the respect of the individuals in it; consequently this society can maintain itself only by force, open or veiled, physical or psychological. When the corporate rulers can no longer respond to challenges except by violence and destruction, they have reached the limits of irrationality and nihilism. A society where even the active affirmation of human life is a crime has precedents in history: all the precedents were self-destructive, and all of them caused unspeakable misery and suffering before they flickered out. An individual who continues to affirm life, rationality and community, who refuses to prostrate his intellect and imagination to the regime devoted to genocide, has less chance of effectively realizing his ideals than in any previous dispensation. All the "avenues of truth" are clogged with big lies, all the means of creation and participation are dedicated to profits and annihilation. The society whose Declaration of Independence spoke of "the right of the people to alter or to abolish [their government], and to institute a new government," has abolished the expression of that right except through revolution. Should a democratic revolution fail once more, the revolutionaries will not again be integrated into an "opposition party." "Democratic America" today provides for its democrats only three terrible alternatives: impotence, exile, and martyrdom.

The terror and its meaning, however, are not yet visible to those within the confines of the corporate society. From the inside, the United States seems to be transforming itself into a rigid and stable society of ants; and in this sub-human form, Corporate America seems yet to be assured of an extended era of unchanging permanence. With men degraded into "hands," with all natural and human resources devoted to the profit of owners, with mind mechanics policing and repairing misfits, the attainment of perfect adjustment and fixity seems to be the goal of Our Way of Life. Looking at the prospects of mankind from within the corporate walls, Roderick Seidenberg, in *Posthistoric Man*, predicted the condition of perfect fixity and rigid changelessness found among insects: "...in a period devoid of change, we may truly say that man will enter upon a *posthistoric age* in which, perhaps, he will remain encased in an endless routine and sequence of events, not unlike that of the ants, the bees, and the termites. Their essentially unchanged survival during some sixty million years testifies to the perfection of their adjustment, internally and externally, to the conditions of life: man may likewise find himself entombed in a perpetual round of perfectly adjusted responses."[64] According to Seidenberg, ants and bees have attained changeless permanence through the perfect integration of instinct; men would reach the same end through rational means. Already visible in the air-conditioned glass cages of the corporate couriers, where endless repetition is life's only task, the "posthistoric" era will be marked by the smothering of creativity and the gradual disappearance of consciousness. "Curiously," writes Seidenberg, "we seem to have returned, via the route of intelligence to the very status from which man departed, aeons ago, under the undivided dominance of the instincts. For here, too, in the conditions of the future, the organism appears suspended within set responses, following interminably the selfsame patterns until altered by the slow processes of biologic mutations.... Consciousness depends upon a state of imbalance, a condition of tension. It is an awareness, in its widest and most intensified aspects, of that unstable equilibrium whose passing phases in the development of man we call history. Thus we are led to perceive that history itself, however inclusive we may conceive its sway, must be counted in reality as a high transitional era of relatively short duration in comparison with the slumbering eternity that preceded it, or the ever more static ages that will follow upon it. Consciousness will gradually evaporate and disappear in this posthistoric period, very much as it condensed step by step into ever sharper focus during man's prehistoric era. In the ultimate state of crystallization to which the principle of organization leads, consciousness will have accomplished its task, leaving mankind sealed, as it were, within patterns of frigid and unalterable perfection. In this consummation we perceive the essential meaning of the posthistoric period of man's development.... Unerringly, his drive toward conformity will guide him into an ever more static condition of fixity and permanence; and the perfection of his adjustment will come to be synonymous with a slow but ultimate fading out of his consciousness. His triumph will be complete, and by that very token his awareness, no longer necessary, will evaporate, leaving only a fixed routine of actions whose perfect suitability will erase all memory of thought."[65] The "posthistoric" society will have no art, no philosophy, no culture, because creative intellectual syntheses will not be "rational" within its confines.

The condition of fixity and permanence predicted by Seidenberg is far from being realized. Though Seidenberg brilliantly depicts the appearance of corporate capitalism with all its goals fulfilled, he commits the fallacy of identifying capitalist goals with human goals and capitalist "reason" with human reason, and thus builds his conclusions on partial premises. The state of permanent fixity will not be attained precisely because of what Seidenberg himself illustrates. Taking the marketing, research, advertising and manipulation as human sense, and taking the irrational cycle of production for corporate profit as the aim of humanity, Seidenberg projects this "rationality" into a future of fixity and permanence. Yet it is precisely the identification of capitalist reason with human reason, of corporate sense with human sense, that will prevent the perfect and unchanging fixity Seidenberg predicts. For, as Paul Baran lucidly observed, Seidenberg is not alone in identifying corporate reason with human reason; his contemporaries too are "afflicted with 'common sense' that is studiously nurtured by all the agencies of bourgeois culture and the principal injunction of which is to take capitalist rationality for granted, ... [and they] can hardly avoid identifying the rationality of buying, selling, and profit-making with reason itself."[66] And since Seidenberg's contemporaries are still human beings—they are not yet manufactured in bottles to fit corporate specifications—they will still react in human ways against corporate "reason," and by reacting they will rebel and thus destroy Seidenberg's fixity. As Baran points out, man's "revolt against capitalist rationality, against the rationality of markets and profits, thus becomes a revolt against reason itself, turns into anti-intellectualism, and promotes aggressiveness toward those who manage to capitalize on the rules of the capitalist game to their advantage and advancement. It renders him an easy prey of irrationality."[67] Many of Seidenberg's contemporaries do in fact obediently "adjust" to the system; if they were the corporate society's only inhabitants, Seidenberg's prediction would no doubt be a good guess. But "adjustment," or submission, is only one possible response to corporate "reason": other possible responses are escape, rebellion, and destruction. Paul Goodman has labeled the responses to corporate absurdity resignation, beat and crime. (All three are negative responses; Goodman would doubtless grant the possibility of a fourth, a positive response, namely creative rebellion.) If beat and crime were responses restricted to a few odd misfits, the misfits could easily be put aside and corporate fixity could still be attained. But these responses are not restricted, because within an irrational dispensation every man is a potential "misfit." In so far as he retains vestiges of human consciousness and imagination, every man in the corporate society can become beat or criminal. It is this fact that prevents the perfect integration and permanent fixity predicted by Seidenberg.

The destructive responses, while preventing the perfect integration and eternization of corporate capitalism in the form of a changeless insect society, do not, however, ensure the survival of humanity. On the contrary, destructive criminality at the top of the corporate society would mean the annihilation of mankind. A criminal response to corporate nihilism is itself a nihilistic response. The criminal, by taking capitalist "reason" as human reason, rejects both simultaneously and turns to irrationality. He finds a model of irrational self assertion at the top of the same corporate structure whose lower-level rationality he rejects. In other words, the criminal rejects the "micro-sense' of the corporate society, and turns instead to its "macro-madness." At this point, American juvenile delinquency and political practice meet: the gangs of juvenile delinquents are miniature mirrors of the Pentagon and the State Department; the young criminals enact on a city block the same "policies" the United States government carries out on a world scale. The top responds irrationally because it takes the "macro-madness" for human sense, the bottom because it rejects the corporate "micro-sense" and seeks salvation in madness. Those at the top take capitalist reason for granted, and in a world where men are throwing out capitalist "reason" for human goals, they fear the collapse of their "way of life"; yet since they identify corporate capitalism with life itself, they can only react with a frantic appeal to nationalist tribalism and its consequent fear, hatred, destruction and terror. Those at the bottom reject human reason along with capitalist reason in a grand irrational sweep, and they can only respond by destroying achievements and annihilating life. When annihilation becomes not only thinkable, but the main goal of human activity, consciously pursued at both the top and bottom levels of the corporate society, then the tempo of criminal breakthroughs increases and destroys all corporate hopes of permanence and fixity. In this sense, Dostoyevsky's fantastic prediction of a resurgence of barbarism in the midst of technological abundance, realized already once in this century, is far more ominous than Seidenberg's prediction, which will remain no more than a self-destructive tendency. What Dostoyevsky foresaw, a century ago, was that the psychological extinction of human beings would have to be preceded by total physical annihilation, and that men would arise to implement this program. "I would not be at all surprised, for instance, if suddenly and without the slightest possible reason a gentleman of an ignoble or rather a reactionary and sardonic countenance were to arise amid all that future reign of universal common sense and, gripping his sides firmly with his hands, were to say to us all, 'Well, gentlemen, what about giving all this common sense a mighty kick and letting it scatter in the dust before our feet simply to send all these logarithms to the devil so that we can again live according to our foolish will?' That wouldn't matter, either, but for the regrettable fact that he would certainly find followers: for man is made like that...."[68] The political "realists," the war experts, the bureaucratic terrorists, have joined hands with the hoodlums and juvenile criminals in capitalism's last grand enterprise, that of "giving all this common sense a mighty kick and letting it scatter in the dust before our feet..."

Nihilist rejection, in the form of gang crime and nuclear barbarism, is the main response to corporate irrationality, and by far the most dangerous. The nihilist mentality grows like an uncontrollable cancer, and spreads with greatest force especially to the chambers where the weapons of death are kept. The greatest danger to human life is the frenzy with which the corporate dominant minority reacts to the growing circle of disaffection and anti-capitalist revolution around the world. The disaffection is the outcome of corporate plunder, yet to cope with it the corporate rulers can resort only to violence; the violence, in turn, increases the number of victims, and thus enlarges the circle of disaffection. As a result, disaffection with corporate capitalism and its "freedom" takes place on all grounds at every turn. Clearly revealed during the Cuban debacle was the fact that the corporate "elite" are fully aware that men will no longer submit to corporate "freedom." Also clearly revealed was the fact that the corporate bosses will not calmly accept a slave rebellion, but will strike out with all the frenzy, the hatred, the destruction, of the caged beast. Capitalists are now aware that it is not merely a few profits that are at stake, but their entire structure of privilege.

Thus while each revolution gives life and hope to an increasing number of men, each defection at the same time aggravates the possibility of total annihilation. Yet, faced with death, and confronted with the choice between continuing submission and revolution, men everywhere are choosing revolution. Most of the rebellions take place within the capitalist-imposed confines of nationalism, bureaucratism and specialism, but they do take place, and they do open to men the possibility to create societies with genuine creative participation. The corporate rulers interpret every revolution as an incursion into their "free world," and with every incursion their frenzy grows. To protect their vanishing privileges, the capitalists increasingly surrender even those very privileges to their military establishment on the delusion that a vast campaign of annihilation will preserve corporate privilege intact.

While the negative, destructive responses are tangible and all-pervading, the positive, constructive responses are as yet intangible, half-formulated, and utopian. In the era of technological barbarism, crime is much easier than revolution, and spreads much further. It took only one American atomic bomb to annihilate Hiroshima, while it takes the ingenuity, wisdom and good will of many men, all intensely aware of the accumulated experience of generations, to build a community where technology is made to serve human ends. It takes far less motion to use a knife for killing than for carving and sculpting. It takes far less ingenuity or intelligence to destroy than to create. It takes far less effort for "realists" to maintain a permanent war economy than for "idealists" to create a peace economy, because it is far easier to submit to criminality than to rebel against it. The history of obedience and submission is a history of outrage and crime; it is a history of war, of military oppression, of police brutality. The history of rebellion and revolution is not without its violence and hatred, but violence is not its aim, and its hatred is short lived. As defined by Camus, rebellion is an affirmation of human life; the recourse to violence is thus the betrayal, not the fulfillment, of rebellion. Oppression gives birth to rebellion; the same oppression, through violence and terror, forces rebellion to defend itself with violence, and thus tinge itself with the very oppression that gave it birth. Yet, clearly, to abolish the violence, it is the oppression that must be eliminated. Men all over the world are at last realizing that obedient submission to oppression only heightens oppression, and they are turning to rebellion to affirm life and community. It is this fact that gives hope to human survival and encouragement to creative action. The radicals* of today are at last divorcing themselves from the conservative "movements" that speak the language of radicalism while clinging to corporate privileges. Whether in Europe or in America, the radicals of today have more in common with the revolutionaries of Cuba, China, India, Africa and Latin America, than they do with the wise and weary old cynics who still call themselves the local Left. Creative rebels aim at the abolition of corporate plunder and the prevention of the capitalist war of total annihilation as

---

*I use the words "radical" and "rebel" to describe those who affirm human life, community, participation. In a recent American usage, the term "radicals of the right" has been used to describe reactionary and neo-fascist groups. If this usage is accepted, I will have to be content to substitute "radicals of the left" for radicals. I would suggest, however, that clarity and precision in communication can better be served by a more conventional usage, namely by calling the "radicals of the left" radicals, and the "radicals of the right" reactionaries.

the prime requirements for regeneration; these rebels have nothing to do with the conservatives of the one-time "American Left," with the British Labour movement, with the European "Social Democrats," with the anti-communist "socialists," with the no-action "pacifists" or with the noisy "liberals" whom C. Wright Mills has called the "NATO Intellectuals."

The circle of disaffection is spreading even within the corporate society itself, in spite of the fact that in "freedom loving" America the choice of radicalism renders one a pariah, an outcast as untouchable as the lowest caste of old India. Thomas Jefferson's advice and warning can now be read as an ominous prophecy in the land where the democratic revolution failed: "Each generation ... has a right to choose for itself the form of government it believes the most promotive of its own happiness.... A solemn opportunity of doing this every 19 or 20 years should be provided by the constitution. This corporeal globe, and everything upon it, belong to its present corporeal inhabitants, during their generation. They alone have a right to direct what is the concern of themselves alone.... If this avenue be shut..., it will make itself heard through that of force, and we shall go on, as other nations are doing, in the endless circle of oppressions, rebellions, reformations; and oppression, rebellion, reformation, again; and so on forever."[69] In America, critics of the ruling class are as unprotected from harassment and persecution as in any tyranny in history; the persecution is not only carried on by the Government, but has now been pronounced "consistent" with the Bill of Rights by the Supreme Court of the land. In America, radicalism which aims to unseat the corporate aristocracy is labeled "communist conspiracy" and is now punishable by life imprisonment or even death. One of the Supreme Court Justices who dissented from sanctioning political persecution made a lucid comparison between the frenzy of capitalists during John Adams' administration and that of today: "...the Federalist Sedition Act ... did not go as far in suppressing the First Amendment freedoms of Americans as do the Smith Act and the Subversive Activities Control Act. All the fervor and all the eloquence and all the emotionalism and all the prejudice and all the parade of horrors ... were not sufficient in 1798 to persuade the members of Congress to pass a law which would directly and unequivocally outlaw the party of Jefferson, at which the law was undoubtedly aimed. The same arguments were then made about the 'Jacobins,' meaning the Jeffersonians, with regard to their alleged subservience to France, that are made today about the Communists with regard to their subservience to Russia."[70] In mid-twentieth century America, there are probably as many "conspirators" and "dangerous ideas," and as many police organizations and "investigatory bodies" to cope with them, as ever in history; censorship, spying and informing have not only become respectable practices, but are among the big expenses of the United States government. Yet the circle of heresy continues to spread.

The old Left in America was effectively emasculated and rendered impotent by the inhuman persecution of the past fifteen years, persecution whose brutality is equalled in recent history by the Nazi persecution of Jews. Communists, though rarely very radical, were chosen as the scapegoats of the persecution. One-time communists and friends of one-time communists were hounded out of their homes and jobs and communities and forced to denounce former comrades. So-called "spies" were persecuted, jailed and murdered in peace-time, and highly respectable scientists and educators were thrown from their posts and ostracized for long-forgotten "associations" with communists. Faced with such vicious persecution, the communists, who are only human, retorted with an inflexible rigidity and held on for dear life to a thoroughly idealized picture of their Soviet Heaven, much as in former times persecuted Europeans had clung to a thoroughly exaggerated picture of "Free, Democratic America." Homeless, the communists could not have survived; yet by placing their faith in an unreal "place" which did, in reality, have a history, and did, after all, confront unsolved human problems, they survived at a tremendous price. The price of survival for American communists was rigidity; in the struggle to stay alive, they lost the great gifts they had inherited from Marx, the ability to think, analyze and clarify. Yet, utterly rejected and ostracized, they could not help but hurl defensive slogans that had long lost content, and frantically affirm everything Soviet as good. The victims of Nazi persecution did not emerge with sharpened intellects and sensitive imaginations either; brutal persecution deadens not only its perpetrators, but its victims as well.

Rendered impotent and rigid by vicious oppression, the communists had yet to suffer the further humiliation of seeing friends and comrades, as well as other "socialists," turn on them with a brutality even greater than the government's. This bizarre phenomenon probably has no equal since the Middle Ages, when men who were labeled "heretics" suddenly found themselves feared and hated even by their one-time friends. Now, as then, the fear of "heresy" and contamination is motivated by an irrational desire to save one's "soul," a fear which is nurtured by organized religion. America is an atheist country in terms of personal hope and faith, in terms of love and brotherhood, it is the world's greatest repository of atheism—yet America has adopted the most brutal institution of organized religion, namely the demonology. In America, a doctrine, as well as its spokesmen, have been attributed to the Devil, and an American does not consider himself "safe" if he does not periodically denounce the Devil's doctrine, and if he does not reserve for its spokesmen a contempt and hatred he does not even express towards animals and things. Anti-communism is the only religion of atheist America, and its practice is not restricted to the "average man," the victim of the propaganda media, but has infected and rendered impotent the remains of the old Left. American "socialists," frightened out of their wits by the persecutions of communists, and deathly afraid to be swallowed up by the rigidity with which their one-time comrades responded to the persecutions, fell into an equally rigid posture and spent the remainder of their careers persecuting communists with greater brutality and intolerance than that of Congressmen. The non-socialist sector of the old Left is also rendered impotent by the anti-communist mania, and is beset as well by "unconditional pacifism." This is a highly refined doctrine which holds that any rebellion is bad because it brings violence, and consequently acquiescence and inaction are the only moral alternatives. Though rarely held in its pure form, the doctrine's greatest function is to pacify so-called "liberals." Since some form of violence will be found everywhere, since even a strike may be defined as a form of sabotage, since no resistance will ever be "pure," the outcome is non-action, which means passive acceptance of existing oppression. Gandhi's precept that it is less cowardly to resist oppression with violence than not to resist at all does not penetrate the cowardly consciousness. This type of "pacifism" is not pacifism; it is self-righteousness masquerading as morality: it is not a rejection of violence, oppression and war, but rather a rejection of all effective resistance to violence, oppression and war. Thus beset by many types of "radicals" who are not radical, the old Left will continue impotent so long as it continues paying attention to the tired conservatives in its midst. Continually confronting the world's biggest problems, the old Left has neither unity, nor program, nor plan of action—nor solidarity nor support—above all, no hope or promise.

A comparison of revolutions leads to the conclusion that every revolution is a break-through: it is unprecedented; its causal sequence is not predictable; it is unique. Radical action can define the objectives and prepare the ground; it can have a program and a plan of action; but it cannot have a blueprint, because a blueprint would be outdated from one day to the next. The patterns of one revolution are applicable to another only symbolically; the accumulated experience of revolutions is susceptible to imaginative analogy, not to transplantation: a tropical plant will not grow in the Arctic. So far, social revolutions have concerned themselves with the technological, educational and cultural development of regions, and have thus been able to pursue their aims within national boundaries and nationalist concepts. There will no doubt continue to be regional, nationalist revolutions so long as the inequality between regions, the political barriers between them, and the contrived national loyalties continue to exist. It is clear, however, that the biggest problems of our time, corporate plunder and the war of total annihilation, cannot be dealt with in nationalist confines. The victims of corporate plunder are not restricted to any region: they are in the United States, in Latin America, in all the world's "underdeveloped nations"; the neutralists of Laos, the social revolutionaries of Cuba are victims of continuing terror and invasion; even the remote and stable Russians and Chinese are forced by corporate militarism into military postures which threaten to overwhelm their achievements. The nuclear war of annihilation is not a problem confined to a region or even a continent: Indonesians, Tahitians and Eskimos, as well as unborn generations, would all be affected. It is no longer clear that the inhabitants of the corporate society have a better opportunity of dealing with these problems than those "outside": the American government now keeps elaborate files on all its "dangerous inhabitants"[71] and has the power to remove and isolate all "dangerous," meaning effective, critics. Is it even clear, for example, that a general strike of all humanity against the corporate war economy could not be organized with greater ease than a general strike of American workers? Early in this century, the international solidarity of radicals was discarded because of historical necessity; yet clearly, when plunder and war are carried out in a National Interest, anti-nationalism becomes once more an aim of revolution; the international solidarity of radicals has now become a historical necessity. The issues are no longer regional but world-wide; from one "nation" to another, the problems differ in degree, not in kind; the degradation of human beings for a few men's privilege, the "protection" of privilege by annihilation, are not parochial institutions that affect only a small sector of the world's population; they are the central concerns of all mankind. Even regional development within nationalist confines cannot effectively be carried out while terrorism and sabotage threaten every accomplishment. Internal disaffection and external defection from corporate "freedom" are not two separate revolutions; they are two facets of the same revolution, and neither can succeed if it betrays the other. Plunder, war, and the nationalism under whose guise they are carried on, cannot effectively be opposed with plunder, war and nationalism. If men are to become fully engaged in the construction of peace, culture and community, they will risk exile, imprisonment and death. The risk will not be taken, it will not be worthwhile, until peace means the recognition of the importance of every human being, until culture is grounded on the equal accessibility of the means of life to every man, until community provides for untrammeled criticism, complete development and creative participation by all, and for all men.

June 1961
New York City

NOTES

Chapter 1
GOLDEN AGE

1. Cervantes, *Don Quixote de la Mancha* (translation by J. M. Cohen).
2. *The Tempest*.
3. Karl Mannheim, *Ideology and Utopia: An Introduction to the Sociology of Knowledge*, p. 213.
4. Quoted in R.H. Tawney, *Religion and the Rise of Capitalism*, p. 74. and p. 90.
5. Quoted in George H. Sabine, *Political Theory*, p. 361.
6. See Sabine, *History*, p 490f.
7. This, and the following quotations, are from Thomas More, *Utopia*, First Book.
8. This, and the following, quotations are from Niccolo Machiavelli, *The Prince* (translation by Luigi Ricci, revised by E.R.P. Vincent).
9. This, and the next two quotations, from More, *Utopia*.
10. Quoted in Sabine, p. 492.
11. Quoted in *Ibid.*, p. 491.
12. Babeuf quoted this statement of the French philosopher Mably to his executioners; quoted in Edmund Wilson, *To The Finland Station; A Study in the Writing and Acting of History*, p.75.
13. Paraphrased in Wilson, *op. cit.*, p. 75.
14. Paraphrased in *Ibid.*, p. 74.
15. Quoted in Sabine, *History*, p. 494.
16. Mark Van Doren, *Shakespeare*.
17. *Twelfth Night*.
18. Quoted in Wilson, *op. cit.*, p. 72.
19. Quoted in *Ibid.*, p. 77.

Chapter 2
DEMOCRATIC EXPERIMENT

1. *Declaration of Independence*.
2. More, *Utopia*.
3. Babeuf; quoted in Wilson, *To The Finland Station*, p. 75.
4. John Taylor of Caroline County, Virginia, *An Inquiry into the Principles and Policy of the Government of the United States* (1950 edition of Yale University Press, New Haven), p. 62, Hereafter cited as "*Inquiry.*"
5. Charles A. Beard, *An Economic Interpretation of the Constitution of the United States*, first published in 1913 (I have used the edition published

by The Macmillan Company in 1954), hereafter cited as "*Constitution*"; and *Economic Origins of Jeffersonian Democracy*, first published in 1915 (I have used the edition published by The Macmillan Company in 1952), hereafter cited as *Jeffersonian Democracy*."

6. James Madison; quoted by Beard in *Constitution*, p. 15.
7. John Adams; quoted by Beard in *Jeffersonian Democracy*, p 303.
8. Quoted in *Ibid.*, p. 320.
9. Quoted in *Ibid*.
10. Quoted in *Ibid.*, p. 306 and p. 304.
11. John Taylor, *Inquiry*, p. 284.
12. *Ibid.*, p. 504.
13. Adams; quoted by Beard in *Jeffersonian Democracy*, p. 304.
14. Taylor, *Inquiry*, p. 65.
15. More, *Utopia*.
16. Madison; quoted by Beard in *Constitution*, p. 15.
17. John Adams; quoted by Beard in *Jeffersonian Democracy*, p. 321.
18. Adams; quoted in *Ibid.*, p. 304-305.
19. Taylor, *Inquiry*, p. 243.
20. *Ibid*.
21. *Thomas Jefferson on Democracy*, p. 87.
22. *Ibid.*, p. 89.
23. Taylor, *Inquiry*, p. 245.
24. *Ibid.*, p. 62.
25. *Thomas Jefferson on Democracy*, p. 30.
26. *Ibid.*, p. 15.
27. *Ibid.*, p. 67-68.
28. See Beard, *Constitution*, p. 35.
29. From the Introduction to *The Constitution of the United States* (edited with notes and charts by William H. Barnes), Barnes and Noble, Inc., New York, 1951.
30. Charles Beard, *Constitution*, p. 324.
31. *Ibid*.
32. *Ibid.*, p. 144.
33. Alexander Hamilton; quoted in *Ibid.*, p. 199.
34. Quoted in Beard, *Jeffersonian Democracy*, p. 288.
35. Alexander Hamilton; quoted in *Ibid*.
36. See Beard's *Economic Interpretation of the Constitution* for a detailed catalogue of the interests, wealth, and views of the members of the Philadelphia Convention.
37. *Ibid.*, p. 324.
38. *The Massachusetts Gazette* of October 26, 1787; quoted in *Ibid.*, p. 302.

NOTES

39. John Marshall, in *Life of Washington*; quoted in *Ibid.*, p. 299.
40. Beard, *Ibid.*, p. 325.
41. *Ibid.*, p. 37.
42. Beard, *Jeffersonian Democracy*, p. 122.
43. John Taylor; quoted by Beard in *Ibid.*, p. 202.
44. Taylor; quoted in *Ibid.*, p. 200.
45. Congressman Jackson of Georgia, *Annals of Congress* Vol. II; quoted by Beard in *Ibid.*, p. 148-9.
46. John Taylor, *Inquiry*, p. 68.
47. Jefferson to Washington, September 2, 1792; quoted by Beard in *Jeffersonian Democracy*, p. 110.
48. Quoted in *Ibid.*, p. 111.
49. Quoted in *Ibid.*, p. 153.
50. Jackson of Georgia; quoted in *Ibid.*, p. 137.
51. Quoted in *Ibid.*, p. 211, footnote.
52. John D. Hicks, *A Short History of American Democracy*, The Riverside Press, Cambridge, Mass., 1946, p. 132-3.
53. John Taylor, *Inquiry*, p. 65-6.
54. Beard, *Jeffersonian Democracy*, p. 323.
55. *Ibid.*, p. 415, footnote. Beard points out, however, that Jefferson's pronouncements did not always have the virtue of consistency, as on another occasion Jefferson endorsed John Adams' *Defence of the American Constitutions*.
56. Taylor has also been called "the most fruitful of Republican intellects." Both titles are mentioned by Roy Franklin Nichols in his Introduction to the Yale University Press edition of Taylor's *Inquiry*. (Incidentally, for those readers who are interested in correlating the page references I give in the *Inquiry* with those cited by Beard, it will be indispensable to know that Beard quoted from the original edition of Taylor's work, whereas I contented myself with a more recent edition, published by Yale University Press, New Haven, in 1950. The edition Beard used has 636 pages, whereas the one I used has only 562 pages, which include a 29 page Introduction by Nichols, a professor of History at the University of Pennsylvania.)
57. Taylor, *Inquiry*, pp. 68-9.
58. *Ibid.*, pp. 82-3.
59. *Ibid.*, pp. 59-60.
60. *Ibid.*, p. 73.
61. *Ibid.*, p. 66.
62. *Ibid.*
63. *Ibid.*, p. 67.

64. *Ibid.*, pp. 67-8.
65. *Thomas Jefferson on Democracy*, p. 23.
66. *Ibid.*, pp. 29-30.
67. Jefferson to Dupont de Nemours, December 1801; quoted in Beard, *Jeffersonian Democracy*, pp. 436-7.
68. *Thomas Jefferson on Democracy*, pp. 69-70.
69. *Ibid.*, p. 100.
70. *Ibid.*, p. 47
71. Taylor, p. 278.
72. Cited previously, p. 40; the next four quotations were also previously cited.
73. Beard, *Jeffersonian Democracy*, p. 267.
74. Alexander Hamilton; quoted in *Ibid.*, p. 406.
75. Hamilton; quoted in *Ibid.*
76. Hamilton; quoted in *Ibid.*, pp. 406-7.
77. Hamilton was murdered by Burr in 1804, in a duel that arose from a later issue. Even later, Burr tried to make certain western territories independent of the United States government. The attempt failed.
78. Jefferson; quoted previously, p, 40.
79. Taylor, Inquiry; quoted previously, pp. 39-40,
80. *Thomas Jefferson on Democracy*, p. 30.
81. John Adams; quoted by Beard in *Jeffersonian Democracy*, p. 320.
82. Taylor, *Inquiry*, p. 68.

Chapter 3
GROWTH OF CAPITALISM

1. George Sabine, *A History of Political Theory*, p. 491.
2. Winstanley; quoted in *Ibid.*, p. 492.
3. Quoted in *Ibid.*, p. 361.
4. *Thomas Jefferson on Democracy*, pp. 79-80; next quotation from p. 68.
5. John Taylor, *Inquiry*, p. 244.
6. *Thomas Jefferson on Democracy*, p. 47.
7. Taylor, *Inquiry*, pp. 268-9.
8. Babeuf; paraphrased by Edmund Wilson, *To the Finland Station*, p.74.
9. Taylor, *Inquiry*, p. 59.
10. *Ibid.*, p. 255.
11. *Ibid.*, p. 67.
12. Lewis Mumford, *The Transformation of Man*.
13. Taylor, *Inquiry*, p. 269.
14. Quoted by Taylor in *Ibid.*, p. 254.
15. C. Wright Mills, *The Power Elite*, p. 95.

NOTES   215

16. Theodore Dreiser, *The Financier*.
17. Quoted in *Monthly Review*, August 1959.
18. J. Raymond Walsh, "The Storm Signals are Flying," *Monthly Review*, June 1953.
19. William Appleman Williams, *The Tragedy of American Diplomacy*, p. 103.
20. Quoted from A.A. Berle, Jr., *The Twentieth Century Capitalist Revolution*, in *Monthly Review*, January 1956.
21. Mills, *The Power Elite*, p. 275.
22. Quoted by Harvey O'Connor in *The Empire of Oil*, pp. 229-30.
23. From the *Declaration of Independence*.
24. Foreword to O'Connor's *The Empire of Oil*.
25. In *The Empire of Oil*.
26. *Ibid.*, p. 99f.
27. *Ibid.*, p. 98.
28. *Ibid.*, pp. 89f.
29. Mills, *The Power Elite*, p. 122.
30. O'Connor, *The Empire of Oil*, p. 73.
31. *Ibid.*, p. 227.
32. *Ibid.*
33. Mills, *The Power Elite*, p. 149.
34. O'Connor, *The Empire of Oil*, p. 3.
35. *Ibid.*, p. 21.
36. Mills, *The Power Elite*, p. 124-5.
37. C. Wright Mills, *White Collar*, pp. 336-7.
38. J.K. Galbraith, *American Capitalism*; quoted by Paul Baran in *The Political Economy of Growth*.
39. Mills, *White Collar*, p. 35.
40. O'Connor, *The Empire of Oil*, p. 57.
41. Mills, *The Power Elite*, p. 111, footnote.
42. Song of the Society of Equals, sung in French cafes in days of betrayal; quoted by Edmund Wilson in *To The Finland Station*, p.72.

Chapter 4
IDEOLOGY AND MANIPULATION

1. At the time of writing, Cuba was on the way toward the realization of a program of agrarian reform, universal education, creative participation—a program which failed in the United States, and which is analyzed more fully in this chapter, in the context of United States experience. Those readers who are interested in seeing interpretations of the Cuban revolution which diverge from the accounts given in the United

States "free press" are urged to study the following analyses:
Paul A. Baran, "Reflections on the Cuban Revolution," A Monthly Review Press pamphlet.
Leo Huberman and Paul M. Sweezy, *Cuba: Anatomy of a Revolution*.
C. Wright Mills, *Listen Yankee*.
James O'Connor, "The Classless Revolution," in *The Second Coming* magazine, July 1961.
J.P. Morray, "Cuba and Communism," *Monthly Review*, July-August, 1961. The entire issue is devoted to articles on Cuba.
Jean-Paul Sartre on Cuba.
2. New York *Times*, April 18, 1961.
3. Thomas More, *Utopia*.
4. Alexander Hamilton; quoted by *Beard, Economic Origins of Jeffersonian Democracy*, pp. 406-7.
5. *Thomas Jefferson on Democracy*, p. 44.
6. Ibid., p. 45.
7. *Maryland Journal* of March 21, 1788; quoted by Beard in *Economic Interpretation of the Constitution of the United States*, pp. 317-18.
8. Patrick Henry; quoted in *Ibid.*, p. 319.
9. John Marshall, quoted in *Ibid.*, p. 299.
10. Quoted in *Ibid.*
11. Quoted in *Ibid.*, p. 298.
12. Beard, *Ibid.*, pp. 251-2.
13. *Thomas Jefferson on Democracy*, p. 47.
14. *Ibid.*, p. 67.
15. Hamilton; quoted by Beard in *Jeffersonian Democracy*, p. 286.
16. Chief Justice John Marshall in 1819; quoted *Ibid.*, p. 299. On that page, Beard puts both quotations of Justice Marshall side by side, the one about the narrow margin by which the Constitution was ratified, and the one about the "government of the people."
17. John Taylor, *Inquiry*, p. 67.
18. *Ibid.*, p. 59.
19. *Ibid.*, p. 255.
20. Thomas Jefferson.
21. Taylor, *Inquiry*, p. 62.
22. Hamilton; quoted in Beard, *Constitution*, p. 199.
23. Taylor, *Inquiry*, p. 255.
24. C. Wright Mills; quoted previously on p. 60.
25. William A. Williams, *The Tragedy of American Diplomacy* p. 105.
26. A.A. Berle, Jr.; quoted previously on p. 64.
27. C. Wright Mills; quoted previously on p. 71.

28. Thomas More.
29. John Taylor, *Inquiry*, p. 66.
30. *Ibid.*, p. 67.
31. Thomas More.
32. Taylor, *Inquiry*, pp. 62-3.
33. C. Wright Mills, *The Power Elite*, p. 317-18.
34. Thomas Jefferson.
35. Gerrard Winstanley.
36. Mills, *The Power Elite*, pp. 317-18.
37. Clay Fulks, "Capitalism Seeks Sanctuary," *Monthly Review*, August 1950.
38. Harvey O'Connor, *The Empire of Oil*, p. 141.
39. See O'Connor, p. 139ff.
40. From H.G. Wells, *The First Men in the Moon*; the passage was quoted by Arnold Toynbee in *A Study of History*, Vol. III, Part III, the chapter entitled "Insect Societies and Human Utopias."
41. *Declaration of Independence*.
42. Article I, Amendments to the *Constitution* of the United States.
43. *Thomas Jefferson on Democracy*, p. 95.
44. Jefferson.
45. *Declaration of Independence*.
46. Alexander Hamilton.
47. This and subsequent quotations are taken from Leo Huberman's article "A Free Press? Free for Whom? John Swinton's Famous Reply," New York *Daily Compass*, May 5, 1952.
48. John Swinton, in Huberman's article.
49. Leo Marx, "Notes on the Culture of the New Capitalism," *Monthly Review*, July-August issue, 1959.
50. *Declaration of Independence*.
51. New York *Herald Tribune*, January 9, 1948; quoted in Frontespiece, and again in Foreword, of O'Connor's *The Empire of Oil*.
52. O'Connor, *The Empire of Oil*, p.137.
53. *Ibid.*, p. 147.
54. *Annual Report* (nineteen hundred sixty) of the Tea Council of Annual the U.S.A., Inc. This "report" is probably untypical; it is probably more restrained and "humane" because its Board of Directors is made up of 6 Asians and 6 Americans, and because it is concerned, not with one particular industry, but with the entire cartel. Interested readers will doubtless find far more blatant illustrations of the minds of manipulators, if they care to devote time and patience to the study of the advertisers' reports of the oil companies, steel companies, aluminum, automobile, fruit companies, and so on. A vast study could be made. Such a study

would show Adolf Hitler to have been a mere child, a rank amateur, in the techniques of mass manipulation.
55. *Ibid.*
56. Leo Marx, *loc. cit.*
57. New York *Times,* June 4, 1957.
58. New York *Times,* October 18, 1960.
59. New York *Times,* April 22, 1961; story by Tad Szulc.
60. New York *Times,* April 26, 1961; story entitled:
    "C.I.A. HELD CHIEFS
    OF CUBAN REBELS
    Miro Cardona Among Exiles
    Kept Incommunicado as
    Landings Were Made."
    Miro Cardona was supposed to he the leader of the invasion as well as president of the "Cuban Revolutionary Council."
61. The CBS (Columbia Broadcasting Company) radio station early revealed the source of the reports on the Cuban invasion—but other radio stations, as well as almost all newspapers, continued to the end to give readers the advertising firm's "news" without telling readers the source of the "news."
62. New York *Times,* April 22, 1961; story by Tad Szulc. Incidentally, some persons clever with initials devised for the. C.I.A. the title "Cuban Invasion Association."
63. New York *Times,* April 22; Szulc Story.
64. New York *Times,* April 22, 1961; story by Max Frankel.
65. *Ibid*; Max Frankel.
66. John Taylor, *Inquiry,* p. 68.
67. C. Wright Mills, *The Power Elite,* p. 253.
68. Harvey O'Connor, *The Empire of Oil,* p. 195.
69. Mills, *The Power Elite,* p. 324.

Chapter 5
CORPORATE DISPENSATION

1. Lewis Mumford, *The Transformations of Man.*
2. *Ibid.*
3. Karl Marx; quoted by Paul Baran in "The Commitment of the Intellectual," *Monthly Review,* May 1961.
4. In *The Need for Roots.*
5. C. Wright Mills, *The Power Elite,* p. 9.
6. *Ibid.,* p. 11.

NOTES 219

7. Jean-Paul Sartre, "Materialism and Revolution," *Politics*, July-August 1947 (translation by Ralph Manheim).
8. Satirist of the Constitution, in *Maryland Journal* of 1788; quoted in Charles Beard's *An Economic Interpretation of the Constitution of the United States*; quoted above p. 80.
9. George Bernard Shaw; quoted in *Monthly Review*, August 1949.
10. From Franz Kafka's *Parables*; quoted in Walter Kaufmann, *Existentialism from Dostoyevsky to Sartre*.
11. A.A. Berle, Jr.; quoted above, p. 64.
12. Edward Hyams in the *New Statesman* of March 18, 1959; quoted in *Monthly Review* for July-August, 1959.
13. See New York *Times*, March 5, 1961; front page stories on official estimates of unemployment.
14. "Review of the Month," *Monthly Review*, April 1961.
15. *Ibid.*
16. *Business Week*, May 17, 1952; quoted by Paul Baran, *The Political Economy of Growth*, p. 100f.
17. Quoted above, p. 80.
18. New York *Times*, June 4, 1957; quoted above p. 115.
19. Quoted by Paul Baran, *The Political Economy of Growth*, p. 57.
20. Quoted in *Ibid.*, p.59, footnote.
21. John Swinton; quoted above p. 108.
22. Those who own shares number 6.5 million, according to the Brookings Institute estimate quoted by Baran and cited above. This and the subsequent percentage estimates are my own, however; and the figures can be larger, or smaller, depending upon the statistitian's tastes and political convictions. The only point, however the figures are revised, is that the number of shareholders in America who own a large number of shares is not very large.
23. Figures cited by Leo Huberman, "The Distribution of Income," *Monthly Review*, July-August 1959.
24. Quoted by Huberman in same article.
25. Alexander L. Crosby, editor of *The Housing Yearbook* in a memorandum quoted by Huberman in same article.
26. Representative John M. Slack, Jr.; quoted by Huberman in same article.
27. Percival Goodman, "Gloomy Glass and the Betrayal of the Bauhaus," *The Second Coming* magazine, July 1961.
28. Robert Jungk, *Tomorrow is Already Here: Scenes from a Man-Made World*.
29. Quoted in "Review of the Month," *Monthly Review*, April 1959.
30. *Massachusetts Gazette*; quoted above p. 27-28.
31. Harrison Brown, James Bonner, John Weir: *The Next Hundred Years*, p. 10.

220   THE NEW FREEDOM: CORPORATE CAPITALISM

32. J.D. Bernal, *World Without War*, p. 143.
33. *Ibid.*
34. "Review of the Month," *Monthly Review*, November 1960.
35. *Business Week*, January 3, 1959; quoted in *Monthly Review*, November 1960.
36. Quoted in *Monthly Review*, July-August 1959.
37. *Wall Street Journal*, June 28, 1960; quoted in Scott Nearing's column, *Monthly Review*, September 1960.
38. Wall Street Journal, March 25, 1958; quoted in Nearing's "World Events" column, *Monthly Review*, May 1958.
39. Quoted by William A. Williams in *The Tradgey of American Diplomacy*, pp. 49f.
40. *Woodrow Wilson*; quoted in *Ibid.*
41. Quoted in *Ibid.*
42. F.D. Roosevelt; quoted in *Ibid.*, p. 130.
43. Williams, *Ibid.*, pp. 128-9.
44. Quoted in editorial in *The Nation*, May 27, 1961.
45. Alexander Hamilton; quoted by Charles Beard, *Constitution*, p. 183.
46. *Business Week*, October 10, 1959; quoted in *Monthly Review*, November 1959.
47. Congressman Jackson of Georgia; quoted by Beard in *Jeffersonian Democracy*; quoted above p. 30-31.
48. Quoted above, p. 146.
49. John Taylor, *Iquiry*; quoted above, p.35.
50. New York *Times*, September 25, 1959.
51. John Adams; quoted by Beard in *Jeffersonian Democracy*, p. 306.
52. Taylor, *Inquiry*, p. 504.
53. *Ibid.*, p.63.
54. John Adams; quoted by Beard in *Jeffersonian Democracy*, p. 320.
55. Taylor, *Inquiry*, p. 492.
56. *Ibid.*, p. 503.
57. *Ibid.*, pp. 505-06.
58. *Ibid.*, pp. 58-9.
59. Robert Hutchins, in an address on receiving the Sidney Hillman Award for Meritorious Public Service on January 21, 1959; quoted in *Monthly Review*, March 1959, back-cover notes.
60. Paul A. Baran, "Marxism and Psychoanalysis," *Monthly Review*, October 1959.
61. N.S. Lehrman, "The Conflict Within Psychoanalysis," *Monthly Review*, February 1960.
62. Paul Goodman, *Growing Up Absurd*, p. 21.

63. Mark Van Doren's description of Caliban in his *Shakespeare*, p. 283.
64. Roderick Seidenberg, *Posthistoric Man*.
65. *Ibid.*
66. Paul Baran, article cited in note 60.
67. *Ibid.*
68. Fyodor Dostoyevsky, "Notes from the Underground" (Translation by David Magarshack).
69. *Thomas Jefferson on Democracy*, pp 65-6.
70. From Justice Black's dissent in *Communist Party v. SACB*; quoted in *I.F. Stone's Weekly*, June 12, 1961.
71. See Frank Donner, "HUAC: The Dossier Keepers," for a documented account of the elaborate "files" on "dangerous citizens" kept by the House Unamerican Activities Committee; *Studies on the Left*, Vol. II, No. 1, 1961.

BIBLIOGRAPHY

A. THE DEMOCRATIC IDEAL

I apologize for the European bias of my bibliography. I understand there are old traditions of profound explorations of democratic polities in Indonesia, India, China, and doubtless elsewhere. I regret not having read the works, and hope that my sketchy expression of the democratic polity is not altogether incompatible with what is best in those traditions.

My articulation of the democratic ideal into four parts, which I have termed social justice, education, communication, participation, can obviously take as many forms as there are men who will undertake the study. Lest some unimaginative reader misunderstand me, it has not been my intention to erect walls, but to open doors. The four principles I have examined do not describe the final shape of a democratic society but the conditions for a democratic experiment. There could be no "final shape" to such an experiment, since these are conditions for each to develop according to his genius and his capabilities. The very uniformity one finds on a trip across the United States—uniform architecture, uniform ideas, uniform hopes—belies the existence of democracy on any part of this vast continent. I have tried to list four conditions which would describe the antithesis of uniformity, mediocrity, and centralization. The threat of uniformity comes from fascism, which openly proclaims uniformity and regimentation as its ideal; from capitalism, which has erected market architecture, market relations, and market mentalities wherever in the world it has penetrated; from a "transitional socialism" in which the "transition" is entrenched as a centralized state and the socialism is forgotten. Looking at the societies of today, I can distinguish more or less misery and suffering, more or less hope and promise; I cannot, here and now, make out a society I would call democratic: i.e., one which gives full play to the creative potentialities of the human being.

I list below some books that cast light on one or another aspect of democracy. These books are merely the dampened sands on the beach I happen to have visited: I have not even begun to explore the vast ocean. But I hope that the storm of rockets and bomb-threats subsides, and that men have the patience and time to begin the exploration.

Georg Büchner, *Danton's Death*. (1835) An extremely powerful, unjustly neglected great play, in which the struggle that defeated the French Revolution, dramatically symbolized in the clash between Danton and Robespierre, is profoundly examined.

Miguel de Cervantes Saavedra, *El Ingenioso Hidalgo: Don Quixote de la Mancha*.

John Dewey, *Human Nature and Conduct, Freedom and Culture*. Dewey assigns a crucial role to education for the attainment of the creative individuals and the experimental social context indispensable to democracy.

Howard Fast, *Citizen Tom Paine*. An exciting and important novel on some of the forces that led to the American revolution.

Thomas Jefferson on Democracy. (Edited by Saul K. Padover.) A collection of writings by the "Father of American Democracy."

Peter Kropotkin, *Ethics*. The anarchist Kropotkin was perhaps the only radical Marxist who recognized that capitalism cannot be effectively destroyed, nor socialist democracy ushered in, until the capitalist medium of repression, the State, is totally abolished.

Leo Lowenthal, *Literature and the Image of Man*. Lucid analysis of reflections in literature on the golden age and the gradual development of capitalism after the disintegration of European feudalism.

John Locke, *An Essay Concerning the True Original, Extent, and End of Civil Government* (1690).

Karl Mannheim, *Ideology and Utopia: An Introduction to the Sociology of Knowledge*. (Translation by Louis Wirth and Edward Shils.) A scholarly history and sociological analysis of the role of utopia in Western political thought.

John Stuart Mill, *On Liberty*. (1859) Still the best defense of untrammeled communication.

John Stuart Mill, *Representative Government*. (1861) Mill, himself a member of the privileged class, is here more worried about the repression of the few by the many, than about manipulation of the many by the few.

Thomas More, *Utopia*. (first published in 1516).

Plato, *Dialogues*. Though Plato's ideal "republic" is not a democracy, he nevertheless examines profoundly the meaning of education, of communication, of justice.

Jean Jacques Rousseau, *Discourse on the Causes of Inequality Among Men*. (1754)

Jean Jacques Rousseau, *The Social Contract*. (1762) The proclamation of the incompatibility between freedom and privilege. Unfortunately, Rousseau is not a logical thinker, and as a result his work contains the entire spectrum of eighteenth, nineteenth, and twentieth century political ideas.

George H. Sabine, *A History of Political Theory*, 1955. A monumental study of political thought from early Greece to twentieth century Europe and America.

Johann Christoph Friedrich von Schiller, *Die Rauber* (The Robbers) (1791) and *William Tell* (1804).

William Shakespeare, *The Tempest*.

Max Weber, *Politics as a Vocation* (in *From Max Weber: Essays in Sociology*, edited by H.H. Gerth and C. Wright Mills). Examination of the responsibility of the polititian.

Wilfred Wellock, *Gandhi as a Social Revolutionary*. Gandhian democracy in theory and practice.

Edmund Wilson, *To the Finland Station: A Study In the Writing and Acting of History*. In places marred by a provincial outlook, Wilson's book is by and large a sympathetic historical study of democrats and socialists from Vico to Lenin.

B. THE HISTORY AND MORPHOLOGY OF CAPITALISM

There is a vast literature on the growth of capitalism, much of it constituting mere footnotes to the pioneering work done by Marx and Engels, much of it containing a great deal of new insight and fact. I cannot here list even a fraction of the books which touch on or cover this topic, and can merely suggest that the reader unfamiliar with the subject matter pursue the footnotes and bibliographies of the books I do list, and thus construct for himself a more thorough bibliography. If I omit important works from the list, this does not mean I do not consider them important; it may merely mean I have not read them. This list is merely meant to be suggestive: readers familiar with the topic will probably not find it useful.

The following books give original interpretations of the capitalism in the context of West European and North American history.

Paul A. Baran, *The Political Economy of Growth*. A brilliant analysis of the ramifications of world capitalism in the middle of the twentieth century. Baran's "morphology of backwardness" lucidly unmasks the persistence of economic colonialism under various changed labels, and clearly lists the requisites for economic development for the "underdeveloped" part of the world.

Charles A. Beard, *An Economic Interpretation of the Constitution of the United States*. First published in 1913.

Charles A. Beard, *Economic Origins of Jeffersonian Democracy*. First published in 1915.

Nicholas Berdyaev, *The Meaning of History*. (1920-22) An attempt to interpret the transition from feudalism to capitalism in terms of the medieval divorce of man from nature.

Bertolt Brecht, *Galileo*.

Erich Fromm, *The Sane Society*. Treats the psychological condition of man in capitalist society.

Arnold Hauser, *The Social History of Art*. A monumental work which tells the history of Western art within the context of changing social, political and economic institutions.

Leo Huberman, *Man's Worldly Goods*.

Erich Kahler, *Man the Measure*. Full of profound historical insights, but Kahler's attempt to show man's "transcendence" from one level to another is not altogether convincing, since at the end man has "transcended" into imbecility and barbarism, as Kahler himself is well aware.

Leo Lowenthal, *Literature and the Image of Man*.

Thomas Mann, *Buddenbrooks*. The entire spectrum of capitalist history, as reflected in the story of one German family, is sympathetically, though ironically, presented in this early masterpiece of the greatest European novelist of the twentieth century.

Karl Marx, *Das Kapital*. The first, and still by far the most profound, systematic analysis of capitalism.

Marx and Engels, *Communist Manifesto*. Primarily designed as a program for revolutionaries, this pamphlet nevertheless contains an excellent summary analysis of nineteenth century capitalism.

Lewis Mumford, *Technics and Civilization*, *The Culture of Cities*, *The Condition of Man*. A brilliant trilogy whose scope and depth vividly demonstrate that one man is still capable of informing himself on every important aspect of the world in which he lives.

Lewis Mumford, *The Transformations of Man*. This small book is a concise and suggestive history of humanity, as well as a summary of Mumford's major historical insights.

John Herman Randall, Jr., *Making of the Modern Mind*. A history of the transition from feudalism to capitalism as reflected in philosophical and political ideas. Randall relates the ideas to the age and its problems, and also explores the implications of the ideas on their own terms. Contains comprehensive bibliographies of each period.

George H. Sabine, *A History of Political Theory*, especially chapters 28 to 34, which tell the history of political theories from Rousseau to Marx.

William Shakespeare, *Twelfth Night*.

R. H. Tawney, *Religion and the Rise of Capitalism*. A concise and brilliant history of the role of religious belief and dogma in the transition from Western European feudalism to capitalism.

John Taylor of Caroline County, Virginia, *An Inquiry Into the Principles and Policy of the Government of the United States*. First published in Fredericksburg, Va., in 1814.

Thorstein Veblen, *The Theory of Business Enterprise* and *The Theory of the Leisure Class*. Veblen systematically unveils the central institutions of capitalist society with sustained irony and biting satire.

Max Weber, *The Protestant Ethic and the Spirit of Capitalism*.

Max Weber, "Class, Status, Party," which is chapter 7 in *From Max Weber: Essays In Sociology*, edited by H. H. Gerth and C. Wright Mills.

William Appleman Williams, *The Tragedy of American Diplomacy*. A concise history of the concepts which guide the American government in its relations with the rest of the world.

C. THE CORPORATE SOCIETY AND THE TWENTIETH CENTURY

Once again I wish to point out that the books listed here do not comprise a complete reading list; they are merely examples. This bibliography is not intended for the student of human affairs, who is doubtless well aware that the specimen I list are a mere taste of the vast literature available. This bibliography should, rather, unmask the wilful and self-inflicted character of the ignorance of the specialist, whether his "field" is poetry or pathology—an ignorance he invokes with the words "Where should I find these things out?" whenever his stereotyped "opinions" are challenged. The question, together with the attitude of sad helplessness with which it is asked, imply that only the chosen few, after a rigorous and mysterious initiation, are capable of understanding the truly gargantuan problems of our distressingly difficult age. This obscurantist attitude is an attempt to escape the responsibility to form one's own judgment, and an effort to justify blind conformism to the views of the "respectable." The books I list here, however, are not only a small fraction of illuminating available books on human affairs; most of them are readily available in all libraries and bookstores. And no special initiation is required for an intelligent reading of these books, except that which is given in the first years of elementary school, namely the initiation into literacy.

Specialists may be shocked to find, on one and the same reading list, books by poets and psychologists, philosophers and economists. That's a problem the specialists will have to resolve. I have worked under the assumption that specialism is a species of ignorance, and that the entire corpus of human knowledge is the legitimate "field" of human concern. These assumptions have been made in all parts of the world for centuries, and they have not, to my knowledge, been disproved. The "insect that has somehow contrived to mock humanity" has not yet convincingly shown that his "incredible exaggeration of some particular feature" is either beneficial to humanity or desired by men.

American Friends Service Committee, *Speak Truth to Power*. "A Quaker Search for an Alternative to Violence."

Paul A. Baran, *The Political Economy of Growth*.

Samuel Beckett, *Waiting for Godot*. A nihilistic masterpiece.

J.D. Bernal, *World Without War*. An excellent book which describes vividly the benefits which all humanity could derive from a cessation of the war economy.

Albert Bigelow, *The Voyage of the Golden Rule*. Description of an attempt by pacifists to resist the lunatic preparations for annihilation by sailing into the atomic testing area.

Bertolt Brecht, *Threepenny Opera*.

Harrison Brown, *The Challenge of Man's Future*. Examines the consequences of the waste of natural resources, and presents thesis that, should the world economy be disrupted by another war, man will not again be able to reconstruct technology, and thus will never again be able to maintain the large number of people, or the concentration of non-agricultural populations in cities, that are possible today.

Harrison Brown, James Real, *Community of Fear*. The destructive capacities of nuclear weapons. Indispensable reading, especially for "optimists" and for "shelter" addicts.

Albert Camus, *The Stranger* and *The Plague*. Two brilliant novels on the predicament of twentieth century European man, the first depicting the nihilism, the second the transcendence of nihilism through continuing involvement without belief or hope.

Albert Camus, *The Rebel*. A history of rebellion, as well as a presentation of Camus' view that rebellion betrays itself when it negates human life and turns to violence. This is not Camus' last position; before his death by automobile he seems to have rejected rebellion altogether. (See, for example, the later essays in *Resistance, Rebellion, and Death*.)

Josué de Castro, *The Geography of Hunger*. Unforgettable description of the misery, the hunger, the suffering and disease, that are a direct consequence of monoculture, plantations, one-crop economies—in short, of western colonial capitalism.

Theodore Dreiser, *Sister Carrie*. American epic of the unsuccessful capitalist.

Theodore Dreiser, *The Financier*.

Fyodor Dostoyevsky, *The Brothers Karamazov*.

Fyodor Dostoyevsky, *Notes from the Underground*.

F. Scott Fitzgerald, *The Great Gatsby*. This novel on the "American dream" and on the content of American "culture," gives part of the answer to the question "What do the rich do with their money?"

Waldo Frank, *The Rediscovery of the Man*. A re-evaluation of Western history.

Erich Fromm, *Escape from Freedom, Man For Himself, The Sane Society*. A trilogy that develops a comprehensive view of the psychological consequences of life in capitalist society.

Paul Goodman, *Growing Up Absurd*.

H. Stuart Hughes, *Consciousness and Society*. A history and critique of the social ideas and philosophies of Europe from the 1890s.

Aldous Huxley, *Brave New World*.

Kenneth Ingram, *History of the Cold War*. A British view of the Cold War which controverts most of the dogmas pushed on Americans by their "avenues of truth."

Paul Johnson, "The Plundered Continent," *New Statement* (London), September 17, 1960. A brief description of North American colonialism in South America; a masterpiece of social analysis.

James Joyce, *Ulysses*. The grand entrance of nihilism into twentieth century literature.

Robert Jungk, *Tomorrow is Already Here*.

Robert Jungk, *Brighter Than a Thousand Suns*. A history of the making of the atomic bomb and the subsequent efforts of the initiating scientists to unmake their Great Gift to Humanity.

Franz Kafka, *Amerika, The Trial, The Castle, Metamorphosis*. Each a masterpiece of "truer than history" fiction. The situations which reduce the human being to a trapped insect, to a cipher, belie the propaganda about Human Dignity sold to the consumers of western "civilization."

Eric Kahler, *The Tower and the Abyss*. Critical evaluation of the intellectual and literary content of twentieth century Europe and America.

Albert E. Kahn, *The Game of Death: Effects of the Cold War on Our Children*.

Harold P. Lasswell, *Propaganda Technique in the World War*. Vividly analyzes the manipulation of communication during World War I.

Liberation magazine. A pacifist monthly that generally contains thoughtful and timely articles on world affairs.

Thomas Mann, *The Magic Mountain*. Set in a sanatorium, this brilliant novel depicts in the form of loose allegory the wave of nihilism and unleashed violence sweeping across Europe early in the twentieth century.

Thomas Mann, *Doctor Faustus*. Based on the original German Faustbuch, this somber masterpiece symbolically represents the history of German nihilism and its final eruption into lunacy, as they are embodied in the composer Adrian Leverkühn.

Karl Mannheim, *Man and Society in an Age of Reconstruction*.

C. Wright Mills, *The Power Elite*. Undoubtedly the best analysis of mid-twentieth century corporate capitalism.

C. Wright Mills, *White Collar*. Sociological and psychological analysis of the roles and ways of life of the "new class" in capitalist society.

C. Wright Mills, *The Causes of World War III*. The war economy, the military posture of the government, and the abdication of responsibility by the public, the intellectuals, the scientists.

Monthly Review magazine, "an independent socialist magazine." In my opinion the best commentary on contemporary history which differs from the official line of the American media of "communication."

Lewis Mumford, *The Transformations of Man*, especially (with reference to this section) chapters 7 to 9, on "Post-Historic Man," "World Culture," and "Human Prospects."

Lewis Mumford, *In the Name of Sanity*.

Lewis Mumford, *The Culture of Cities*. (I had not, unfortunately, read this book before setting out.)

Gunnar Myrdal, *Rich Lands and Poor*.

The Nation magazine. A Liberal weekly which, despite its title, makes consistent pleas for international cooperation and understanding in its editorials, and occasionally carries excellent analyses of world events

New Left Review magazine. A British journal which voices the present young generation's desire to stay alive and create a world where participation, creativity and originality are possible to every man.

Friedrich Nietzsche, *Thus Spoke Zarathustra*. The work from which twentieth century racism, barbarism, nihilism have taken many of their slogans, yet at the same time a work in which a courageous if irresponsible thinker tries to transcend nihilism and barbarism.

Philip Noel-Baker, *The Arms Race: A Programme for World Disarmament*.

F.S.C. Northrop, *The Meeting of East and West. An Inquiry Concerning World Understanding*.

Harvey O'Connor, *The Empire of Oil*. A fascinating and highly documented analysis of the workings of the gigantic oil corporations, from their wells around the world to their "clean rest rooms" in the local gas stations.

George Orwell, *1984*. A vision of the world after a few more decades of the regimentation, centralization, and military metaphysic of the present day.

Linus Pauling, *No More War*. A chilling, and it is hoped sobering, description of the effects of nuclear fallout and the destructive potentialities of nuclear weapons.

Luigi Pirandello, *Six Characters in Search of an Author, Right You Are If You Think You Are*. Moral relativism here makes its debut on the stage, and contributes to the making of some of nihilist Europe's best drama.

John Herman Randall, Jr., *The Making of the Modern Mind: A Survey of the Intellectual Background of the Present Age*. Especially Book IV, on "Thought and Aspiration in the Last Hundred Years."

David Riesman, Nathan Glaser, Reuel Denney, *The Lonely Crowd*. The different forms of resignation to the White Collar world.

Bertrand Russell, *Common Sense and Nuclear Warfare*.

George H. Sabine, *A History of Political Theory*, chapter 35 on "Fascism and National Socialism."

G.B. Sansom, *The Western World and Japan*, especially the introduction entitled "Europe and Asia."

Jean-Paul Sartre, *Nausea* and *No Exit*.

Frederick L. Schuman, *The Commonwealth of Man: An Inquiry into Power Politics and World Government*.

Roderick Seidenberg, *Posthistoric Man*.

Upton Sinclair, *The Jungle*. The classic on the Civilizing and Humanizing mission of American capitalism.

Pitirim Sorokin, *The Crisis of Our Age*.

John Steinbeck, *The Grapes of Wrath*. The greatest twentieth century American novel.

I.F. Stone's Weekly. Newsletter of very high journalistic and intellectual quality, covering world events and presenting information that does not find its way into the big-circulation American press.

I.F. Stone, *The Truman Era*. Collection of Stone's writings during the Truman administration, in which the origins of the Cold War are seen through an observer contemporary with the events it describes.

Henry David Thoreau, "On the Duty of Civil Disobedience." (1849) One of the relevant answers to the question "What Should I Do?"

Arnold J. Toynbee, *A Study of History*, especially, in this context, Part 9, on the "Contacts Between Civilizations," and Part 12, on "The Prospects of Western Civilization." Toynbee brings his views of Western Civilization up to date in Volume 12 of the same work.

Alfred Weber, *Farewell to European History*. A re-evaluation of European history in the light of the eruption of Nazism and the Nazi war. Weber's guiding concepts are the loss of what he calls transcendence, and the growth of nihilism.

Simone Weil, "Reflections on War," in *Politics*, February 1945; appeared originally in November 1933 issue of *La Critique Sociale* (Paris). John Taylor had observed that usurpers gain nothing from each other. Weil observes that armies gain nothing from each other. In both cases, the victims are always the same; they are the majority of the people.

Richard Wright, *A Report on the Bandung Conference*.

Richard Wright, *White Man, Listen!*

Publication History

This edition of *The New Freedom: Corporate Capitalism* reproduces the entire text of Fredy Perlman's first book, self-published in 1961 in an edition of 91. The text of this edition is based on copy 7, currently in the possession of the Library of Congress. A publication note contains the following information about the production:

> "Mimeographed and proofread by Lorraine and Fredy Perlman at 133 Henry Street, New York City, from July to November 1961. Woodcuts stamped, and books stapled and bound by John Ricklefs and Fredy Perlman at 53 West 24 Street, New York City. First copy completed in November 1961."

At the end of the book, there is this:

> "The materials that went into the making of this book include mimeograph paper, heavy paper, fiber-board for the covers, and a small hand-cranked silk-screen mimeograph machine. Each chapter is held together by large staples, and the chapters are held to each other (bound) by cloth adhesive tape. The cuts were hand printed from relief wood blocks. The choice of materials was influenced by the extremely limited financial means of author and artist, but both hope their attempt to make a book whose outward shape was consistent with its content has been successful enough to encourage others to follow their example."

Copy 7 has since been rebound in a red library binding with LOC endpapers. Many of the woodcuts by John Ricklefs are reproduced in this edition, which was prepared in Ithaca, Indiana, PA, and Queens, and printed at Bookmobile in Minneapolis.

Southpaw Culture

"poetry to politics, pedagogy to planning"